A HISTORY OF MEDIEVAL ISLAM

A HISTORY OF
MEDIEVAL ISLAM

by
J. J. Saunders

Routledge and Kegan Paul
LONDON AND NEW YORK

First published 1965
by Routledge and Kegan Paul Ltd
11 New Fetter Lane
London EC4P 4EE
Published in the USA by
Routledge & Kegan Paul Inc.
in association with Methuen Inc.
29 West 35th Street, New York, NY 10001

Reprinted 1972
Reprinted and first published
as a paperback in 1978
Reprinted 1980, 1982 and 1987

Printed in Great Britain by
Redwood Burn Limited
Trowbridge, Wiltshire

© *J. J. Saunders 1965*

ISBN 0 7100 2077 5 (c)
ISBN 0 7100 0050 2 (p)

Contents

Maps

Preface

DR. JOHNSON, commenting in one of the *Ramblers* on the oblivion which overtook Richard Knolles' *Generall Historie of the Turkes* (1603), despite its literary merits, explained this neglect on the ground that the author 'employed his genius upon a foreign and uninteresting subject' and recounted 'enterprises and revolutions of which none desire to be informed.' Indifference to Oriental history among the educated public of the West still exists, but is diminishing, and more 'desire to be informed' of the relations between Europe and Islam throughout the ages. Such recent works as Dr. Norman Daniel's *Islam and the West* (1960) and Professor R. W. Southern's *Western Views of Islam in the Middle Ages* (1962) provide striking evidence of the wider perspectives now being opened up, and as our historians cease to be Europe-centred and devote more attention to the nature and evolution of non-European societies, we may expect the history of the Muslim East to be studied with increasingly critical care.

It is true that the task confronting scholars in this field is enormous. The language barrier alone is not easily surmounted. Many relevant texts remain unpublished, and many of the problems to be solved have scarcely been formulated, much less seriously tackled. Thus, for example, the social and economic history of medieval Islam has only just begun to be investigated. The unfamiliarity of the subject daunts some prospective students. The rhythms of Muslim history are not our rhythms. To give but one instance, the memorable struggles of Church and State, from which emerged the Western theory and practice of civil and political liberty, had no counterpart in Islam, which knows no distinction between secular and ecclesiastical, and is puzzled by our concepts of representative government and a free society. In this book I have aimed to provide a brief sketch of a vast theme, a rough outline which may serve as an introduction for those wishing to acquire a general view of the Muslim world during the Middle Ages. It would be absurd to claim it as a work of original research; it does not profess to trace the development of Islam as a religion, and it omits all but the briefest mention of Muslim Spain and India. I have tried to indicate the main trends of Islamic historical evolution down to the Mongol conquests, to avoid a mere recital of facts and names and dates, and to explain rather than to narrate. Hence I have exercised a rigid selection of material; much of moment has been left out, and the picture presented may often be unavoidably over-simplified.

I wish to express my deep obligation to Professor C. F. Beckingham, Professor of Islamic Studies in the University of Manchester, and to Dr. J. A. Boyle, Head of the Department of Persian Studies in the same University, who kindly read the typescript and made many valuable suggestions for improving it. I am also grateful to the editors of *Cahiers d'Histoire Mondiale* and *History Today* for permission to reproduce portions of articles which have appeared in these periodicals. Perhaps I may also be allowed to say how much my understanding of Islamic history has been deepened by the writings of Sir Hamilton Gibb and Professor Bernard Lewis, whose influence will be easily detected in these pages.

In facing the perennial problem of the transliteration of Oriental names, I can claim no consistency. Place-names like Mecca, Medina and Cairo have been left in their familiar English form, together with such words as 'Koran' and 'Caliph'. For the rest, I have usually followed the spelling given in the *Encyclopedia of Islam,* omitting the diacritical points and the long-vowel markings (which are restored, however, in the index entries), and substituting 'j' for the Frenchified 'dj.'

Glossary

(A) = Arabic;   (P) = Persian;   (T) = Turkish.

Abd (A): slave, servant. *Abdallah:* slave of God.

Abu (A): father of.

Agha (T): chief, master.

Ahl (A): family, household, people. *Ahl al-Kitab:* people of the Book, i.e. Jews and Christians possessing their own scriptures.

Ain or Ayn (A): eye, spring, fountain.

Ak (T): white.

Alp (T): hero.

Amir (A): commander, governor, prince. *Amir al-Mu'minin*, commander of the faithful (Caliph's title).

Ansar (A): helpers, Medinans who supported Muhammad.

Ata (T): father. *Atabeg:* 'father-chief', guardian.

Bahr (A): sea. *Bahr al-Rum:* the Roman Sea, i.e. the Mediterranean.

Banu (A): sons of, followed by name of tribe, e.g. *Banu-Hilal.*

Bait or Bayt (A): house, tent. *Bait al-Mal:* house of wealth, i.e. the Treasury.

Barid (A): post service.

Bey or Beg (T): lord, chief.

Bi'r (A): well.

Dagh (T): mountain.

Da'i (A): missionary, propagandist.

Dair or Dayr (A): Christian monastery.

Dar (A): house, dwelling, abode. *Dar al-Islam:* the abode of Islam, where Islam is the established religion, as opposed to *Dar al-Harb*, the abode of war, non-Muslim lands.

Dawla (A): dynasty, "State."

Dhimmis (A): protected people, i.e. Jews and Christians under Muslim rule.

Dihkan (P): village headman, small farmer.

Din (A): religion, faith, often found in name-compounds, e.g. *Nur al-Din* (*Nureddin*), light of the faith.

Dinar (A): Arabic gold coin (from Latin denarius).

Dirham (A): Arabic silver coin.

Diwan (A): office, register, government department, also a collection of poetry or prose.

Fay' (A): land belonging to Muslim community.

Fida'i (A): assassin, agent of Nizari Isma'ilis.

Farangi (*Frank*) (A): common Arabic word for a Western European.

Ghazi (A): champion, great fighter.

Hadith (A): tradition.

Hajj (A): pilgrimage to Mecca.

Hijra (*Hegira*) (A): emigration, flight, withdrawal.

Ibn (A): son of, usually abbreviated 'b.'

Ijma (A): consensus of the Muslim community.

Ikhshid (P): prince.

Ikta (A): fief, estate whose rents are used for the payment of civil or military officers.

Ilm (A): science, learning.

Imam (A): leader.

Isnad (A): chain of witnesses.

Jabal (A): mountain.

Jahiliyya (A): 'times of ignorance' before Islam.

Jazirah (A): island.

Jihad (A): holy war.

Jinn (A): beings distinct from men and angels, capable of inflicting injury.

Jizya (A): poll-tax levied on non-Muslims.

Jum'a (A): day of worship (Friday). *Jum'a Masjid:* principal mosque where Friday service is held.

Jund (A): army, military district.

Kabilah (A): tribe.

Kadi (*cadi, qadi*) (A): judge.

Kafir (A): infidel.

Kara (T): black.

Kasr (A): castle.

Katib (A): secretary.

Khan (T): chief, prince.

Kharaj (A): land-tax.

Khatun (T): queen.

Khutba (A): mosque sermon.

Kiblah (A): direction of Mecca.

Kuds (A): holy. *Al-Kuds:* the holy (city), i.e. Jerusalem.

Kul (T): lake. *Baikal:* rich lake.

Madrasa (A): college.

Maghrib (A): the west.

Mahdi (A): the guided one, supposed to appear in the last days.

Malik (A): king. *Mulk:* kingdom.

Mamluk (A): slave.

Masjid (A): mosque.

Mawla (A): client, helper, freed slave. Plural 'Mawali.'

Mihrab (A): niche in mosque, showing direction of Mecca.

Minbar (A): mosque pulpit.

Mi'raj (A): Muhammad's journey to heaven.

Muharram (A): first month of Muslim year. The 10th Muharram is the anniversary of Husain's death at Karbala in 680.

Mulhid (A): heretic, deviator.

Nabi (A): prophet.

Nahr (A): river.

Nasara (A): Christians, Nazarenes. Singular 'Nasrani.'

Rasul (A): messenger, apostle.

Ridda (A): apostasy.

Rum (A): the Roman or Byzantine Empire, later the Seljuk State in Asia Minor.

Salat (A): ritual prayer, divine service.

Sarai (P): palace.

Shah (P): king.

Shahid (A): witness, martyr.

Shari'a (A): religious law.

Shi'a (A): party (of Ali).

Sira (A): traditional biography of Muhammad.

Sufi (A): mystic.

Sultan (A): power, authority, sovereign ruler.

Sunna (A): custom, practice of the Muslim community. *Sunnites:* those who follow the sunna, as distinct from heretics or deviators.

Sura (A): chapter of the Koran.

Ta'rikh (A): history, chronicle.

Umma (A): people, community.

Ushr (A): tithe.

Wadi (A): non-perennial river.

Wakf (A): pious endowment, land or property set aside for religious purposes.

Wazir or vizier (P): chief minister.

Zindik (P): heretic, freethinker.

Dates

711–714	Arabs overrun Spain.
712	Arabs cross the Jaxartes and advance to Kashgar.
713	Arabs invade Indus Valley and take Multan.
717–718	Arab siege of Constantinople fails.
732	Arabs defeated by Franks in Gaul near Tours.
739–742	Berber anti-Arab revolt in North Africa.
750	Omayyads overthrown by Abbasids.
755	Omayyad refugee escapes to Spain and sets up independent amirate there.
763	Baghdad founded.
786–809	Harun al-Rashid Caliph.
800	North Africa becomes independent under the Aghlabids.
813–833	Ma'mun Caliph.
827–902	Arab conquest of Sicily.
861–870	Turkish mercenaries create state of anarchy in Baghdad.
868	Turkish viceroy Tulun makes himself independent in Egypt.
869–883	Zanj revolt in Basra.
875	Karmathian (Isma'ilian) movement begins about this time.
900–999	Samanid dynasty in Khurasan fosters revival of Persian culture.
909	Fatimid anti-Caliphate set up in North Africa.
928	Karmathians break into Mecca and carry off Black Stone.
945	Buyids occupy Baghdad and put an end to the political power of the Abbasids.
956	Seljuk Turks embrace Islam.
969	Fatimids conquer Egypt.
996–1021	Hakim Fatimid Caliph.
997–1030	Mahmud of Ghazna.
1040	Seljuks defeat Ghaznavids at Dandankan.
1055–58	Seljuks overthrow Buyids, occupy Baghdad and "protect" the Abbasid Caliphs.
1071	Seljuks defeat Byzantines at Manzikert.
1072–91	Normans recover Sicily for Christendom.
1085	Spanish Christians regain Toledo.
1090	Assassins seize Alamut.
1095	Pope Urban II launches Crusading movement.
1099	Crusaders take Jerusalem.
1141	Seljuk Sultan Sanjar defeated by pagan Kara-Khitay near Samarkand.

DATES

1144	Zengi drives Crusaders from Edessa.
1169–93	Reign of Saladin.
1171	Saladin overthrows Fatimid Caliphate in Egypt.
1187	Saladin recovers Jerusalem from the Crusaders.
1206–27	Reign and conquests of Chingis Khan.
1219–24	Mongols ravage Transoxiana and Khurasan.
1250	Mamluks seize power in Egypt.
1256	Mongols destroy Assassins of Alamut.
1258	Mongols sack Baghdad and kill the last Caliph.
1260	Mamluks defeat Mongols at Ain Jalut in Palestine.

I

Arabia and Her Neighbours

THE peninsula of Arabia may be described as a vast rectangle of
more than a million square miles in extent, placed between Africa
and the main land-mass of Asia. The Red Sea, which forms its
western boundary, is part of the great rift valley which continues
northwards through the Gulf of Akaba, the Dead Sea, and the
River Jordan; the huge convulsions which produced it have piled
up mountain ridges which rise steeply along the coast from the
Hijaz to the Yemen, and the land thus slopes down from west to
east towards the gentle declivity of the Persian Gulf. On three sides
Arabia faces the sea; her only land frontier is the Syrian Desert,
and as the crossing of these sandy wastes was at least as difficult
as landing on her almost harbourless coasts, she long remained an
isolated and inaccessible country, whose inhabitants aptly styled
her *Jazirat al-Arab*, the *island* of the Arabs.

The climate of Arabia is distinguished chiefly by high tempera-
tures and the absence of moisture. The autumn monsoon deposits
heavy showers on the coastline of Oman and the Yemen, but the
steep hills force the rain-laden clouds to ascend rapidly and dis-
charge their contents before they have passed over the inland
slopes; the winter and spring rains of the Mediterranean region are
scattered sparsely over the northern deserts, the *Nufud*, where the
wilderness blossoms like a rose for a short season, but the southern
interior is beyond their range, and is in consequence a dreadful,
waterless waste, the *Rub al-Khali*, the Empty Quarter, which until
recent times has rarely been crossed by European travellers. Arabia
is destitute of lakes, forests and prairies; scarcely a perennial stream

1

is found in the land; the *wadis* or rivers, which become raging torrents in the short wet period, are for most of the year dry and empty, and a man might cross their beds without being aware of their existence. Except in the high country, the heat of the summer is intense, yet the climate is not on the whole injurious to human health. The dryness of the atmosphere mitigates the strength of the sun's rays; the nights are cool; in winter snow often lies in the highest valleys of the Jabal Shammar, a chain of hills immediately south of the Nufud, and frost is not unknown in the highlands of the Yemen.

Western Arabia, the mountainous region fronting the Red Sea, consists of three clearly defined areas: a hot, narrow coastal plain, known as the *Tihama,* or lowland; hills, with peaks rising to several thousand feet, which bear the name of *Hijaz,* or barrier, and beyond these, a great plateau which dips eastwards to the central deserts. In the north, the land of Midian, the mountains are wild and desolate, but in the Yemen, the Arabia Felix of the ancients, the hillsides receive a substantial rainfall, and grain crops and (since the sixteenth century) the coffee bean are grown in the fertile valleys. Here, in the extreme south-west corner of the peninsula, arose the earliest civilisations of old Arabia, those of the Minaeans and Sabaeans. Southern Arabia presents an inhospitable front to the Indian Ocean; its long coastline has few natural harbours, and its inhabited valleys lie inland and free from prying strangers. Its principal division, the Hadramawt, was famous in remote antiquity as the land of incense; the gum from the incense-trees was a prized article of commerce, and vast quantities of it were bought and burnt on the altars of Egyptian and Babylonian temples. Eastern Arabia is a land of contrasts. The shores of the Persian Gulf are flat, barren and humid, the natives deriving a scanty living from fishing and pearl-diving, but the province of Oman is filled with well-watered vales which run back to the foothills of the Jabal Akhdar, or Green Mountains, and whose palm-groves and fruit-orchards support a substantial population. The interior of Arabia is by no means all desert: many oases provide food and water for considerable settlements; springs and wells afford refreshment to the traveller, and some large fertile depressions, such as the Wadi Hadramawt in the south and the Wadi Sirhan in the north-west, have served for ages as channels of commerce.

The name 'Arab,' which may possibly be connected with the Hebrew root, *abhar*, to move or pass, has been often restricted to the desert-dwellers, the *Badw* or Bedouins, and repudiated by the townsmen and peasants, a practice which reminds us that the majority of the inhabitants of the peninsula have since historic times been pastoral nomads. The pattern of their life has remained unchanged through the centuries since the days of Abraham. Prisoners of the seasonal cycle, they spend the four summer months from June to September around the wells of their tribal territory, patiently enduring heat, thirst and choking sand-storms; in October, when the first rains fall, they strike their camps and depart for their grazing-grounds, which in a few weeks are covered with plants and coarse grasses. After seven or eight months of wandering over and consuming these pastures, they converge in May on their wells, to await with the stoic fatalism of their race the approach of another summer. Their hunger is barely appeased by a single daily meal of rice, dates and camel's milk; their clothing, consisting of a long shirt, a flowing upper garment and a headdress held in position by a cord, is worn till it rots, and their habitation is a tent of coarse cloth made of goat's hair or sheep's wool, sparsely furnished with mattresses, cooking-pots and water-skins. Every Bedouin tent shelters a single family; several families constitute a *kawm* or clan, and clans linked by blood relationship make up a *kabilah* or tribe, to whose particular name is commonly prefixed the word *Banu*, sons of. To no authority outside his tribe does the Bedouin acknowledge any allegiance; his *shaikh* or chief is merely a first among equals, chosen by the elders from the adult males of the ruling house, whose business is to govern his people according to ancient custom and to defend them against their enemies. For inter-tribal war is endemic in such a society: the fierce competition for the possession of wells, sheep, camels and pastures, the only wealth of a nomad people, constantly incites one tribe to launch a *ghazw* or raid on the territory of another. As no supreme public authority is recognized, a crime committed by a member of one tribe against a member of another, unless purged by a compensatory payment, may produce a vicious blood-feud that persists for years.

The manners and morals of the Bedouins reflect the conditions and needs of desert life. Hospitality is perhaps the chief virtue of the nomad: in a land where man is engaged in a perpetual struggle against nature, food and shelter are never withheld from the travel-ler, and even a fugitive fleeing from the vengeance of his foes has but to touch the tent-ropes of a family to be assured of temporary sanctuary within its domain. Bedouin women enjoy more freedom than their urban sisters, and the heavy physical toil of the camp is shared by both sexes. Pride of descent is strong among the tribes-men, who carry in their heads long and complicated genealogies: to preserve the unity and purity of the family, they commonly marry first cousins. Divorce is easy: a wife is usually repudiated for childlessness. Large families are common, but dirt and ignor-ance account for the high infant mortality. The threat of famine al-ways hung over Bedouin society; the nomads often refused to be burdened with extra mouths to feed, and the horrible custom of burying alive female babies was abolished only by the humane edict of the Prophet.

Whether the Bedouins were the original inhabitants of the coun-try, whether the ancestors of the Arabs migrated from Africa or Mesopotamia, and whether the land was first peopled by Semites or non-Semites, are questions at present beyond the reach of solution. The national tradition proclaimed a duality of descent: the Arabs of the North were descended from Adnan, those of the South from Kahtan. This tradition is of great antiquity, since Kahtan is evidently the Joktan of the Old Testament, and the famous 'table of races' in the tenth chapter of Genesis, which dates from about 900 B.C., makes the South Arabians his sons. The language of the South was different from that of the North, and was written in a different alphabetic script. The northerners were mainly nomads, the souther-ners settled agriculturists. Whether the two groups belonged to dif-ferent racial stocks, we do not know. What is fairly certain is that Arabia entered history with the domestication of the camel some-where around 1000 B.C.

The dromedary or one-humped camel has been aptly styled 'the ship of the desert'. In pre-historic days, the only form of animal transport in Arabia was the donkey. The coming of the camel effec-ted a social and economic revolution. It was admirably suited both for riding and as a beast of burden: its speed over long distances is three times as fast as a horse; it can go for seventeen days without water and can consume thirty gallons at a time; it can carry a weight of 450 pounds; its flesh and milk are edible; its hair is used for tent-covers and its dung for fuel, and a caravan party, caught in the desert far from wells or springs, may save their lives by slaughtering a camel and drinking the water from its stomach. Once tamed, the animal increased enormously the mobility of the nomads and gave a powerful stimulus to commerce, since goods could now be carried over Arabia faster and in larger quantities than ever before. As early as 854 B.C., an Assyrian inscription records that 'Gindibu the Arab' (the first of his race to be named in history) led a troop of a thousand camels against Shalmaneser III in fighting along the border of the Syrian Desert, while the visit of the queen of Sheba (Saba, in the Yemen) to Solomon, which if historical must have occurred in the tenth century B.C., indicates that camel caravans were already travelling at that date, laden with the products of the East, between South Arabia and Palestine.

From this time onwards Arabia was drawn into the stream of international trade, and the first civilized societies appeared in the peninsula. It is possible that the disorders in Egypt, which followed the fall of the 'New Empire' in the eleventh century B.C. and led to the loss of its overseas territories, enabled the South Arabians to secure naval control of the Red Sea and establish a virtual monopoly of the incense traffic from the Hadramawt and the spice trade with India. At some time between 1000 and 500 B.C., two strong kingdoms rose to prominence in the Yemen, those of Ma'in and Saba.[1] The former sent their caravans northwards towards the Mediterranean markets; a big Minaean colony was settled at Dedan or Daydan in the Tihama, and Minaean inscriptions have been found as far afield as Memphis in Egypt and Delos in the Greek archipelago. The latter expanded westwards towards Africa; their ships controlled the Straits of Bab al-Mandab; they colonized Abyssinia (whose name is said to be derived from Habashat, an Arabic word perhaps meaning a confederacy), and for many ages poured a silent stream of Arab migration into the African coastlands from Cape Guardafui to Sofala, which have retained to this day a strongly

---

[1]The chronology of these South Arabian kingdoms is still a matter of controversy. Mlle J. Pirenne has recently attempted (*La Grèce et Saba*, Paris, 1955) to synchronize it with that of Greece, there being some evidence that the South Arabian alphabet was derived directly from the Greek and not through the Phoenician. If her theory be correct and it seems now to be fairly generally accepted, a much lower date than the tenth century B.C. must be assigned to the emergence of Ma'in and Saba as organised States.

marked Semitic character. Saba ultimately absorbed Ma'in and two smaller principalities, Aswan and Kataban; her kings, known as *mukarribs*, combined the functions of prince and priest, and her wealth was largely expended in the beautifying of her capital Ma'rib, which lay at the junction of caravan routes nearly four thousand feet up in the Yemen hills. Ma'rib was celebrated not only for its temples and palaces, but above all for the dam which was built a few miles outside its walls to catch and distribute the waters of its local river, the Wadi Dhana, and so to irrigate a broad expanse of the surrounding countryside. So remarkable a feat of hydraulic engineering argues a high degree of technical skill among the Sabaean people.

The prosperous trade of Arabia excited the cupidity of the Assyrians, who built up the first great world empire in Western Asia. The records of their kings (Shalmaneser III, Tiglath-Pileser III, Sargon II, Sennacherib, and Esarhaddon) contain frequent references to fighting in the Syrian Desert, with the object of suppressing marauding Bedouins and securing control of caravan routes, particularly the road through the Wadi Sirhan, which linked the markets of Syria with those of Mesopotamia. The overthrow of the Assyrian Empire in 612 B.C. brought the Chaldaeans to power in Babylon : under their rule, relations with the Arabs were more friendly, perhaps because the newcomers were themselves of Arab stock. The last Chaldaean king, Nabonidus, actually took up his residence at Tayma, an oasis and important caravan station in North Arabia, familiar from the references to it in the book of Job, and left his son Belshazzar to act to regent in Babylon. The Persians who succeeded the Chaldaeans apparently maintained this pacific policy during the two centuries of their domination (539-337 B.C.), but when their empire was destroyed by Alexander and his Greeks, the political and economic condition of the Near East underwent some significant changes.

First, the Greeks reached India itself, and Alexander's admiral Nearchus sailed down the Indus out into the Indian Ocean and up the Persian Gulf, thereby presenting a potential threat by sea to the Sabaean monopoly of the Indian trade. Secondly, in the confusion following the dissolution of the Persian realm, a North Arabian tribe, the Nabataeans, seized around 320 B.C. the rock fortress of

Petra and the oases of the Wadi Sirhan, ejected the Minaean-Sabaeans from Daydan, and placed themselves athwart the principal roads running across North-West Arabia to the Mediterranean ports. For the next four centuries the Nabataeans were a power to be reckoned with in the politics of the Near East, and the wonderful ruins of Petra, the 'rose-red city half as old as Time,' have kept their memory alive to this day. Thirdly, when after Alexander's death in 323 B.C., the Ptolemies established themselves in Egypt, a vigorous attempt was made to restore Egyptian naval power in the Red Sea. The ancient canal between that sea and the Nile was re-opened; Egyptian ships passed through the Straits of Bab al-Mandab and made direct contact with Indian ports, bringing back cargoes of pepper and cinnamon, and the discovery attributed to one Hippalus of the periodicity of the monsoons greatly facilitated navigation in the Indian Ocean.

These developments sapped the economic strength of Saba, provoked unrest and discontent, and led to a revolution in or about 115 B.C., when the ancient monarchy was overthrown by the Himyarites, a tribe whose original home was perhaps in the Hadramawt and who under the name 'Homerites' were familiar to the Greeks and Romans for the remainder of the classical period as the lords of Arabia Felix. The new rulers of the Yemen were soon called upon to defend their land against something more serious than mere trade competition. The shadow of Rome was falling across the Near East; after the battle of Actium (31 B.C.), Augustus landed in Egypt and turned the country into a Roman province; the Nabataean kingdom was reduced to the status of a Roman satellite, and plans were set on foot to seize the incense-lands of Arabia. In 24 B.C. Aelius Gallus, the prefect of Egypt, landed an army on the North Arabian coast and pushed down the Hijaz as far as the Wadi Najran, within a few days' march of Ma'rib. At this point something went wrong and the expedition was forced to return. Either the Romans were unable to cope with the hazards of desert warfare, or they were betrayed by Nabataean spies and agents they had brought with them. The Himyarites thus escaped subjection to Rome, but they never regained the monopoly of the Indian trade which their Sabaean predecessors had so long enjoyed.

For the first two centuries of the Christian era, Western, that is to say, Roman-Egyptian, shipping plied regularly to and fro across

7

the Indian Ocean. Details of this sea traffic have been preserved in a handbook for merchant captains compiled about A.D. 50 and known as the *Periplus of the Erythraean* (Red) *Sea*. Large hordes of Roman coins have been dug up in southern India, and at least one Roman trade mission reached China. The land routes across Arabia lost a good deal of their importance, and Trajan in 106 A.D. was able to annex Petra and abandon the Wadi Sirhan, which the Nabataeans had so long controlled, to Bedouin anarchy without risking economic loss. In the third century, however, the situation was transformed by the emergence of three new factors, the breakdown of the Roman peace, the rise of the powerful Sassanid kingdom in Persia, and the emergence of the kingdom of Axum in Abyssinia.

After the death of Marcus Aurelius in 180 A.D., the Roman Empire was subjected to a series of barbarian assaults which nearly brought it to ruin, and in 226 the new Sassanid dynasty came to power in Persia. Persian attacks on the Roman positions in the Near East multiplied, at a time when the emperors were struggling with foes elsewhere. Trade and commerce suffered, and almost certainly the volume of Roman shipping in Indian waters sharply declined. This circumstance revived the importance of the desert caravan roads. Petra and the Nabataeans were no more, but a new commercial centre arose at Palmyra, halfway across the Syrian Desert, a meeting-place for merchants from Damascus, Mesopotamia and Arabia. Palmyra was a very old settlement in a fertile oasis, known in Biblical days and still known to the Arabs as Tadmor, but fame and prosperity only came to it when it took over much of the trade that had once flowed through Petra. A self-governing city under the protection of Rome, its mainly Arab inhabitants used its wealth to construct a magnificent imitation of a Greco-Roman metropolis, with temples, fora, porticoes and colonnaded streets, whose vast ruins, starting up out of the desert wilderness, still amaze the traveller. For a time the Palmyrenes loyally defended Rome against Persia, but after the capture of the Emperor Valerian by the Sassanids in 260, the city, under its chief Odenathus, resolved to make a bid for the sovereignty of the East. For several years Odenathus and later his widow Zenobia ruled a kingdom which stretched over Syria, North Arabia, part of Asia Minor and even Egypt, but when the military strength of Rome was restored by Aurelian, the brief glory of Palmyra was ended. In 272

Palmyra was captured by the Romans, and Zenobia was taken prisoner. The city went the way of Petra, but the example of both the Nabataeans and the Palmyrenes showed that communities of Arab stock were capable of attaining a high degree of civilization under the stimulus of contact with advanced peoples. Petra and Palmyra may be regarded as local forerunners of the mightier culture of Islam.

Far more significant for the subsequent history of Arabia was the rise of a new military State in the highlands of Abyssinia. When the Ptolemies brought Greek culture into Egypt, some knowledge of it reached the Abyssinians through the Red Sea port of Adulis, which was frequented by Egyptian shipping. A few miles inland from Adulis arose the city of Axum or Aksum, which became the capital of the kingdom of that name. Its sovereigns professed sympathy for Hellenic civilization, and their decrees were issued in both Greek and Ethiopic. Axum emerges into the full light of history after the Roman occupation of Egypt: it seems to have been accepted as an ally of Rome, and the two Powers had a common interest in repelling the incursions of the Blemmyes or Bejas, a savage tribe who roamed the regions of the middle Nile. Axum doubtless had her share of the Indian trade, and when in the third century the Roman Empire fell into anarchy and Sassanid Persia became a Great Power, she perhaps saw her interests threatened by a possible extension of Persian naval control over Arabian waters, and reacted by attempting to gain a foothold in the Yemen. Early in the fourth century, the Axumites invaded and conquered Himyar, and their kings for a time style themselves 'kings of Axum, Himyar and Hadramawt.' Some time before 378 (when the royal title changes again), a national reaction must have ejected the intruders, but the freedom of Himyar was never again secure, and from now until the rise of Islam South Arabia was a bone of contention between Axum and Persia, with Rome, or rather Byzantine Constantinople, occasionally intervening from a distance. The situation was complicated by the rapid spread of Christianity over the Near East after the conversion of Constantine, which dragged Arabia deeper than ever into the vortex of international politics.

The primitive religion of the desert was restricted to the worship of trees and streams and stones in which the deity was supposed to reside. The nomad, at the mercy of a seemingly capricious and hostile Nature, was impelled to believe in personalized elemental forces, whose protection was invoked and whose anger was averted by appropriate rites and ceremonies. Yet the authority of the gods was local and limited: vast tracts of the earth were delivered over to strange, supernatural beings known as *jinn* (the 'genie' of the European translations of the *Arabian Nights*), whose activity, though sometimes beneficent, was more commonly evil and malicious. The *jinn* were conceived of as corporeal creatures who haunted thickets, graveyards and waste places, and assumed the form of snakes or wild beasts; they appeared and disappeared with mysterious suddenness, and ruthlessly inflicted death or madness on those who offended them. Nomads had naturally no temples or priesthoods; they usually carried their gods with them in a tent or tabernacle, and consulted them by casting lots with arrows, while their *kahins* or soothsayers delivered oracles in short rhymed sentences. When a nomadic tribe adopted a more sedentary manner of life, its gods were placed within a *haram,* or sacred enclosure, usually a circle of stones, and sacrifices were there offered to them: thus the Nabataeans at Petra worshipped their deity in a square block of unhewn basalt, over which the blood of offerings was poured. In short, Bedouin religion was part and parcel of ancient Semitic paganism, many traces of which are to be found in the beliefs and practices of the early Hebrews as recorded in the Old Testament

In the more advanced and civilized kingdoms of the South a higher type of religion developed. Instead of sticks and stones, the heavenly bodies were the object of a worship curiously akin to that of the Babylonians, a circumstance which has led some inquirers to seek a direct connection between the Sabaeans and ancient Sumer. Stone temples, often consisting of big sanctuaries flanked by private chapels, were erected in the principal cities, and endowed with the revenues of incense-forests and other landed estates, and a sacrificial priesthood, whose members in early days at least combined both civil and ecclesiastical functions, enjoyed great wealth and power in the State. In the South Arabian pantheon, the primacy was held by the moon-god, who was venerated under a variety of names. He was Almakah to the Sabaeans, Wadd to the Minaeans, while in the Hadramawt he was known as Sin, the same name as in Babylon. Northern influence is also clearly visible in the case of Athtar, the planet Venus, whose name is obviously a variant of the Phoenician Astarte and the Babylonian Ishtar. The sun-god Shams, so prominent among the northern Semites, oddly changed his sex in Arabia, and was found under different local designations, but always in a female form. A few towns or oases, such as San'a, Najran and later Mecca, possessed temples or shrines of wide repute, which attracted pilgrimages from afar. It is doubtful if the pre-Islamic Arabs had a very clear or firm belief in a future life. Is is said that a camel was often tied by its owner's grave and left to die there, so that he might ride the animal in the next world, but it is likely that an other-worldly existence was envisaged as little more than a gloomy land of shadows similar to the Sheol of the Hebrews.

An isolated people may preserve unchanged for centuries their primitive faith, but as soon as they are subjected to pressure from an external and more advanced civilization, the old pattern of life is disrupted and ancient beliefs and institutions crumble away. From the fourth century onwards, Arabian paganism was exposed to a mounting challenge from a Christianity which was now the official religion of Rome and Axum. This was not indeed the first monotheistic creed with which the Arabs were acquainted. Jewish communities had long been settled in Arabia: it is possible that the oldest of them were founded by refugees who fled from Palestine after the destruction of Jerusalem by Nebuchadnezzar in 586 B.C. Jews were found in the Yemen towns, in northern oases like Tayma and Khaibar, and three clans in Medina professed the Jewish religion. They rarely indulged in proselytism, kept severely to themselves, and were viewed by their Arab neighbours with some suspicion and dislike. No doubt Arabs out of curiosity strayed from time to time into synagogues, but the impact of Judaism on them was far feebler than that of Christianity.

The gospel first entered Arabia from the north, through the medium of the Nabataean kingdom, which in the apostolic age controlled Damascus, the scene of St. Paul's conversion. The beginnings of Arabian Christianity are quite obscure, though legend attributed its foundation variously to the Wise Men from the East (who were held to have come from Saba), to the apostle Bartholomew, and to the eunuch of Queen Candace mentioned in *Acts*.

Episcopal lists testify to the existence of numerous though small Christian groups in north-west Arabia from the third century, and the Romanized *shaikh*, Philip the Arab, who reigned as emperor from 244 to 249, is doubtfully claimed as a Christian convert. Constantine's acceptance of Christianity gave a powerful impetus to evangelization in lands bordering upon the Roman Empire. Axum became Christian in the reign of Ezanes (c.320-360), whose change of faith is proved by his coins and inscriptions, and a certain Theophilus 'the Indian' was sent by the Emperor Constantius to preach the gospel in Himyar and perhaps at the same time to negotiate a Roman-Arab alliance against the Persians. How successful his mission was we do not know but what is certain is that the violent controversies which rent the Church in the fifth century had repercussions all over Arabia.

Since the days of Arius and the Council of Nicaea, theologians had been trying to settle the thorny question of the precise relation of Christ to the Godhead. The Greeks tended to take the lead and to impose their own solution of these difficulties. The Councils which debated and decided these matters all met in Greek lands, but their findings were often repudiated by the non-Hellenic Christians of the East, who had created what were virtually national Churches in Egypt and Syria and were in revolt against Greek ecclesiastical domination. In 431 the Council of Ephesus condemned Nestorius for exaggerating the humanity of Christ, and in 451 the Council of Chalcedon declared heretical the belief that Christ had only one nature, his human nature being wholly absorbed in the divine. The 'one-nature' Christians ('Monophysites') had a large following among the Egyptians and Syrians; they rejected the decrees of Chalcedon, and were subjected to spasmodic bouts of persecution. Axum followed its mother-Church of Egypt in accepting the Monophysite position. The Nestorians were driven out of the Roman Empire altogether, and sought refuge in Persia, where they conducted a vigorous missionary drive all over Western Asia. It was these unorthodox forms of Christianity which now gained a lodging in Arabia, and particularly in the Yemen. Monophysite and Nestorian preachers helped to undermine Arab faith in the old gods and unwittingly contributed to the political upheavals which ruined the ancient civilization of the South, but they surprisingly failed to create a Christian Arabic literature or to translate the Bible into the language of their converts, an achievement which would have given solidity and permanence to their church.

At the beginning of the sixth century, the kingdom of Himyar was far gone in decay. Already it had experienced one attack and temporary conquest by the Axumites; the foundation of Constantinople had revived Roman commerce with the East, which had fallen off badly during the troubles of the third century, and Rome's ally Axum was now trading as far afield as Ceylon. The spread of Christianity alarmed the Himyar rulers, who, ill-versed in Christian heresies, probably discerned in the missionaries the crafty agents of Roman and Axumite imperialism. Himyar's last king, Dhu-Nuwas, resolved on desperate measures. He saw that the old paganism was moribund and that his State required a new faith to strengthen its moral basis, but unwilling to adopt the religion of his powerful neighbours, he proclaimed his adhesion to Judaism, possibly at the instigation of his mother, who is said to have been a Jewish slave-girl. He then set to work to root out foreign influences from his kingdom, and a number of Roman and Axumite merchants were put to death. Ela-Asbeha, the king of Axum, resolved to punish this outrage; he landed an army on the Arabian coast, and drove Dhu-Nuwas into the hills. When the invader had re-crossed the seas, the Himyar king reconquered his realm, and wreaked a savage vengeance on the Christians of Najran, who had probably collaborated with the Axumites. Their churches were demolished, and several hundred Najranis, who refused to apostatize, were burnt alive in a trench or moat outside their principal settlement. This occurred in the year 523, and the 'martyrs of Najran' are commemorated in the liturgies of the Greek, Latin and Oriental Churches. This time the Abyssinians determined on a final reckoning, and with some naval help from the Romans, they led a veritable crusade against the persecutor. The Himyarite forces were routed; Dhu-Nuwas perished, and South Arabia was turned into a province of the Axumite monarchy. Thus ended the independence of Arabia Felix.

This was not, however, the end of the story. In circumstances which are obscure, the Axumite commander or viceroy, Abraha, seems to have mutinied against his government and to have set himself up as an independent ruler. For thirty years or more (c.535-570), he was the most powerful man in Arabia. The Emperor Justinian solicited his help in the struggle against Khusrau of Persia, and he was hailed by his co-religionists everywhere as a great Christian champion. He rebuilt the ruined churches, erected a big cathedral at San'a, and in order to open up direct communication with the Mediterranean world, he invaded the Hijaz about 570 and attacked Mecca, the last independent stronghold of Arabian paganism. A hundred legends have gathered round this famous expedition, which is said to have taken place at the time of Muhammad's birth in the 'Year of the Elephant,' so-called because Abraha brought an African elephant with his army, a beast never before used in Arabian warfare. The invasion failed: probably a pestilence destroyed the bulk of the Abyssinian forces and saved the city. Abraha did not long survive this setback; the natives of the Yemen rose in revolt and sought aid from Persia. Khusrau sent a fleet and army, and in 575 the land passed under Persian control. The naval power of the Sassanids was extended to the Straits of Bab al-Mandab, with disastrous consequences to Axum, and Christian hopes of converting all Arabia were blasted. Had Abraha taken Mecca, the whole peninsula would have been thrown open to Christian and Byzantine penetration; the Cross would have been raised on the Kaaba, and Muhammad might have died a priest or monk. As it was, paganism gained a new lease of life, and Christianity was discredited by Abraha's defeat and its association with the Axumite enemy.

The confusion and disorder in the Yemen precipitated the final economic collapse of this once flourishing land, a disaster symbolized by the bursting of the dam of Ma'rib. According to an inscription of Abraha's, the dam was last repaired in 542: soon afterwards its walls must have been finally breached and the waters run to waste. The event was mournfully commemorated in Arabian song and legend. The sixth century has been called the 'Dark Age' of Arabia, because there is evidence of a general movement of population from south to north, marking not on this occasion the spread of urban, civilized life but the reversion of hitherto sedentary tribes to nomadism. Yet this same century saw the birth of Arabic literature, a momentous development apparently associated with the short-lived kingdom of Kinda, which arose in north-central Arabia about 480 and disappeared about 550. The Kinda were former vassals of Himyar from Hadramawt who built up a tribal confederacy stretching from the Rub al-Khali to the fringes of the

14

Syrian Desert. One of their kings, Imr'ul-Kais, was a poet and a patron of poets; his desert court became a literary centre, whose productions attained a wide fame and helped to fix the dialect in which they were composed as the classical tongue of Arabia, as Luther's Bible did for German. Almost every Bedouin tribe had, of course, long had its *sha'ir* or bard, who sang of his people's victories in battle, but this sudden flowering of poetic talent was as unexpected as the appearance in their day of Homer and the Chansons de Geste. These poems, the most famous of which were known as the 'seven golden odes,' give a vivid if idealized picture of desert life, and may have helped to build up something like a national sentiment among the Arabs, a sentiment deepened and intensified by Islam.

This same age is memorable in Arabian history for the bitter duel between the Lakhmids and the Ghassanids, two peoples who had settled respectively on the eastern and the western fringes of the Syrian Desert. The Lakhmids came up from the south into the lower Euphrates valley, were recognized around 300 A.D. as clients by the Persian Government, who employed them to keep the Bedouins of the interior in order, and their camp at Hira grew into a considerable town. As allies or vassals of the Persians, they took part in the incessant wars between Rome and the Sassanids by making destructive raids on Roman Syria. By 500 the imperial government at Constantinople was driven to create a rival Arab power and to entrust the Banu-Ghassan, another southern tribe who had moved northwards into the territory once occupied by the Nabataeans, with the defence of the Syrian frontier. The Ghassanids never completely shed their nomadic habits or reached the level of their Nabataean predecessors; no Petra glorified their reign, and their kings resided, not in city palaces, but in movable camps. Their greatest chief, Harith (Aretas) the Lame, was a contemporary of Justinian, and for forty years (c.529-569) was a loyal ally of Rome. Arabian legend has made much of his lifelong struggle with al-Mundhir of Hira, who captured Harith's son and sacrificed him to his goddess al-Uzza and was at last killed by the bereaved father with his own hands in 554.

Yet both Rome and Persia found these Arab client-States expensive and unreliable. The Ghassanids went the way of the Nabataeans, their principality being suppressed about 584: not long

15

after, Khusrau of Persia about 602 put an end to the Lakhmid regime and installed a Persian governor in Hira. The northern frontiers of Arabia were abandoned to Bedouin licence and anarchy, and at some time during the first decade of the seventh century, in the lifetime of Muhammad, a group of Arab tribes routed a Persian army at Dhu-Kar on the Euphrates. The affair was doubtless a mere skirmish, but was hailed as a great triumph in Arabia, and was well remembered when thirty years later, the Muslim armies marched out to do battle both with the Roman Emperor and the Sassanid Shah.

Arabia's millennium and more of recorded pre-Islamic history ended with the country still on the fringes of civilization. She was no Tibet, shut off from the rest of humanity; foreign influences—Hellenic, Persian, Christian, Jewish—had streamed in, but as yet she had been a mere passive recipient, and had given nothing to the world. Now she seemed to be sinking back into barbarism. The old civilized lands of the south were decayed, depopulated, and under alien domination; their dialects were dying out, and were being replaced by forms of Arabic spoken by the more backward peoples of the north and written in a new script possibly devised by Christian missionaries from Hira. In many regions the pastoral nomad was replacing the townsman and the peasant. What suddenly pulled the Arabs out of themselves and thrust them on the path of world empire was a combination of two factors: the appearance among them of a man of genius, the founder of a new religion, and the mutual exhaustion of their great neighbours in the north, Rome and Persia, who at the end of a war of nearly thirty years (603-629) were utterly incapable of stemming the onrush of the hordes of Islam.

BOOKS FOR FURTHER READING

AIGRAIN, R., Art. 'Arabie' in *Dictionnaire d'histoire et de géographie écclesiastique*, tom. 3, Paris, 1924. The most erudite account of Arabian Christianity.

ARBERRY, A. J. *The Seven Odes*, London, 1957. A translation of and commentary on these famous poems.

DOUGHTY, C., *Arabia Deserta*, Cambridge, 1888. See also *Passages from Arabia Deserta selected by E. Garnett*, 1931. Still the most vivid picture of Bedouin life before the changes of recent years.

DUSSAUD, R., *La pénétration des Arabes en Syrie avant l'Islam*, Paris, 1955. *Encyclopaedia of Islam*, new ed. 1954, arts. 'Djazīrat al-Arab' and 'Badw.'

HOURANI, G. F., *Arab Seafaring in the Indian Ocean*, Princeton, 1951. A good short account of the sea commerce of old Arabia.

O'LEARY, DE L., *Arabia before Muhammad*, London 1927. Now somewhat out-of-date.

PHILBY, H. ST. J., *The Empty Quarter*, London, 1933. The story of the crossing of the Rub al-Khali. All Philby's travel books are worth reading.

ROBERTSON SMITH, *The Religion of the Semites*, Cambridge, 1889. 3rd ed. 1927. A classic on ancient Semitic religion.

ROBERTSON SMITH, *Kinship and Marriage in Early Arabia*, Cambridge, 1903.

ROSTOVTZEFF, M., *Caravan Cities*, Oxford, 1932. A scholarly history of Petra, Palmyra and other desert cities in the light of archaeology.

RYCKMANS, G., *Les religions arabes préislamiques*, Louvain, 1951.

RYCKMANS, J., *L'institution monarchique en Arabie Méridionale avant l'Islam*, Louvain, 1951.

THESIGER, W., *Arabian Sands*, London, 1959.

THOMAS, B., *Arabia Felix*, London, 1932. A brilliant record of travel and exploration in South Arabia.

VIDA, G. DELLA, 'Pre-Islamic Arabia,' in *The Arab Heritage*, Princeton, 1946.

Archaeological work in Arabia is still in its infancy. For some account of what has been done in the South in recent years, see *Archaeological Discoveries in South Arabia*, published by the American Foundation for the Study of Man, Baltimore, 1958.

II

The Prophet

T HE great world faiths may be divided into two groups: the polytheistic religions of India and the monotheistic religions of Western Asia. Hinduism, while postulating the existence of a single divine principle, conceives this principle as personalized in a multiplicity of gods and goddesses; Buddhism, a Hindu heresy, while in theory agnostic about the gods and the human soul, has in its popular forms descended to the level of a crude polytheism. The Indian view has been that the world is *maya*, illusion, and that the wise man must strive to free himself from its enveloping corruption till he attain the bliss of *nirvana*, spiritual serenity. The West Asian religions have, by contrast, envisaged the universe as an absolute monarchy, created and sustained by a single, all-powerful Deity, Ahura-Mazda, Jehovah, God, Allah; they have grappled with but moderate success with the difficulty of reconciling the illimitable might of a just and beneficent God with the existence of manifold evil, and they have all professed belief in a future life, heaven and hell, and a last judgment. The more rigid monotheism of Judaism and Islam has been modified in the religions of Zoroaster and Christ, in the former by a system of dualism, in which the power of Ahriman the Evil One balances that of Ahura-Mazda, in the latter by the conviction that God became incarnate in a man who walked the earth in the days of the Emperor Tiberius. Islam was to carry monotheism to its utmost limits: Allah has no rival and no son, nor are his attributes shared by the members of a Trinity, and the unfathomable gulf between heaven and earth has never for the Muslim been bridged by a God-Man.

Islam was described by Renan as "an edition of Judaism accommodated to Arab minds", but though the Jewish influence is unmistakable, the Christian element can in no wise be disregarded. It is of some significance that the career of Muhammad fell during the period of the great Christological controversies which shook the Church between the Council of Nicaea in 325 and that of Constantinople in 680. The belief that Jesus of Nazareth was God in human form inevitably aroused perplexities which the subtlest theology could scarcely settle; the modes of this union were ardently canvassed, disputes developed into schisms, and the seamless robe of Christianity was rent apart. Arius pronounced the Son inferior to the Father; Nestorius denied that Mary could be the mother of God but only of the man Jesus; the Monophysites (*monos*—one; *phusis* —nature) claimed that the human nature of Christ was wholly absorbed in the divine, and the Monothelites (*thelema*—will) that he possessed but a single divine will. A series of Church Councils condemned these teachings as heretical and cast those who professed them out of the orthodox fold. Two consequences of historical moment followed. First, many heretics sought refuge in Arabia and spread their doctrines there, and secondly, Eastern Christendom was so completely disrupted by these quarrels that it was in no condition to oppose a strong resistance to the forces of Islam.

To describe, still less to account for, the rise of Islam is a matter of peculiar difficulty. Renan's claim that Islam was the only religion to be born in the full light of history can hardly be sustained in view of the fact that we have virtually no contemporary witness. Our knowledge of Muhammad is derived from the Koran, the *hadith* or traditions, and the *sira* or formal biography. Concerning the first, no non-Muslim scholar has ever doubted that it was his personal composition, the revelations he claimed to have received from God during the last twenty years of his life; it is therefore the most authentic mirror of his career and doctrine, but its figurative style, obscure allusions, and uncertain dating of its *suras* or chapters, make it highly unsatisfactory as a biographical source. The second consists of an enormous mass of sayings and stories attributed to the Prophet, and guaranteed by an *isnad*, or chain of witnesses, framed on the pattern: 'I heard from A, who heard from B, who heard from C, that the Prophet said . . .' But memory is fallible, and *isnads* may be forged, and the desire of parties or groups in

19

Mediterranean Sea

° Palmyra

Ctesip

Damascus

BYZANTINE EMPIRE

Syrian Desert

LAKHMIDS

Hira

Euphr

Jerusalem

GHASSANIDS

Mu'ta

Wadi Sirhan

Ka'b

° Dumat-al-Jandal

Petra

Gulf of Akaba

Tabuk

Nufud

Tayma

Daydan °

Jabal Shamm

Khaibar

Uhud

A R

Medina

Badr °

H I J A Z

Red Sea

Hudaibiya

Mecca

Ta'if

KINGDOM

OF

AXUM

Adulis

° Axum

K

Sa

Stra

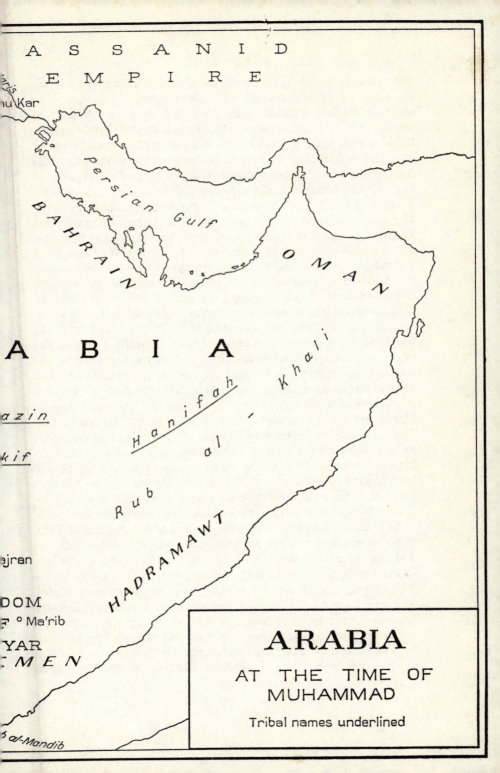

A S S A N I D
E M P I R E

aris
hu Kar

persian Gulf

BAHRAIN

OMAN

A B I A

Hanifah

al - Khali

azin

kif

Rub

HADRAMAWT

ajran

DOM
° Ma'rib

YAR
MEN

ARABIA

AT THE TIME OF
MUHAMMAD

Tribal names underlined

al-Mandib

later years to justify their particular beliefs or practices by citing the authority of Muhammad for them undoubtedly produced an alarming amount of falsification. To base a life of the Prophet on the *hadith* is to build on sand. The *sira* is a more valuable and reliable source, since it gives a full account of Muhammad's career in narrative form, but the earliest of these compositions which has come down to us, the *Sirat Rasul Allah,* or Life of the Apostle of God, by Ibn Ishaq, was put together well over a century after his death, and the portrait is already tinged with miracle and legend. Nor can we rely on foreign witnesses. The records of the Persian kingdom perished in the Arab conquest, and the oldest historical account of Muhammad by a Byzantine Greek is that of the monk Theophanes, who wrote when the Prophet had been dead nearly two hundred years. Every sketch of his life must thus be fragmentary and defective, and the many gaps must be filled by speculation.

Muhammad (the name means 'worthy of praise') was born sometime between 570 and 580, according to tradition in the Year of the Elephant, when Abraha was repulsed from the walls of Mecca. His father Abdallah died before his birth, and his mother when he was six, and the orphan was brought up, first by his grandfather Abd al-Muttalib, and then by his uncle Abu Talib. He grew to manhood the citizen of a flourishing trading community. The early days of Mecca are quite obscure: it was known to the second-century Greek geographer Ptolemy as 'Macoraba', and owed its importance to its position on the incense-road linking the Yemen with the markets of Syria and Iraq and to its sanctuary or Kaaba, which had been erected near a deep well called Zamzam and had long been a place of pilgrimage. Business and religion went hand in hand. The town was built in a narrow, sterile valley, surrounded by bare hills; its food supply was drawn from the gardens and corn-fields of Ta'if, some seventy-five miles to the south-east, and its livelihood depended entirely on the profits of trade and pilgrimage. Its wealth was increasing in the sixth century, perhaps because the decay of the Yemen gave the Meccans a stronger grip on the caravan routes. The people of Mecca claimed descent from a common ancestor Kuraish (Quraysh), and the government of the city was vested in a *mala'* or council, comprising the heads of the leading families. Regular caravans travelled northwards to Damascus and Gaza carrying not only Arabian products like incense but silks from

China, spices from India, and slaves and ivory from Africa. If modern interpretations are correct, rising prosperity was producing a social crisis within the town. The big fortunes made by merchants and bankers roused resentment among the small men, the artisans, craftsmen and poorer shopkeepers, and the old ties of tribal group loyalty were being weakened by the growth of a narrow and selfish individualism.

However this may be, it is certain that Muhammad did not belong to the 'aristocracy' of this commercial republic, but to a socially inferior clan, that of Hashim. He probably accompanied his uncle on trading journeys to Syria: legend later recounted how, on one of these trips, the boy was singled out by a Christian monk named Bahira, who told Abu Talib that his nephew was destined to be a prophet and should be protected against the plots of the Jews. At twenty-five he married a well-to-do widow Khadija, several years his senior, who was in business on her own account and had employed him as her agent. Of the 'hidden years' of Muhammad's youth and early manhood, before his 'call' to prophethood at the age of forty, the compilers of *hadith* and *sira* know no more than the gospel-writers of the early life of Jesus. One anecdote of this time has, however, the ring of truth. Mecca contained a number of pious men who had grown dissatisfied with the existing pagan cults and who, without accepting either Judaism or Christianity, had come to a belief in one God. They were known as *hanifs*. One of them, Zaid b.Amr, once encountered the young Muhammad on the road to Ta'if, and was offered by him some meat which had been sacrificed to idols. The offer was scornfully rejected; Zaid upbraided his companion, and told him decisively: 'Idols are worthless: they can neither harm nor profit anybody.' The words sank deeply into Muhammad's mind. 'Never again', he is reported as declaring, 'did I knowingly stroke one of their idols nor did I sacrifice to them until God honoured me with his apostleship.'

Tradition relates that the call of God came to Muhammad during solitary retreats he was in the habit of making in a cave on Mount Hira, a hill just outside Mecca. He had two dreams or visions of a mighty Being in the sky whom he first identified with God himself but later with the angel Gabriel and who commanded him to recite what all Muslims believe to be the oldest passage of the Koran, the one beginning:

Recite, in the name of the Lord who created

(*Sura* 96; *verse* 1)

At first so terrified that he was driven almost to suicide, he became convinced, perhaps by the assurance and encouragement of his wife, that the experience was a genuine message from heaven, and the visions were followed by a series of auditory 'revelations' which continued at intervals until the end of his life. On such occasions, he was gripped by a kind of ecstasy and the sweat poured from him even on the coldest day, as he uttered the words which (in his conviction) Gabriel ordered him to transmit from God to his people. The earliest revelations appear to have been short sentences or ejaculations in praise of the majesty and unity of God, to whose name the titles of the Compassionate and the Merciful are invariably added, and in warning of the terrors of the Last Judgment, when the earth will give up its dead and the Lord will return to reward and punish each according to his deserts. To escape the divine wrath and eternal fire, the sinner must repent and throw himself upon the mercy of God, a submission (*islam*) which gave its name to the new religion.

Muhammad's message was first communicated to a private circle of relations and friends. Among his earliest converts are reckoned his wife Khadija, his cousin Ali, a son of Abu Talib and then a lad of nine or ten, his closest companion Abu Bakr, an honest and upright merchant of substance, and Othman b.Affan, a member of the powerful clan of Omayya, whose adherence to the new faith was to place his descendants for a hundred years on the throne of the greatest monarchy on earth. But when Muhammad began, perhaps around the year 613, to preach in the streets of Mecca, he was met with scorn and ridicule, which turned to anger on the part of the Kuraish chiefs when his reiterated attacks on idolatry threatened their interests as guardians of the Kaaba. His uncle's protection saved him from personal injury, but some of his followers were reviled and ill-treated, and eighty-three of them, including Othman, crossed the sea and sought temporary asylum in Abyssinia. A powerful recruit was obtained soon afterwards in the person of Omar b. al-Khattab, a vigorous, forthright young man who like St. Paul had once persecuted the faith which finally conquered him. But the generality of Meccans held aloof and scoffed at Muhammad's pretensions. The growing opposition of the pagans depressed him, and led to the strange affair of the 'abrogated verses.' Among the most popular deities of Mecca were three goddesses, al-Lat, Manat and al-Uzza, and the Prophet suddenly announced that he had received a revelation legitimizing their worship. So startling a concession to those whom he had been denouncing as sinful idolators bewildered his disciples and exhilarated his enemies, but after a short interval, he confessed that he had been deceived by Satan into uttering false-hood and that the 'satanic' verses had been cancelled by a genuine revelation confirming the divine unity.

From this time onwards the Kuraish were his sworn foes and his position in Mecca rapidly deteriorated. The deaths of his wife and uncle about 619 left him lonely and defenceless, for the new head of the Hashimite clan, Abu Lahab, withdrew the protection which Abu Talib had conferred on his nephew, and Muhammad could thus be killed or injured without provoking a blood feud. He began to look beyond Mecca, and tried to gain support in Ta'if, but its inhabitants would have none of him. He had better success with some men from Medina, who came to Mecca for the pilgrimage of 620. Medina, whose original name was Yathrib, was a place very different from its sister-city, from which it was separated by a dis-tance of 250 miles. Situated in a fertile oasis, it was largely self-supporting, and took but a small part in commerce. It was at one time under Jewish dominance, but the three Jewish clans—the Nadir, the Kuraiza, and the Kainuka—were now overshadowed by eight Arab clans, of the tribes of Aws and Khazraj. Feuds between these tribes kept the city in a state of tension and disorder, and in 617 or 618 there was a violent battle at a place called Bu'ath. The more responsible citizens were anxious to put an end to these troubles: the most hopeful method, often resorted to in Arabia, was to bring in an arbitrator from outside, who would act as judge and keep the peace. Who better, some of them now asked, than the man in Mecca who was claiming to be a prophet of God? In 620 six men of the Khazraj met Muhammad and professed Islam; the next year five of these returned, bringing with them three of the Aws, and at Akaba, near Mecca, they solemnly pledged themselves to foreswear idolatry. At the pilgrimage of 622 seventy-five Medinans entered into a compact by which they recognized Muhammad as the Apostle of God and promised to defend him as they would their own kin. He was assured of a welcome in their city, and the stage was set for the famous *Hijra,* emigration or withdrawal, which closed the first period of his career.

Had the Kuraish been united and resolute, they could probably have disposed of their disturber. But though the killing of the Prophet was apparently discussed, no course of action was decided on, and in September 622 Muhammad and his loyal friend Abu Bakr slipped quietly out of Mecca, eluded pursuers sent belatedly to capture them, and reached the safety of Medina. Many of his followers, the *Muhajirun* or Emigrants, travelling in small groups, had got there before them. Shortly after his arrival, Muhammad drew up a treaty or constitution (the original text is uncertain, the one we have being a conflate of several documents of different dates) which may be recognized as the earliest sketch of the Islamic theocracy. All Muslims, whether Meccans or Medinans, were to form a single *umma* or community; they were to stand united against unbelievers, and disputes among them were to be referred to 'God and his Apostle.' Such compacts were not unknown in pagan Arabia, but here for the first time loyalty to tribe or political confederacy was replaced by loyalty to a community of religious believers. A distinction, never to be obliterated, was drawn between *Dar al-Islam,* the house or abode of Islam, and *Dar al-Harb,* the abode of war, of those who rejected Allah and his Prophet and were therefore deemed to be in state of enmity with those of the true faith.

Muhammad's position at Medina was for a time uncertain. The Emigrants were probably fitted with some trouble into Medina society; the Medinan converts, the *Ansar* or Helpers, doubtless soon included many who joined the *umma* from interest rather than conviction, and whose loyalty was therefore suspect; the pagans held sullenly aloof, and the Prophet was surprised and irritated to find his claims contemptuously repudiated by the Jews. In Mecca, at the outset of his mission, he perhaps scarcely distinguished between Jews and Christians, but he had gradually acquired an imperfect knowledge of the Bible, and the Koran contains references to Adam and Noah, Abraham and Moses, and the kings of Israel, while a whole *sura* is devoted to the story of Joseph and his brethren. Aware of the existence of prophets among the Jews of old, he conceived of himself as the last of a series of messengers of God, chosen to bring mankind a final and perfect revelation, the completion of the Jewish system. At Mecca he commanded his followers to face Jerusalem when they prayed, and soon after his arrival in Medina he instructed them to observe the Jewish Day of Atonement as a solemn fast. These measures failed to secure for him recognition from the Jews, whose rabbis taunted him with ignorance of their faith, and the Prophet's attitude changed to bitter hostility. The *kibla* or direction of prayer was altered from Jerusalem to Mecca, and for the single day's fast of the Atonement was substituted the month of Ramadan, during which all food and drink was interdicted between the hours of sunrise and sunset. For a time he dissembled his wrath, but the Jews of Medina were destined to pay heavily for their refusal to accept the Koran as the new scripture and himself as the *Rasul Allah* or Apostle of God.

During his early months in Medina, the Prophet was engaged in organizing his community, settling his family (it was at this time that he married A'isha, the daughter of Abu Bakr, and gave Fatima, his own daughter by Khadija, to his cousin Ali), converting the wavering heathen, and silently expanding his civil and religious authority. In Mecca, the Kuraish, relieved at his departure, made no move, but Muhammad was resolved to punish the idolators who had cast him out, and in characterisic Arab fashion he did so by launching a series of *razzias* or raids against their caravans, thereby striking at their principal source of livelihood. A Koranic revelation urged the Muslims to 'contend' with their pagan adversaries, and the word *jihad*, striving or contending, acquired the meaning of 'holy war'. The Prophet's *maghazi* or campaigns opened in January 624 with the ambushing of a caravan at Nakhla, between Mecca and Ta'if, in which one Meccan guard was killed and two captured, a trivial affair which nonetheless caused much searching of conscience among the Muslims because it took place during one of the 'sacred months' when peace was supposed to be observed. The Meccans decided to provide their next caravan with an armed escort of nearly a thousand men; Muhammad was able to collect a bare 300, but he displayed some military skill in forcing the enemy to fight him on ground of his own choosing, at Badr, eleven miles south-west of Medina, and in the skirmish which followed (March 624), although the caravan escaped, the guards were routed, and fifty or more of them were left dead on the field. Islam emerged with surprising success from its first ordeal by battle; the Koran pronounced that the army of unbelievers had been put to flight by

God himself; the victory was compared with the delivery of the children of Israel from Pharaoh; the *umma* was united as never before, Emigrants and Helpers alike having fought and fallen in defence of the Faith; the authority of the Prophet was immensely strengthened, and in later years no Muslim was treated with more respect by his co-religionists than one who could say: 'I was present on the day of Badr!'

Encouraged by this (to him) signal mark of divine approval, Muhammad proceeded to take action against his Jewish critics. The Banu-Kainuka were the first victims; besieged for fifteen days in their fortified quarter of the town, they received no help from their fellow-Jews, and were obliged to surrender. They were driven into exile, and their property, consisting chiefly of armour and goldsmiths' tools, were distributed among the gratified Muslims. Meanwhile, Mecca was plotting revenge for Badr. Her trade was suffering badly, since it was now a hazardous business to send caravans northwards to Syria or Iraq. In March 625 a powerful force of 3000 men, 700 of whom were clad in coats of mail, and 200 of whom were mounted on horseback, set out for Medina, and encamped near Uhud, a hill a few miles from the city. The younger Muslim warriors, eager to repeat the success of the previous year, refused to stand on the defensive and rushed forward to the attack. For a moment, their impetus carried all before it, but the Meccan cavalry, under the command of Khalid b. al-Walid, later to gain fame as the most brilliant of Arab captains, then intervened with decisive effect, and rode down the Muslim infantry. Seventy-four believers (the 'martyrs of Uhud') were killed and Muhammad himself was wounded. Yet the Kuraish strangely enough made no attempt to exploit their victory and capture Medina, but withdrew back to Mecca, perhaps feeling that they lacked the equipment and resources to besiege the town. In so doing, they missed their best chance of crushing Islam in its cradle.

The defeat of Uhud disheartened the Prophet's disciples, who argued that if Badr were a sign of God's favour, this setback must indicate that he was no longer on their side. The skill and statesmanship of Muhammad were equal to the occasion. The Muslims were reassured by a revelation that Uhud was at once a divine punishment for their sins and failings and a test of their faith and steadfastness in adversity. To occupy their minds with other things, the Prophet struck a fresh blow at the Jews, this time at the Banu Nadir, who were ordered to quit Medina within ten days on pain of death. After a brief resistance, the clan gave in, and was permitted to depart for Khaibar, seventy miles to the north, with as much property as they could load upon their camels. To demonstrate that Uhud had not impaired his military strength and perhaps to harass the trading communications of Mecca, he led in 626 an expedition to Dumat al-Jandal, an oasis on the borders of Syria, only five days' march from Damascus, where he may have first envisaged the expansion of Islam beyond the bounds of Arabia. The astonishing march of nearly 400 miles in the hot season must have startled the neighbouring nomads and disinclined them to join the grand alliance which the Kuraish were forming in order to annihilate the power of their adversary.

In all their dealings with Muhammad, the Kuraish displayed neither unity nor energy nor resolution. The situation which confronted them was beyond their experience, and they fumbled helplessly in their efforts to master it. Divided and weak in leadership, sluggish and hesitant in action, and untrained in war, they were perhaps impelled to a supreme attempt by the importunities of the exiled Nadirites at Khaibar, and they at last assembled a force of 10,000 men, probably the biggest force ever seen in Arabia. To this formidable confederacy, Muhammad could oppose only 3,000, comprising nearly all the able-bodied males of Medina. Learning by the example of Uhud, he decided to risk no open battle, but on the advice of a Persian convert, who was familiar with the military techniques of civilized nations, he defended Medina by an earthen trench and rampart, a simple device which baffled the Meccan besiegers when they arrived outside the city in March 627. Even Khalid's cavalry were unable to clear the ditch, and as the Muslims remained entrenched behind their defences, the Kuraish after a fortnight ran short of food and were obliged to retire. With this fiasco, Mecca shot its last bolt. It was clear by now that Muhammad would never be crushed by military force, and unless the Kuraish were prepared to face economic ruin, some kind of accommodation would have to be reached with him.

This final failure sealed the fate of the Banu-Kuraiza, the last remaining Jewish clan in Medina. They had failed to succour their fellow-Jews, but during the siege of Medina their conduct had been ambiguous and suspicious, and the Prophet undoubtedly believed that they had been guilty of treasonable relations with his pagan foes. Blockaded in their quarters, they surrendered unconditionally, and no doubt expected that they would be expelled like the Banu-Nadir. Their old allies, the Aws, pleaded for leniency for them, and the Prophet allowed their punishment to be decided by an Aws chief, Sa'd b.Mu'adh. This man was, however, their bitter enemy, and he decreed that all the men of the clan should be put to death and the women and children sold into slavery. The bloody sentence was instantly executed, and 600 or 700 unhappy Jews were led out in batches and beheaded. Since their treason seems not to have been definitely proved, no act of the Prophet's has been more severely condemned by the opponents of Islam or defended with more embarrassment by his apologists.

Muhammad was now undisputed master of Medina; his prestige was mounting among the Bedouin tribes, and he boldly resolved to make the pilgrimage to Mecca during the sacred month when hostilities were forbidden. Since his break with the Jews, he had come to hold that the religion God had called on him to preach was the same as that revealed in early ages to Abraham, the first true Muslim, and which had been corrupted by the novelties of rabbis and priests. His followers were commanded to face Mecca at prayer because the Kaaba, it appeared, had been built by Abraham and later given over to idol-worship, from which it was now the Prophet's duty to purge it. Mecca and its temple were thus skilfully fitted into the system of Islam, a fact which doubtless did much to placate some of the Kuraish. But for the moment the latter were not minded to permit his entry into the city, and would only consent, by a treaty drawn up in 628 at Hudaibiya, on the outskirts of Mecca, to a ten years' truce and the admission of Medinans as unarmed pilgrims for three days in the ensuing year. These were, however, important concessions: if the Meccans could freely resume their trading journeys without fear of attack, they had been obliged to recognize the political status of their enemy.

War with Mecca having been suspended, the Prophet turned to destroy the last stronghold of Jewry in Western Arabia, that of the wealthy oasis of Khaibar, where the exiled Banu-Nadir were allegedly inciting the neighbouring Arab tribes against the Muslims. As usual, the defence was negligible, and the place was stormed with little loss in the spring of 628. Muhammad used his victory with moderation, the Jews being retained as tenants on their lands, which passed into Muslim ownership. The fall of Khaibar was followed by the capitulation, on the same terms, of the smaller Jewish settlements in the Hijaz. Thus closed a tragic chapter in the history of Arabian Jewry, of a people who had sought refuge in the freedom of a desert land from Babylonian or Roman oppression and who, although removed from the main stream of Judaism, preserved the purity of their faith, whose silent influence, when reinforced by that of Christianity, contributed to the overthrow of the ancient gods of Arabia. Muhammad was deeply impressed by their antiquity, their God, their sacred books, and the ritual of their worship; the Koran abounds in rabbinic lore, and his title of Prophet (*nabi*) is visibly borrowed from the Old Testament. Their repudiation of his claims was perhaps the most grievous disappointment of his life; he was easily persuaded that by their blindness and unbelief they had forfeited the protection of the Almighty, and he could not feel that his mission was safe until these dangerous opponents had been removed from the scene. Had the Jews accepted Islam, they might have become partners with the Arabs in a mighty world empire, but they would have forsworn their past and their principles and have been swallowed up in the *umma* of the Muslim faithful. They chose, not for the first or last time, the path of consistency and danger; they rejected Muhammad as they had rejected Jesus, and were exposed to the eternal enmity of the two religions which had themselves sprung from the soil of Judaism.

When the proper season arrived, Muhammad prepared to accomplish, in accordance with the terms of the treaty of Hudaibiya, the delayed pilgrimage to Mecca. He travelled with a cavalcade of two thousand men; the Kuraish retired to the hills as the Prophet re-entered the city from which he had fled more than six years before; he performed his devotions at the Kaaba, and after instructing the Abyssinian negro Bilal, who regularly filled this office at Medina, to summon the Muslims to worship from the roof of the temple, he conducted a service of prayer and thanksgiving. Resistance to him was crumbling: among the noteworthy new converts at this time was the soldier Khalid, who had routed the Muslims at Uhud, and Amr b.al-As, the future conqueror of Egypt. Tradition recounts that Muhammad had already sent messengers to kings and rulers within his ken urging them to embrace Islam: the kings of Axum and Persia, the governor of Egypt, even the emperor Heraclius himself, are said to have been among the recipients. Did he now envisage Islam as a universal faith, something more than the national religion of the Arabs? It is impossible to be sure, but in the autumn of 629 an expedition, under the command of his adopted son Zaid b.Haritha, was despatched to the Syrian border and was cut to pieces by Roman frontier guards at Mu'ta, a village on the slopes of Hawran. The object of this raid is obscure: perhaps it was designed to secure the submission of the local Arab tribes and unexpectedly ran into a Roman border patrol. At all events, it was the opening shot in the conflict between Christendom and Islam which was to rage throughout the centuries.

Early in 630 Mecca capitulated. Since the failure of the siege of Medina in 627 it had been clear that peace would have to be made with Muhammad, and with the tide now running strongly in favour of Islam, the Kuraish leader, Abu Sufyan, the head of the Omayya clan, undertook to arrange for a peaceful occupation of the city by the Muslims. An army of 10,000 men marched on Mecca; Abu Sufyan offered his submission, and apart from a minor clash, no blood was shed, and the Prophet took possession of his birthplace in placid triumph. He demolished the idols of the Kaaba and dedicated the building afresh to the worship of the one true God. To his former foes he displayed the tact, moderation and humanity of a born statesman, and most of the Kuraish chiefs, who had so bitterly opposed him, were won over to his side. Almost immediately he found himself in the odd position of having to defend Mecca against attack from two tribes, the Hawazin and the Thakif, who were probably alarmed at the growth of this strange new power in Arabia. Khalid won his first victory for Islam when he crushed this confederacy at Hunain, a few miles east of Mecca, a battle which convinced Arabia that resistence to the new religion was vain. Delegations poured into Medina (whither Muhammad returned after the submission of Mecca) from all quarters of the land; the chiefs of distant Oman and Bahrain accepted Islam; even the Persian governor of the Yemen is said to have accorded some form of recognition to the Prophet. The pagans of Ta'if were among the last to give in. They offered to submit if their chief deity, the goddess al-Lat, were spared for three years. 'Three years!' exclaimed Muhammad, 'no, not for a day!' and with a single blow of the axe, the great image was smitten to the ground. Its fall sounded the death-knell of the antique faith of Arabia. At the pilgrimage of 631 the Prophet proclaimed that in future no pagan would be permitted to approach the Kaaba, and a Koranic revelation urged the faithful: 'Fight against them that believe not in God!'

By this time Muhammad had become the dominating power in Arabia. He entered into agreements with all the leading tribes: those who accepted Islam received most favourable treatment, those who were Christians or Jews and wished to remain so were taken under Muslim protection (*dhimma*) and guaranteed security of their goods and property and the free exercise of their religion, on condition that they paid the *jizya,* tax or tribute. Among those who acquired the status of *dhimmis* or protected people were the Christians of Najran, whose annual payment was fixed at 2000 cloth garments. Gradually the Prophet reached out to extend his control over the tribes on the Syrian and Iraqian frontiers, not unaware, in all probability, that such a policy involved the risk of conflict with the Byzantine and Persian Governments. From Persia he had little to fear: in 628 she had sustained a crushing defeat at the hands of Heraclius, and the State was slipping into anarchy and ruin. But Byzantium was a formidable Power, and Heraclius in 630 celebrated his victory over the Persians by replacing the Holy Cross in Jerusalem, this revered relic having been for long in enemy hands. Yet it was at this very moment that Muhammad assembled a great military force of 30,000 men and launched it against Syria with the intention of avenging the affair of Mu'ta in the previous year. It got as far as Tabuk, near the Gulf of Akaba, but no Roman army appeared, the men complained of the heat and difficulties of the campaign, and the Prophet was compelled reluctantly to retire. He had, however, clearly indicated the line of future Arab expansion, and he was sufficiently shrewd to realize that if peace was enforced within his *umma,* the warlike energies of his people must be employed in raids against the neighbouring lands of the north.

In March 632 Muhammad led the *hajj,* or greater pilgrimage to Mecca, commonly called 'the pilgrimage of farewell', for it was to be his last. Every detail of his actions on this occasion was carefully noted and imitated by his disciples: the rites and ceremonies which he had endorsed by his example and presence became standard

Muslim practice. He was now over sixty years of age, and his health was failing. On his return to Medina, he fell ill and requested Abu Bakr to lead the prayers in his place. On June 8, 632, he died in the house of A'isha, the best loved of his wives. The faithful were stricken with grief and incredulity, and the violent and impetuous Omar threatened to cut off the hands and feet of anyone who dared assert that the Prophet was dead. This wild ranting was rebuked by the calm good sense of Abu Bakr, who told the people: 'If anyone worships Muhammad, Muhammad is dead, but if anyone worships God, he is alive and dies not.' As the Prophet left no son or any obvious heir, the question at once arose: who was now to lead his community? An attempt by the *Ansar* to elect one of their number was forestalled: Omar seized the hand of Abu Bakr and called on the people to obey the man whom the Prophet had appointed to lead the prayers in his absence, and the venerable friend of Muhammad, who had rarely left his side, was saluted as the *khalifa* (caliph), vicar or successor of the Apostle of God.

To delineate the character of this extraordinary man is a task of extreme difficulty. No contemporary descriptions have reached us, and the oldest portraits which have survived are hagiographical in tone. We are told that the Prophet had a stately and commanding figure, with sad and piercing eyes, that his manner was normally kind and gentle, that he loved children and animals, that his habits were so simple that even in his last days in Medina, when he governed Arabia, he mended his own clothes and cobbled his own sandals. His piety was sincere and unaffected, and his honest belief in the reality of his call can be denied only by those who are prepared to assert that a conscious impostor endured for ten or twelve years ridicule, abuse and privation, gained the confidence and affection of upright and intelligent men, and has since been revered by millions as the principal vehicle of God's revelation to man. He disclaimed all pretension to sinlessness and miracle-working (when asked for a sign, he pointed to the Koran as the greatest miracle), discouraged superstitious veneration for his person, and insisted, insofar as was compatible with his claim to be the Apostle of God, that he was but a man amongst men.

Yet it would be idle to deny that the Arab prophet has never been viewed with sympathy and favour by Christians whose ideal has naturally been the milder and purer figure of Jesus. The losses which

Islam inflicted on Christendom and the propaganda disseminated during the Crusades were not conducive to an impartial judgment, and down almost to recent times Muhammad has been portrayed in controversial literature as a lying deceiver and a shameless lecher. Absurd stories were circulated and long believed, such as that he trained a dove to pick seeds of corn from his ear so as to persuade the people that he was receiving communications from the Holy Ghost, and that his iron coffin at Mecca (he was really buried at Medina) was suspended in midair by the action of powerful load-stones! To the charges that he 'induced' revelations to suit his purposes, that he propagated his creed by the sword, and that he used religion as a cloak for the satisfaction of his sensual desires, reasonably convincing answers may be returned. Our modern psychologists, who have explored the dark recesses of the human mind or rather of the unconscious, are slow to question the integrity of men of the type of Muhammad. Notwithstanding his war with Mecca, which was in the ancient tradition of Arab tribal conflict, he never countenanced the forcible conversion of Christians or Jews, and laid it down as a principle that 'there is no compulsion in religion,' in consequence of which Islam has been, on the whole, one of the most tolerant of creeds. The fiercest censure has been reserved for his sexual conduct, but it may be observed that so long as Khadija lived, he took no other wife, and that of the ten or twelve women he subsequently married, the majority were widows whose husbands had fallen in his cause and for whom he might feel obliged to provide. The four lawful wives permitted to the Muslim believer is, in fact, a restriction on the licence of pagan Arabia, which set no legal limits of polygamy. Yet his love of women is not denied by his biographers, and his personal preferences are artlessly revealed in the Koranic picture of a paradise where the pious faithful are refreshed with delicious fruits and caressed by *huris,* black-eyed girls of eternal youth and beauty.

The religious system which he constructed was the purest and most uncompromising monotheism. Islam rests upon 'five pillars,' the *shahada,* or profession of faith, 'There is no god but God and Muhammad is his Apostle,' the *salat,* or daily worship, ultimately fixed at five prayers, the *sawm,* or fast of Ramadan, the *zakat,* or alms, one-tenth of the believer's income being payable to charitable purposes and the *hajj,* or pilgrimage to Mecca, to be undertaken at least once in a lifetime. His God is an almighty Creator, an arbitrary though merciful despot, who has revealed himself to man successively through the *Tawrat*, or law of Moses, the *Zabur*, or psalms of David, the *Injil*, gospel or evangel of Jesus, and finally and completely through the Koran of Muhammad. Allah, the embodiment of mighty will rather than of moral righteousness, demands no sacrifice or atonement for sin; no mediator, redeemer or saviour interposes between him and man, and Islam knows no sacraments or priesthood. Jesus is venerated as a noble prophet, miraculously conceived and endowed with the power of raising the dead to life, but the crucifixion is a myth, a substitute having been nailed to the cross in his place, and on the Day of Judgment he will repudiate those who have perversely treated him as divine.

At Medina Muhammad was, like Moses, at once prophet, prince and legislator. The distinction between civil and religious authority was unknown in the Semitic East, and the Koran is both a body of doctrine and a code of regulation. The life of the Muslim, like that of the Jew, was guided by the Law (*shari'a,* or path), which being divinely revealed, could never be repealed or modified, and the reforms which the Prophet enacted in the name of Allah in seventh-century Arabia, are now, thirteen centuries later, a hindrance to the progress of the Muslim nations. The withdrawal of liberty of divorce from women and the use of the veil might be calculated in their day to raise the level of public morality, but they have survived into a different age, along with such ancient institutions as concubinage and slavery, which also received the sanction of the Koran.

The inquirer who seeks an explanation of the great revolutions of history is often driven to attach almost equal weight to the personalities of the leading actors and the peculiar circumstances of their time, which favoured the fullest deployment of their talents, and he may well accept the conclusion, that vast changes are produced neither by the operation of blind forces nor by the genius and will of great men, but by a subtle and unpredictable combination of the two. Without Muhammad, there would have been no Arab Empire; yet in a different age and situation, the Prophet of Islam might have lived and died in impotent obscurity. Had he been born a century earlier, the powerful empire of Justinian would have opposed an impenetrable barrier to the onrush of the Arab hordes: had he flourished a century later, Arabia might have already accepted the Christian faith and the realms of Caesar and Khusrau might have recovered from the effects of their mutual antagonism. His lot was cast in a period most fortunate for the realization of his hopes, and his success was assured by the social unrest of Mecca, the civil strife of Medina, the ruin of the Himyar kingdom of the south, the defeat of Abraha and the decay of the military strength of Axum, the familiarity of his countrymen with the idea of one God, the prostration of the Sassanid monarchy and the exhaustion of the Roman Empire, whose power was sapped by religious discord, the withdrawal of the Syrians and Egyptians from active loyalty to the imperial government, and the strains and losses of the Persian wars. Yet the man is not dwarfed by these events: he towers above his countrymen and contemporaries as a religious genius and a practical statesman, and his creations, more enduring than bronze, have survived the vicissitudes of the thirteen centuries and been adapted to the style and requirements of people he never knew. In the wider perspectives of universal history, we may discern in Muhammad, the greatest of the sons of Ishmael, the belated response of the restless and long-submerged East to the challenge of Alexander; the Greek tide, which had overspread these lands for a thousand years, was rolled back, Christianity from Mesopotamia to Morocco was levelled to the status of a despised and tolerated sect, and Islam, the executioner of Hellenism, broke forever the unity of the Mediterranean world.

BOOKS FOR FURTHER READING

ANDRAE, TOR, *Mohammed, the Man and his Faith*, London, 1936. A subtle and illuminating character study.

BLACHÈRE, RÉGIS, *Le Problème de Mahomet*, Paris, 1952. A brief but interesting analysis.

BUHL, FRANTS, *Das Leben Mohammeds*, Leipzig, 1930. The standard modern life, originally published in Danish in 1903. There is no English translation, but a summary of Buhl's views may be found in his article 'Muhammad' in the *Enc. of Islam*.

MUIR, SIR WILLIAM, *The Life of Mohammed*, 4 vols. 1858-61; revised ed. one vol. Edinburgh, 1912. Now rather antiquated, but still the fullest biography in English. Strongly Christian in tone.

THE PROPHET

WATT, W. MONTGOMERY, *Muhammad at Mecca*, Oxford 1953; *Muhammad at Medina*, Oxford, 1956. The most recent treatment, with special emphasis on the social and economic background. Dr. Watt has published a shortened version of these two books under the title *Muhammad Prophet and Statesman*, Oxford, 1961.

For Muhammad's debt to Judaism, see C. C. Torrey, *The Jewish Foundation of Islam*, New Haven, 1933; for his debt to Christianity, see R. Bell, *The Origin of Islam in its Christian Environment*, London, 1926 and Tor Andrae, *Les Origines de l'Islam et le Christianisme*, Paris, 1955.

TRANSLATED SOURCES

THE KORAN. There are translations by Sale, Rodwell, Palmer, Bell, Pickthall and Dawood. Perhaps the best is Arberry's *The Koran Interpreted*, London, 1955.

IBN ISHAQ, *The Life of Muhammad*, tr. A. Guillaume, Oxford, 1955. The oldest surviving biography, composed by a man who died in Baghdad in A.D. 768.

For a general view of the *hadith*, see A. Guillaume, *The Traditions of Islam*, Oxford, 1924.

III

The First Conquests

THE creation within the space of a single century of a vast Arab
Empire stretching from Spain to India is one of the most extraordinary marvels of history. The speed, magnitude, extent and permanence of these conquests excite our wonder and almost affront our
reason, but the historian who seeks to explain them is impeded by
the deficiency of the evidence at his disposal. Few revolutions of
such gigantic import are worse documented: the conquerors were
an unlettered people; the archives of Persia perished in the general
ruin of the Sassanid State, and the Greek side of the story is revealed
only in chronicles put together nearly two centuries after the irrup-
tion of Islam into the eastern provinces of Byzantium.

In a general view, the Arab conquests may be conceived as the
southern counterpart of the Germanic invasions which in the fifth
century overwhelmed the power of Rome in the lands of the West.
In each case the imperial defences were shattered by the powerful
assault of a barbarian foe, and the Empire was shorn of vast territories, on which, after a long and painful interval, a new social order
was constructed out of the wreckage of the old. There was, however,
one fundamental contrast between these two attacks on Greco-
Roman civilization. The German peoples entered the Roman world
either as pagans, like the Franks and Anglo-Saxons, or as Christians,
like the Goths and Vandals; all were in the end gathered into the
fold of the Catholic Church, and the Roman and the Teuton, the
conquered and the conquerors, combined to produce the Christian
society of the Middle Ages. The Arabs broke into the Empire neither
as pagans nor Christians, but as the adherents of a new religion,

39

which imposed an insurmountable barrier between themselves and their opponents; the Arabic language, raised by the Prophet to the exalted status of the vehicle of divine revelation, triumphed over every other tongue in the lands where Islam gained a footing, and a new and distinct Muslim culture and pattern of society emerged to challenge the beliefs and values of Christendom.

According to the pious convictions of the Arabs, their victories and conquests were attributable to the aid and favour of God, whose divine interposition scattered the armies of the infidels and bestowed the most fruitful lands of the earth upon his loyal and zealous people. Modern historians seek more mundane explanations, but they are at variance concerning the relative weight to be attached to religious and secular causes. By some the Arabs are envisaged as fanatical devotees of the new faith, riding forth from their deserts resolved to carry the message of their Prophet to all mankind, their natural courage in battle stiffened by the belief that the soul of the believer who fell fighting for Islam was instantly conveyed to paradise. By others they are depicted as animated chiefly by the lure of plunder and booty and goaded by the prick of poverty and hunger: a desiccated peninsula, it is suggested, could no longer support a growing population, and shortage of food and grazing-land was more potent than the mandates of Allah. It is reasonable to assume that Islam supplied an element of cohesion, a stimulus which welded a congeries of tribes into a nation, and gave them a drive and unity they would not otherwise have possessed; it is also reasonable to hold that the conquests would not have been launched but for the peculiar situation in which the Muslim leaders found themselves on the morrow of the Prophet's death and would not have encountered so little resistance but for the political and religious weaknesses of the rival Great Powers of Byzantium and Persia.

The death of Muhammad threatened the dissolution of the Muslim community. The submission of the intractable Bedouins to him had been extorted by a mixture of fear and superstition; their pride and independence were injured by the exaction of tribute under the name of alms and by the obligation of systematic religious worship; their nomadic instincts recoiled at the prospect of being subordinated to the men of Medina, and as soon as they learnt that the Prophet was no more, tribe after tribe proclaimed that their compact

with him, being of a personal nature, was now ended and they refused allegiance to his successor Abu Bakr, in whose election they
had had no part. This repudiation is known as the *Ridda* or Apostasy, though in fact many of the tribes involved had never formally
adopted Islam. Some had listened to the teaching of rival prophets,
of whom several appeared in the last year or two of Muhammad's
life, among them one Musailima, who won a large following in the
powerful tribe of Hanifa in central Arabia. Had the disaffected tribes
made a concerted attack on Medina, Islam would probably have
been destroyed. But united action of this kind was not in their line,
and Abu Bakr in this crisis displayed all the marks of a cool and
vigorous leader. His powers as Caliph were new and undefined; he
would not claim any religious authority, believing as he did that the
stream of divine revelation had ceased with the death of Muhammad, but he was prepared, like a tribal shaikh, to assume responsibility for the military defence of his community. Summoning all
able-bodied Muslims to take up arms against the rebels, he divided
them into eleven columns, and entrusted each with the subjugation
of a particular region, the redoubtable Khalid being given command
of the expedition against Musailima and the Banu-Hanifa. For several months there was fighting over the greater part of Arabia; at last
unity triumphed over discord, and the victory of Khalid at Akraba
in 633, where the Banu-Hanifa were crushed and the 'false prophet'
Musailima killed, established for all time the dominance of Islam
in the land of its birth. Following the example of the Prophet, Abu
Bakr treated with leniency those who submitted, and dismissed them
as reconciled brothers of Islam.

The *Ridda* is connected by a clear chain of cause and effect with
the launching of the mighty offensive which in two or three generations left the vicars of the Prophet the masters of a world empire.
To overcome a perilous defection, the Caliph and his associates
were obliged to raise and equip a more numerous military force than
Arabia had yet seen; in the hazards of domestic war, its commanders grappled with problems of strategy and tactics, transport and
communication, supply and discipline, of a magnitude undreamt of
by the chiefs of the petty kingdoms of old, and they were eager and
qualified, when the rebellion was over, to employ their talents on a
wider theatre. When the last insurgents had surrendered, Arabia
was an armed camp, yet Abu Bakr could not be insensible to the

dangerous instability of the situation. His punitive columns had penetrated every quarter of the land; the last remnants of idolatry were extirpated, but the defeated tribes were sullen and resentful, the natural turbulence of the Bedouins might easily reassert itself, and the unity of Islam might be imperilled by the revival of ancient feuds and jealousies. To attach the recent, tepid and unstable converts to the cause of Islam by powerful and permanent interest, to seek a safe outlet for the Bedouin passion for war and rapine, to remove from the land dangerous, restless and possibly disloyal elements, and to unite the nation in a common enterprise under the banner of the Faith, was a policy clearly dictated by the exigencies of the internal situation. In the summer of 633 the momentous decision was taken to employ the armies which had overcome the apostates in a continuation on a larger scale of the raids which the Prophet had inaugurated on the northern borders. That the raids developed into conquests was most probably a surprise to the Arabs themselves and was certainly a proof of the disunity and feebleness of their civilized neighbours.

Of the two Empires of Byzantium and Persia, the latter was by far the more vulnerable. Shaken by its defeat at the hands of Heraclius, its throne the sport of a dozen competitors, its army and administration disorganized, the Sassanid State was in no condition to cope with a violent assault from the Arabian deserts. The Zoroastrian State Church was disliked by the non-Persian minorities. The peasants were oppressed by heavy taxation and the exactions of their landlords. The long war with Rome, which had dragged on from 603 to 628, had exhausted the nation. Social discontent was widespread: a hundred years earlier a religious communist named Mazdak had acquired a large following by urging the poor to plunder the rich, and it is possible that the movement he set on foot had never been completely suppressed but had gone underground. The capital and centre of government was at Ctesiphon in Iraq, a province whose population was mainly Semitic, and where no national Persian resistance to an invader could be expected. The Byzantine or East Roman Empire was a much stronger edifice. Its army and civil service had inherited the traditions of old Rome; the power of the urban middle class balanced that of the landed aristocracy; its capital Constantinople was virtually impregnable; its navy controlled the Mediterranean; and it had emerged the victor in its recent struggle with its deadly rival. But the Persian war had stretched its resources to their utmost limit; it was faced by the aggressions of the Slavs and Avars in the Balkans and the Lombards in Italy, and its authority over the provinces of Syria and Egypt had been undermined by the temporary Persian occupation and the persistent religious strife between the Chalcedonians and the Monophysites. During the few years that the Persians were in possession of Rome's eastern lands, the Monophysite heretics had enjoyed toleration: when the imperialists came back, they restored the Orthodox Church and embarked on a ruthless persecution of the Copts and Jacobites. To add to the disorder and confusion, there was a violent outburst of anti-Semitism in Palestine, the Jews being accused of having worked for the Persians and betrayed Jerusalem to them in 616, when the Holy Cross was carried off to Ctesiphon. Never was the imperial government more unpopular with its Syrian and Egyptian subjects than it was on the eve of the Arab invasions.

One thing could have blocked the path of Islam in the Near East: the existence of a Syriac-speaking national Church. Had the Semitic peoples who resented and resisted the domination of the Christian Church by the Greeks, united in a strong community, they might never have abandoned their ancestral faith and turned Muslim. But non-Hellenic Christianity was sharply divided between the Monophysites and the Nestorians, who shared indeed a common language but who detested each other as heretics worse than the Greeks. The majority of the inhabitants of Egypt, Syria and Armenia clung to the Monophysite creed, but the Christians of Iraq were mostly Nestorian and during the Persian occupation of the Yemen their co-religionists had probably got control of the Monophysite churches in Arabia and imposed on them their particular beliefs. This fatal schism divided and weakened the Christianity of the East in the face of Islam and in time reduced it to the pathetic fragments which alone survive today.

Early in 634 Abu Bakr issued the summons to a holy war, and in his speech to the eager volunteers who answered it, he told them (if he be truly reported) to do no harm to women, children and old people, to refrain from pillage and the destruction of crops, fruit-trees, flocks and herds, and to leave in peace such Christian monks and anchorites as might be found in their cells. The army was divided into three corps, commanded respectively by Amr b.al-As,

Shurahbil b.Hasanah, and Yazid, the son of Abu Sufyan, whose instructions were to advance into Syria. Another force under the great Khalid was sent to raid lower Iraq, where it routed a small Persian detachment and received the submission of the Arab Christians of Hira. Amr entered Palestine and near Gaza cut to pieces a local body of Roman troops under the governor Sergius. Realizing that Heraclius would soon understand that this was no mere Bedouin raid but a full-scale attack and that he would order the main imperial army into action against the invaders, Abu Bakr instructed Khalid to move the bulk of his troops from Iraq to Syria. After an extraordinary march across almost trackless and waterless desert, Khalid suddenly descended into the vale of Damascus and effected a junction with his colleagues. Heraclius, who was at Emesa in northern Syria and in ill-health, sent his brother Theodore with a large army which caught up with the intruders at Ajnadain, some twenty miles west of Jerusalem, where Khalid's skill and valour inflicted on it a decisive defeat (July or August 634). The discomfited imperialists retired into the fortress of Jerusalem; the stronghold of Gaza, cut off from all succour, was obliged to surrender; the victorious Arabs roamed freely over Palestine, and by Christmas the Patriarch Sophronius was lamenting that owing to the insecurity of the roads, the customary pilgrimages to Bethlehem could not take place.

The news of the victory of Ajnadain cheered the last days of Abu Bakr, who died a few weeks later (August 23) in the sixty-third year of his age. Wiser than his master, he dictated on his death-bed, with the concurrence of his associates, a statement naming Omar as his successor. 'None of my own kin have I chosen,' he told the people, 'but Omar. I have tried to choose the fittest: do you obey him loyally.' His last words were: 'Let me die a true believer!' The memory of the first Caliph was always cherished by the faithful as a man of simple loyalty and gentle kindliness, whose steadfast calm was never ruffled by the most furious gale. His reign was short but its achievements were momentous: his cool firmness surmounted the crisis of the *Ridda* and reclaimed the Arabian nation for Islam, and his resolve to subjugate Syria laid the foundation of the Arab world empire.

Omar's accession to power appears to have been unchallenged either by Ali or by the *Ansar*. The new Caliph, whose career and conversion have been likened to St. Paul's, is a classic example of the persecutor turned zealot. Ardent, loyal and impulsive, he won the esteem of Muhammad, who married his daughter Hafsa and is said to have observed that if God had willed there should be another Prophet after him, Omar would have been he. He rose to prominence without any advantage of birth (for his clan, the Banu-Adi, were among the meanest in Mecca) or of military valour, for although he was present at Badr and Uhud, tradition ascribes no deeds of fighting prowess to him. He made his mark by sheer force of will, shrewd judgment of men and motives, and a political acumen which rendered his counsel invaluable in times of crisis or difficulty. Abu Bakr relied on him implicitly, and Omar never failed to treat the elder man with respectful deference. On succeeding to the leadership of the *umma,* he proposed at first to style himself 'Caliph of the Caliph of the Apostle of God', but this clumsy title was soon dropped, and to the simple and single name he later added the designation *Amir al-Mu'minin,* Commander of the Faithful, which continued to be borne by his successors down to the last age of the Caliphate. In the Arabic language, the word *amir* signifies military command, and the Prophet's deputy might now be considered the supreme overlord of a rapidly expanding realm. As such his government insensibly acquired a more secular and military character, which foreshadowed the monarchy of the Omayyads. The decade of Omar's rule (634-644) is the most glorious in the annals of the Arabs: Egypt and Syria submitted to their arms, and they overturned with miraculous ease the empire of the Sassanids. The responsibilities of office sobered Omar's impetuous character and brought out the full quality of his statesmanship, for the soldier must be followed by the administrator and to the second Caliph fell the task of deciding on what principles the conquered territories were to be governed.

The Roman defeat at Ajnadain left the open country of Palestine and Syria exposed to the Arab invaders. Ignoring strongly fortified places like Caesarea and Jerusalem, they moved swiftly northwards, compelled Heraclius to fall back from Emesa to Antioch, and laid siege to Damascus, which, isolated in the desert, was obliged after six months (March—September 635) to capitulate from lack of food. The treaty which Khalid concluded with the Damascenes is typical of the arrangements that were to be made by the score in many different lands during the next decades. 'This is the treaty which Khalid b.al-Walid makes with the people of Damascus, on his entry into the town. He assures to them their lives and goods, their churches and the walls of their town. No house will be pulled down or taken away from its owner. To guarantee this, he takes God to witness and promises them the protection of the Prophet, of his successors and of the faithful. He will do no ill to them, so long as they pay the tribute.' In this way the Arabs managed to create the impression that they were warring only with the Greeks and their Emperor: the native Syrians, Christians and Jews, were freed from Orthodox persecution, regained their religious liberty, and felt no desire for a restoration of imperial rule. As a Nestorian bishop put it: 'The Arabs to whom God has in our day accorded the dominion, have become our masters, but they do not war against the Christian religion, rather they protect our faith, respect our priests and holy men and make gifts to our churches and convents.'

After strenuous exertions, Heraclius assembled at Antioch an army drawn from the depots and garrison-centres of Asia Minor and reinforced by contingents from Armenia and the Christian Arab tribes of Syria. With this he hoped to clear the 'desert vermin' out of his dominions, and in face of this threat, Khalid prudently withdrew to the south, abandoning even Damascus, and fell back to the line of the Yarmuk, a stream which flows into the Jordan a few miles south of the Sea of Galilee. From this position the Arabs could maintain communication with Medina, receive fresh supplies of men and arms, and in case of defeat, slip back into the recesses of the desert. They were heavily outnumbered, but the morale of their opponents was low. The Emperor's bad health prevented him from taking personal command of the army, which no doubt weakened its spirit, and there were quarrels and dissensions among the various nationalities which composed it. At the banks of the Yarmuk, on a hot summer's day (August 20, 636), as a strong south wind blew clouds of dust and sand into the faces of the imperialists, Khalid ordered the attack, and to the cry of 'Paradise is before you, the devil and hellfire are behind you!' Islam's warriors threw themselves on the unbelievers. The enemy lines wavered and broke; the cavalry galloped off across the plains, while the infantry fell victims to the deadly Arab lances, and the rocky defiles of the river were choked with their corpses. When the tidings of the disaster reached Antioch, the sick Emperor abandoned the struggle in despair, and returned to Constantinople. Syria was irretrievably lost on the day of Yarmuk; town after town was occupied without resistance, and within a few months the conquered province, in Khalid's words, 'sat as quiet as a camel.'

The victory of Yarmuk brought Omar himself into Syria to settle the innumerable problems connected with the civil government of the land which the Arabs had often raided but had now conquered. Leaving Ali in charge of affairs in Medina, the Caliph proceeded to Jabiya, the base in the Hawran from which the military operations had been conducted. His first step was to remove Khalid from his command and to appoint Abu Ubaida, a close friend of his who had distinguished himself in the campaign, as viceroy or governor. The dismissal of the great general, the 'Sword of God' as Muhammad had called him, on the morrow of his most brilliant victory, wears the appearance of gross ingratitude, but it would seem that Khalid had a bad reputation for cruelty and corruption, and Omar, a man of rigid honesty, was resolved to enforce the highest standards from his subordinates. He next framed a series of fiscal regulations designed to provide an adequate revenue for the State without oppressing and alienating a nation of cultivators and citizens upon whose continued goodwill the conquerors must depend. The custom of the Prophet condemned the enemies of Islam, who had been overcome by force of arms, to the forfeiture of all their rights and possessions: one-fifth of the spoil was set aside for the service of God and the *umma,* and the rest, whether land, captives or chattels, was divided among the Muslim warriors. Omar forbade, however, his soldiers to acquire landed property outside Arabia, confined them in time of peace to military camps or cantonments where their intercourse with the natives was reduced to a minimum, and in lieu of the booty of war, assigned them fixed pensions from the public treasury. The landowner or peasant was relieved of the fear of lawless extortion or confiscation by the levying of a regular *kharaj,* a tax in money or kind, graded according to the productivity of his fields; the crown lands, forests, wastes, and the estates of landlords and officials who had fled before the conquerors, property styled *fay',* were treated as the domain of the State, whose rents were paid into the exchequer, and the non-Muslim was probably exempted from military service and accorded protection of life, goods and religion by the payment of the *jizya,* or tribute. In this way the new Islamic

State defrayed the growing expenses of its administration and met the cost of the pensions which partly silenced the murmurs of an army of nomads deprived of its ancient and traditional claim to the spoils of conquest. The Jabiya ordinances are evidence of a shrewd and enlightened mind, and Omar saw to it that as little interference as possible was made in the life of the country. The existing civil service, with its records and registers, was preserved, and Greek continued to be for more than fifty years the language of the administration.

While Omar was at Jabiya, he received the gratifying news that Jerusalem was prepared to surrender on condition that he came in person to accept its submission. The city had been blockaded for many months and had lost all hope of relief. To the pious Muslim it was a spot scarcely less holy than Mecca or Medina, for it had been the first *kibla* of Islam and the scene of the *mi'raj,* the supposed journey of the Prophet to heaven as related in the Koran and embellished by tradition.[1] Omar set out with lively emotions, and his visit to Jerusalem was the most dramatic event of his life. He was received by the Patriarch Sophronius, who had been given charge of the city by Heraclius and whom the Caliph greeted with the courtesy of an Arab gentleman. He was shown round the sites and streets associated with the life of Jesus: it is said that as he and the Patriarch stood together in the Church of the Resurrection, Sophronius muttered, in the words of the Prophet Daniel: 'The abomination of desolation standeth in the holy place!' On the spot where Solomon's temple was believed to have stood, the Muslims later erected the splendid mosque called either the Dome of the Rock[2] or the

---

[1] The *mi'raj,* or ascent of Muhammad to heaven, is based on the passage in the Koran (17: 1): 'Praise to him who travelled in one night with his servant from the Masjid al-Haram to the Masjid al-Aksa, whose surroundings we blessed, in order to show him our signs.' Masjid al-Haram ('sacred mosque') is the Kaaba at Mecca, and Masjid al-Aksa ('the farthest mosque') is traditionally said to be Jerusalem, though it is possible that the identification had not been made so early as Omar's time. Two miracles or legends, the Ascent and the Night Journey, were combined: the Prophet was supposed to have been carried in one night on a mysterious animal called the Burak from Mecca to Jerusalem, from which he was caught up into the seventh heaven and appeared before the throne of God. See the article 'Mi'rādj' in the *Enc. of Islam.*

[2] So-called from the rock sixty by fifty feet in extent and rising to a height

Mosque of Omar. To them Jerusalem was never known by any other name than *al-Kuds*, 'the Holy (City)'.

Jerusalem most probably fell at the end of 637 or the beginning of 638. Less than ten years before, Christendom had rejoiced in the recovery of the city from the Persian fire-worshippers: now it had been lost again, this time to the 'Ishmaelites.' Heraclius nerved himself to a last effort. In 638 he issued a theological edict called the *Ecthesis*, in which he tried to win back the loyalty of the Monophysites by proclaiming that Christ had a single will, though not a single nature, and he landed some troops by sea on the Syrian coast near Antioch. Omar sent Abu Ubaida to drive them out, a task he accomplished with little trouble. In the same year Caesarea, the last remaining Roman fortress in Palestine, fell to the Arabs, in consequence, it was said, of the treachery of a Jew, who revealed to the besiegers an entrance through a disused aqueduct. With this the Syrian war ended, but the rejoicings of the Muslims were soon quenched by a dreadful outbreak of bubonic plague which claimed 25,000 victims. Among those who died was Abu Ubaida, who was widely thought to have been chosen by Omar as his successor. Had Abu Ubaida lived to reign as the third Caliph, in place of the weak and vacillating Othman, the Arab Empire might have escaped the strife and bloodshed into which it was plunged when the strong hand of Omar was removed. To supply his place as governor of Syria, Omar selected the Omayyad Mu'awiya, the younger brother of Yazid, who had also died of the plague, and that able and ambitious statesman entered upon the career which in little more than twenty years was to raise his family to the lordship of the Muslim world.

The conquest of Syria ran parallel with that of Iraq, the most westerly province of the kingdom of Persia. The anarchy into which the Sassanid realm had fallen after the defeat and death of Khusrau Parves in 628 had been partially overcome by the elevation to

---

of five feet above the ground, over which the building was erected. Innumerable Jewish, Christian and Muslim legends are associated with this rock. A Muslim belief is that it is the rock from which Muhammad ascended to heaven: it tried to follow him, but was restrained by the angel Gabriel, and remained suspended in mid-air. This is probably the source of the tale that Muhammad's *coffin* was so suspended by means of powerful magnets! See p. 35.

the throne in 632 of his grandson Yazdegerd, a boy of eleven and the last surviving male of the reigning house, but only a long period of peace could have restored the health of the enfeebled State, whose weakness was well known to the Arabs. Within a year of Yazdegerd's accession, the Arab invasion began. The attackers were led by Muthanna, a Bedouin chief of the Bakr tribe who had reclaimed Bahrain from the apostasy of the *Ridda* and whose racial pride and ambition were perhaps stimulated by the memory of the day of Dhu-Kar some twenty or thirty years before. After advancing along the shores of the Persian Gulf, he was joined by Khalid, and together they routed a mixed force of Persians and Christian Arabs at Ullais, a victory stained by a brutal butchery of prisoners. This was followed by the capitulation of Hira, on the lower Euphrates and once the centre of a Christian border kingdom, and of the fortress of Anbar, halfway up the river. From this point the invaders were in a position to threaten Ctesiphon, a few miles away across the Tigris, but at this crucial juncture Khalid was called away to take charge of the Syrian war, and Muthanna's depleted forces were inadequate to deal with a vigorous Persian counter-offensive led by the Sassanid general Rustam. Near the ruins of Babylon he fell upon the Arabs striving to cross the river; the Persian elephants spread terror among the Arab cavalry, and 'the Battle of the Bridge' (November 634), as it was styled, ended in a disastrous setback to the Muslims, Muthanna receiving wounds of which he soon afterwards died.

It was a mark of Omar's statesmanship that he refused to permit any steps to be taken to avenge this defeat so long as the issue of the Syrian war remained in doubt, but once the resistance of the Greeks had been finally broken at the Yarmuk, the Caliph called for a holy war against the Persian infidels and gave the command to Sa'd b. Abi Wakkas, a seasoned warrior who had fought at Badr and Uhud. Rustam marched out of Ctesiphon and met the new invading army on the plain of Kadisiya, near Hira: the battle, which was probably fought in the spring of 637, lasted four days and resulted in an overwhelming Arab victory, largely because the Arab archers had discovered how to deal with the Persian elephants by firing at their eyes and trunks. Rustam was killed; the wreck of his army retreated on Ctesiphon, but the capital was ill-fitted to stand a siege; the young king and his court fled to Hulwan, in the Zagros mountains, and the Arabs occupied almost without opposition one of the finest cities in Asia. The untutored Bedouins revelled in a fairyland of riches, gold and silver, silks and jewels; in their ignorance they mistook sacks of camphor for salt and were astonished at its bitter taste, and the story goes that a tribesman who sold a jacinth for a thousand dirhams, on being asked why he did not demand more for it, replied that he was unaware that there was a bigger number than a thousand! Sa'd pursued the enemy across the Tigris, beat a new hastily levied Persian force at Jalula, and drove Yazdegerd from Hulwan. His advance had carried him beyond Iraq, and he asked Omar's permission to press forward into the heart of the Persian kingdom and attack the rich but distant province of Khurasan. The Caliph, whose judgment was not impaired by these dazzling victories, wisely forbade a campaign in the mountainous country beyond Iraq, where the Muslims might be trapped in a hostile environment far from their bases, and he shrewdly suspected that to conquer the Iranian plateau, whose inhabitants would oppose a national resistance to the Arabs, would be a much tougher task than the subjugation of Iraq, a Semitic province which had never displayed intense loyalty to the Sassanids. Disturbed at the possible demoralizing effect on his people of the wealth of Ctesiphon, he ordered the bulk of the Arab army to be concentrated in two cantonments in lower Iraq, at Basra and Kufa, camps which in a few years grew into populous cities.

Kadisiya had done for Iraq what the Yarmuk had done for Syria, and the short pause which now ensued before Medina decided whether or not to attempt the total destruction of the Sassanid monarchy was filled by the conquest of a third land, that of Egypt. Throughout the greater part of recorded history, the fortunes of Egypt and Syria have been commonly linked, and the Persians themselves had recently shown how easy it was, from bases in Syria, to seize the valley of the Nile. The Egyptians were hardly likely to fight with ardour in defence of their Byzantine masters, for the life of the country had long been poisoned by racial and religious strife. The native Copts had repudiated almost to a man the decrees of Chalcedon; every church, every monastery, was a focus of anti-Greek feeling, and the Patriarch Cyrus, appointed viceroy by Heraclius in 631, pursued the Monophysite heretics with floggings, tortures and executions, until the persecuted sect was only too glad to receive relief from any quarter. The peasants were oppressed by tyrannous and often alien Greek landlords, whose vast estates were coming to resemble feudal fiefs. The Persian occupation, which lasted from 617 to 627, undermined the whole basis of imperial rule: the Arab invasion finally toppled it over.

After the fall of Caesarea in 638, Amr urged Omar to allow him to march across Sinai into Egypt, which he represented as a country both rich and defenceless. With some reluctance, Omar sanctioned the enterprise, and late in 639 Amr made a swift raid on the Delta to test the strength of the defences, and after receiving reinforcements, routed the main Roman army at Heliopolis in July 640. The Arabs easily overran the open country, but they did not possess as yet the siege-engines and technical equipment requisite to take the strongly-fortified city of Alexandria, the centre of Egyptian Hellenism, or the massive citadel of Babylon, which had been built by Trajan and whose ruined site now forms part of Old Cairo. Fate came, however, to their assistance. The Patriarch Cyrus, a strange character who seems to have been as timid and craven in adversity as he was harsh and haughty in prosperity, cherished the hope that the Arabs could be bribed into withdrawing from the country, and entered into negotiations with Amr. His arrangements were indignantly repudiated by Heraclius, but the Emperor died in February 641, his son and successor Constantine III a few months later, and the weak regency set up to govern in the minority of his grandson Constans, then a boy of eleven, was incapable of inspiring loyalty or pursuing a decisive line of action. The lack of a strong lead from Constantinople undoubtedly hastened the loss of Egypt. Two months after the death of Heraclius the garrison of Babylon surrendered. The Copts began to desert the imperial cause; the high command of the army was riddled with feuds and jealousies, and in November 641 Cyrus secretly agreed with Amr on an eleven-months' armistice, during which the imperial troops would evacuate Alexandria. Amr spent the interval establishing a permanent military settlement near the fort of Babylon: it was named Fustat, presumably from the Latin *fossatum,* a fortified camp, and later grew into the metropolis of Cairo, the capital of Muslim Egypt as Alexandria had been of Hellenic Egypt. In September 642 there was a wholesale exodus of Greek troops, officials, merchants and landowners from Alexandria, and Amr's men marched into the desolate city, whose temples and palaces, theatres and baths, attested the luxury and culture of a millennium of Hellenism.[3]

Thus the reign of Christ and of Caesar came to an end in the land of the Nile. The Copts viewed without regret the departure of their persecutors: their Patriarch Benjamin, who for thirteen years had been hiding in remote convents from the imperial police, was welcomed by Amr in Alexandria and assured that his people would in future enjoy full religious liberty, and when in 645 the Byzantines landed an army in the Delta and tried to reconquer the country, the native Christians actively joined in repulsing them.

The surprisingly rapid conquest of Egypt may have influenced the momentous decision of Omar to allow the Muslim armies to advance beyond Iraq into the Persian homelands. The battle of Kadisiya had inflicted a shattering blow on the Sassanid regime, and had virtually dissolved the unity of the State. But the growing Arab threat to their independence was beginning to arouse the Persian people, and centres of resistance sprang up in the provinces under local leaders. King Yazdegerd had retired to Ray, a holy city of the Zoroastrians, at the foot of Mount Damavand, and there summoned the nation to a crusade against the enemies of their faith. It was soon obvious that a determined Persian counter-attack might imperil the Arab position in Iraq and drive the invaders back to their deserts. Had the fighting in Egypt been prolonged, the Sassanid monarchy might have been saved, but the armistice of Babylon in 641 probably enabled larger forces to be diverted to the Persian

---

[3]With the Arab occupation of Alexandria is associated the famous story of the burning of its library. According to this tale, Amr asked Omar what should be done with the thousands of books there, and received the answer: 'If these volumes of which you speak agree with the Koran, they are useless and need not be preserved: if they disagree, they are pernicious and should be destroyed.' They were therefore fed to the furnaces of the city baths. Modern critics are almost unanimous in rejecting the story, which is found in no author, Muslim or Christian, who wrote within 550 years of the Arab conquest. It is first referred to in a description of Egypt by Abd al-Latif, (1162-1231), compiled about 1202. There is some evidence that the Arabs burnt the Zoroastrian sacred books in Persia, which to them would be heathen writings, unlike the Jewish and Christian scriptures, and out of this in some confused way the Alexandrian story may have arisen. See E. A. Parsons, *The Alexandrian Library*, London, 1952.

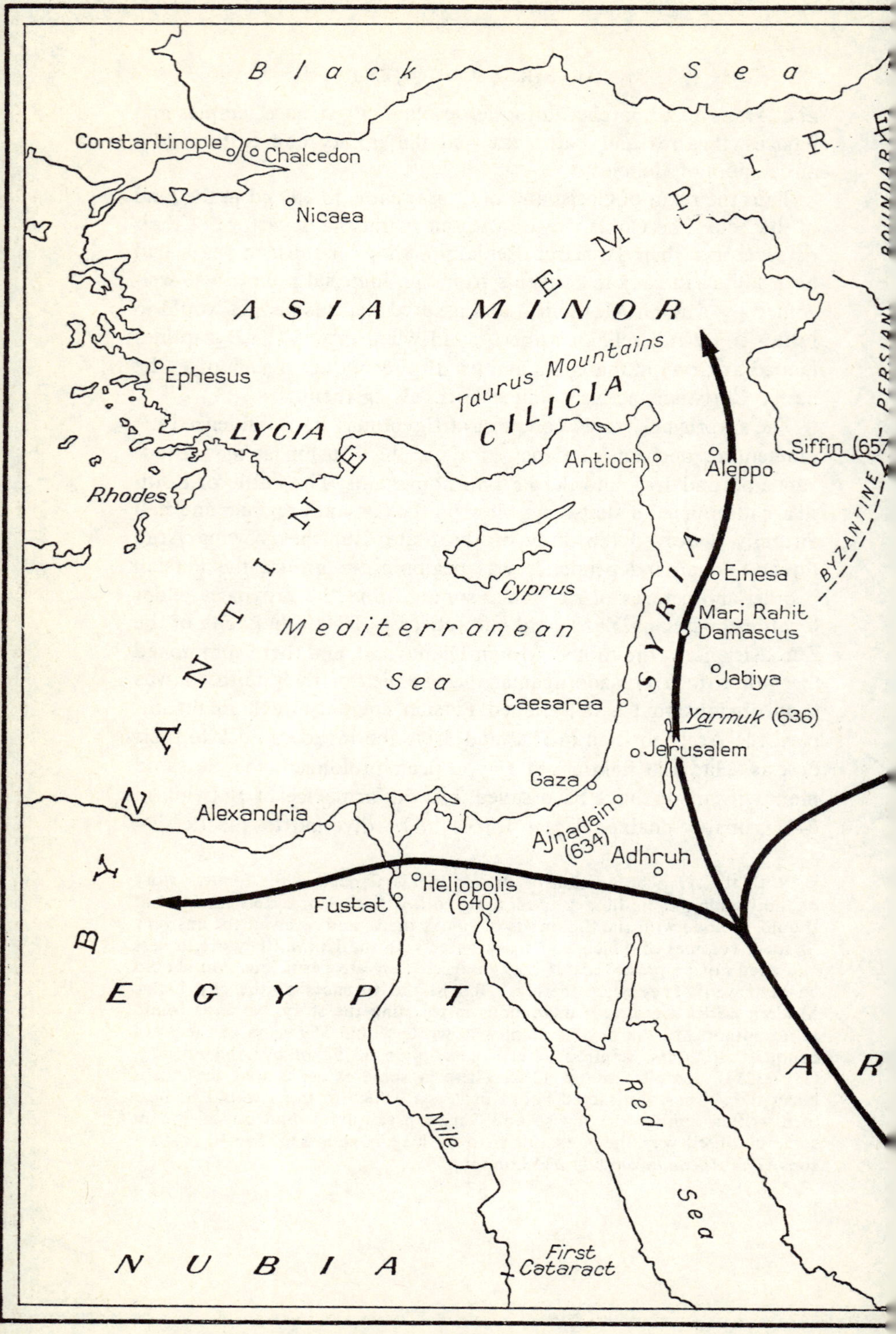
Black Sea
Constantinople
Chalcedon
Nicaea
BYZANTINE EMPIRE
ASIA MINOR
Taurus Mountains
CILICIA
Ephesus
LYCIA
Rhodes
Antioch
Aleppo
Siffin (657
PERSIAN - BYZANTINE BOUNDARY
Cyprus
Mediterranean Sea
SYRIA
Emesa
Marj Rahit
Damascus
Jabiya
Yarmuk (636)
Caesarea
Jerusalem
Gaza
Ajnadain (634)
Alexandria
Adhruh
Heliopolis (640)
Fustat
EGYPT
AR
Nile
Red Sea
NUBIA
First Cataract

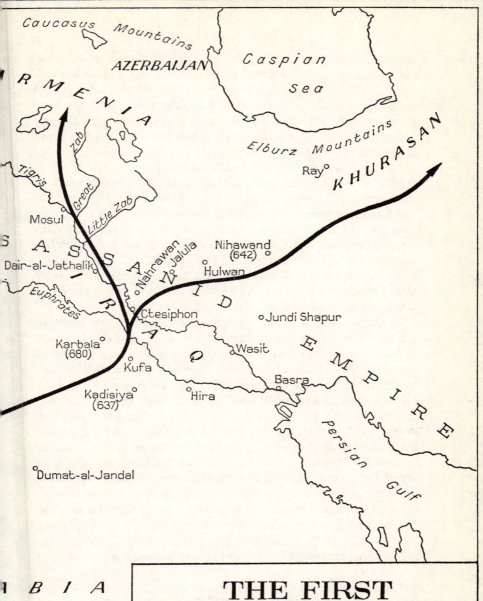

Caucasus Mountains

AZERBAIJAN

Caspian Sea

ARMENIA

Elburz Mountains

Ray

KHURASAN

Tigris

Great Zab

Little Zab

Mosul

S A S S A N I D

Dair-al-Jathalik

Nahrawan

Jalula

Nihawand (642)

Hulwan

Euphrates

Ctesiphon

Jundi Shapur

Karbala (680)

Wasit

Kufa

Basra

Kadisiya (637)

Hira

Persian Gulf

EMPIRE

Dumat-al-Jandal

A B I A

Medina

THE FIRST ARAB CONQUESTS

SHOWING THE MAIN THRUSTS

Figures in brackets indicate dates of battles

campaign at the critical moment when a new Persian army was moving from Ray through Hamadan towards the Tigris. At Nihavand, some forty miles south of Hamadan, it encountered a strong Arab force drawn from the garrisons of Kufa and Basra, and was completely routed. This engagement, which really determined the fate of Iran, was probably fought in 642.[4] There was no longer any doubt in Medina that Persia must be completely occupied. Yazdegerd fled eastwards to make a last stand at Merv in Khurasan. The northern regions of the kingdom were easily subdued; Mosul or Mawsil, on the Tigris, had perhaps fallen even before the battle of Nihavand, and from this base Azerbaijan was overrun in a single campaign. Elsewhere hard and stubborn fighting was needed before the Arabs were in full control, for here they were dealing, not with a disaffected province but with a proud nation. Yet after Nihavand the ultimate outcome was not in doubt, even though it was many years after Omar's death before the Muslim armies reached the River Oxus, the eastern boundary of the Persian kingdom.

By the conquest of Persia, the Arabs may be said to have achieved a fatal victory. Had they contented themselves with the dominion of Syria, Egypt and Iraq, they might have built between the Nile and the Tigris a solid and enduring Semitic kingdom. Such a State would, however, have been imperilled, like the Roman Empire, by constant Persian aggression, and less fitted than its predecessor to repel it; Omar's decision to annihilate rather than defeat the Sassanids may be justified on the score of this danger, and many benefits accrued from the throwing down of the barrier which, since the days of the Macedonian kings, had made the Euphrates the frontier of two eternally hostile Powers. But Persia, though subjugated, could not be assimilated; her people, mindful of their imperial past, resented their subjection to a barbarous race of 'lizard-eating Bedouins'; such Persians as embraced Islam as *mawali* or clients of the Arabs chafed at the humiliating inferiority of their status; and the nation clung tenaciously to its culture and language as its badges of

---

[4]The chronology of the conquest of Persia is as confused as that of Syria. Some Arabic historians place the battle of Nihavand in the year 639: others fix it at 642, and this latter date is accepted by the great Italian Arabist Caetani, in his *Annali della Islam*, vol. 4, Milan, 1911, pp. 474-504. If the earlier year be correct, the co-relation with events in Egypt suggested in the text cannot, of course, be sustained.

distinction. In course of time, Persian civilization triumphed over Arab barbarism; the Persians contributed more than any other race to the building of Muslim culture; the story of Greece and Rome was repeated, and to adapt Horace's famous line, 'Captive Persia took prisoner her conquerors.'

The first revenge of Persia for her political and military downfall was the death of Omar himself. A Persian Christian, one Abu Lu'lu'a, who had been taken prisoner in the fighting in his country, was sent as a slave to Medina, where he worked at his trade of a carpenter. As he watched the captives from the battle of Nihavand filing through the streets, he was filled with shame for his country and with hatred for her victorious conquerors. On November 4, 644, when the congregation was assembled for worship in the mosque and Omar entered and took up his position as *imam* to lead the prayers, Abu Lu'lu'a rushed forward and stabbed him six times in the back with a sharp dagger. The wounded Caliph was carried across the courtyard to his house; fully conscious, he calmly observed that his injuries were mortal, expressed satisfaction on being told that his assassin was not a Muslim, and appointed a *shura* or electoral college of six persons, including Ali and Othman, to choose his successor with due sense of responsibility to God and the Faith. After lingering some hours, he died in the fifty-third year of his age. Omar was the real founder of the Arab empire. His youthful asperity had long mellowed with age and office; his administrative measures, designed as they were to solve problems outside all his previous experience, were wise and prudent; his sagacious firmness repressed the licence of tribal armies and the quarrels of factious clans, and the simple homeliness of his manner was never altered even when the spoils of nations were laid at his feet. The disorders which followed his death were a measure of the loss which Islam suffered by his untimely end.

BOOKS FOR FURTHER READING

BECKER, C. H., *Cambridge Medieval History*, vol. 2, 1912, chap. xi. The best general sketch of the Arab conquests.

BUTLER, A. J., *The Arab Conquest of Egypt*, Oxford, 1902. A classic work, which did for Egypt what de Goeje did for Syria.

CHRISTENSEN, A., *L'Iran sous les Sassanides*, 2nd. ed. Paris, 1944. Standard work on Sassanid Persia.

GLUBB, J., *The Great Arab Conquests*, London, 1961. Expert military appraisal by the former commander of the Arab Legion.

DE GOEJE, M. J., *Mémoire sur la conquête de la Syrie*, 2nd. ed. Leiden, 1900. The first scholarly work to straighten out the tangled chronology of the subject.

HITTI, P., *A History of Syria*, London, 1951.

LAMMENS, H., *La Syrie, précis historique*, 2 vols. Beyrouth, 1921.

LANE-POOLE, S., *A History of Egypt in the Middle Ages*, London, 1901; 3rd. ed. 1924.

SPULER, B., *Iran in Früh-Islamischer Zeit*, Wiesbaden, 1952. Covers the history of Persia from 633 to 1055. An English translation is announced.

SYKES, P., *A History of Persia*, 2 vols. London, 1930. A compilation from secondary sources.

WIET, G., *L'Égypte arabe*, Paris, 1937.

The principal original source available in English is al-Baladhuri, *The Origins of the Islamic State*, tr. Hitti and Murgotten, 2 vols. New York, 1916-24. Baladhuri was probably of Persian origin: he lived and wrote in Baghdad, and died in 892. Although he is one of the earliest historians of the conquests whose work has come down to us, he lived 200 years after the events he describes.

IV

The Civil Wars

THE unity and concord of Islam were dissolved by the death of Omar. Every great movement of expansion must after a time lose its momentum: the conquerors must consolidate, their opponents, recovering from the initial shock, will stiffen their resistance, and internal dissension, long masked, will break out in open quarrels. The rapidity of the early conquests, from the invasion of Syria to the battle of Nihavand (633-642), probably astonished the Arabs themselves, but in the second decade the rate of advance was slowed down and grave problems emerged which might well have taxed the statesmanship of Omar and were certainly beyond the capacity of his successor to solve. The young Arab Empire hastened towards a crisis which left a permanent division in Islam and whose effects are visible to-day.

The *shura* or electoral college nominated by the dying Omar was faced by an invidious choice: the strongest candidates were Ali and Othman; neither would forego his claims in favour of the other, and they agreed at last to accept the decision of a third member, Abd al-Rahman, who himself disclaimed all ambition for the succession. He pronounced for Othman, perhaps in order to propitiate the powerful house of Omayya, perhaps in the hope of securing a more pliant and less exacting ruler than Omar. Wealthy, handsome and elegant, the new Caliph was an elderly man in his sixties; as the first convert to Islam of high social standing, he had been accorded the favour and friendship of the Prophet, two of whose daughters he married, but his indolent and easygoing nature precluded him from playing a valiant and active part in the wars and politics of the heroic age. But if the man were unimpressive, his family were numerous, rich and influential, Meccan patricians who despised Medina and those who under Abu Bakr and Omar had filled the offices of administration. The election of Othman passed without challenge, though the friends of Ali were grieved that he should be set aside for a third time, and the old Companions found it difficult to reconcile themselves to the rise to power within the Community of Muhammad of the progeny of Abu Sufyan, notorious for its long persistence in idolatry.

The twelve years' reign of Othman (644-656) was far from devoid of military success. A Byzantine attempt to recapture Alexandria was beaten off in 645. Othman's foster-brother, Abdallah b. Sa'd, who replaced Amr as governor of Egypt, led a big raid on Byzantine Africa in 647 and routed the forces of the Exarch Gregory at Sbaitla, in southern Tunisia, though no attempt was made to follow this up by permanent conquest. The Caliph's cousin, Mu'awiya, whom Omar had made governor of Syria, received permission to construct a fleet, in order to guard against Byzantine naval attacks and to carry the holy war into the heartlands of the enemy: the ships were built in the dockyards of Syria and Egypt, and manned mostly by native Christian crews who being Copts or Jacobites felt no compunction in serving against the Greeks. Naval expeditions were launched from Syrian ports against Cyprus, which was occupied in 649, and Rhodes, which was captured in 654, and where the Arabs sold to a Jewish dealer the metal fragments of the famous colossus that once bestrode the harbour. A Byzantine counter-attack was crushed in a battle off the coast of Lycia in 655, called Dhat al-Sawari, 'that of the Masts', the biggest sea-fight in the Mediterranean since the days of the Vandals. On land, Mu'awiya was able to occupy Armenia in 653-655, the religious schism again aiding the invaders: the Armenians, being mostly Monophysites, did not welcome help from the Emperor, and came to prefer Muslim to Greek rule, though here there was a stronger tradition of national freedom than in Syria, and the country was never a docile province of the Caliphate. In Persia fighting went on, though organized resistance collapsed when King Yazdegerd, the last of the Sassanids, was killed while hiding in a miller's hut near Merv in 651. He had sought to rally support in the eastern regions of his kingdom, and had even appealed for succour to the Chinese. Othman's cousin Abdallah b.

Amir, who had been appointed governor of Basra, led an army into the rich province of Khurasan, which he subdued in 651-653, receiving the surrender of Herat, Merv and Balkh. The boundary of the Caliph's dominions had now been pushed as far as the Oxus.

These victories were, however, of a different character from those of the first decade, which had seen the lightning conquests of Syria, Iraq and Egypt: they were more dearly purchased, involving as they did heavy loss and heavy expense. The stream of wealth which had poured in from the subjugated territories began to dwindle; since Omar had spent as he received, disdaining to accumulate a reserve lest so profane a measure should cast doubt on the willingness of God to provide for his people, the State exchequer under Othman found difficulty in maintaining the pension payments, and a growing army received diminishing stipends. The circulation of money from the looted treasuries of the East far outstripped the production of goods and services it could buy: prices rose, and popular discontent rose with them. Othman had already excited criticism by promoting his Omayyad relatives to high office and letting to them lucrative contracts for the supply of food and clothing to the army. Medina complained of the rapacity of the Meccans. The Bedouin tribesmen resented the centralized control exerted over them in the camp-cities of Kufa, Basra and Fustat. Pious believers were scandalized by the banishment of one Abu Dharr, a Companion who practised the asceticism of a Christian monk and who had declaimed against the growing wealth and luxury of the ruling class, and by Othman's attempt to provide a definitive text of the Koran and to destroy all non-authorized copies, a sensible measure which was twisted into an accusation of tampering with the sacred book.

The Caliph's authority gradually sank. His indolence increased with age; his capacity for grappling with the problems of empire declined as their magnitude grew; he reacted to arrogant opposition by timid concessions, and he complained with the bitterness and frustration of a weak man, that reproaches were levelled against him by accusers who would never have dared to bring such charges against Omar. Disaffection in the garrison camps broke out into open mutiny. The hatred of the tribal warriors, irked by the restraints of an unaccustomed discipline, was concentrated on the representatives of the Meccan aristocracy whom Othman appointed to govern them. A more adroit prince might have curbed the licence of the Bedouins by confronting them with the united strength of the townsmen, but Othman's policy antagonized the bulk of the Companions, the Ansar, the Emigrants and the Hashimites, and in his hour of peril he could reckon on no positive support save from his kinsmen in Syria. Kufa gave the signal of rebellion by shutting its gates against Othman's governor; the sedition spread to Egypt, where it was probably encouraged by Amr, resentful of his dismissal, and in Medina itself two Companions, Talha and Zubair (the latter a son-in-law of Abu Bakr), with the backing of the Prophet's widow A'isha, intrigued against the Caliph and undermined his position. Alarmed by the growing unrest, Mu'awiya urged his cousin to remove to Damascus and put himself under the protection of the loyal Syrian army, to which Othman replied that he would never leave the land where the Prophet had lived and the city where his body rested. In 656 bands of mutineers from Egypt appeared before Medina, demanding a reform of the government; the sovereign of the mightiest empire on earth was virtually defenceless in his own capital, and was obliged to parley with the rebels. Some accommodation appeared to have been reached, when the Egyptians claimed to have intercepted a letter from Othman to his governor in Fustat ordering him to put the ringleaders to death on their return. Confronted with this missive, the Caliph swore it was forged: to truculent demands for his abdication, he answered with dignity: 'I will not put off the robe with which I have been invested by God!' Puzzled and disheartened, the Medinese stood aside while the rebels besieged him in his house and loudly called for his resignation or death. When the news of these tumults reached Damascus, Mu'awiya set out to rescue his kinsman, whereupon the insurgents resolved to force the issue before the arrival of the Syrian army. On June 17, 656, they broke into Othman's house and found the old man sitting in an inner apartment with the Koran spread open on his lap. His wife heroically strove to shield him, and had several of her fingers cut off; the assassins thrust their swords into his body, and the blood of the murdered Vicar of the Prophet flowed over the pages of the sacred volume. So great was the terror inspired by the mutineers that Othman's family did not dare to bury him until the third day, and then by night in a common field. In his grave was buried also the peace and unity of Islam.

The murder of Othman was one of the most fateful events in

Islamic history. To adapt the phrase of Tacitus, the secret of empire was disclosed, that the Caliphate was no sacred office, but a prize to be snatched by violence; the swords of believers, hitherto employed only against infidels, were turned against each other, and Muslim blood was spilt by Muslims in the second holiest city of Arabia. In the ferocious civil war which followed, the seat of government was removed from Arabia (Othman was the last Caliph to reside in Medina), the rival parties sought the support of the non-Arab converts, the great schism of the Shi'a opened which still divides Islam, and the faithful were troubled by painful moral questions of the nature and limitation of political authority.

To shield themselves from the wrath of Mu'awiya, the regicides resolved, on the morrow of Othman's assassination, to offer the throne to the most distinguished of the surviving Companions: if Ali accepted the dangerous honour, his stature in the Community might stop the hand of the outraged family, and from motives of gratitude he might be reluctant to punish those to whom he owed his elevation. The character and career of Ali, whose reputation in his lifetime fell far below his posthumous fame, present many puzzling features. As a boy, he accepted with loyal ardour the prophetic mission of his cousin; as a youth, he displayed at Badr, Khaibar and Hunain the dash and gallantry of a born fighter. His marriage to Muhammad's daughter Fatima was a union of love and esteem; during her lifetime he took no other wife, and their sons Hasan and Husain, who were often fondled in the Prophet's lap, might have appeared as the natural successors, after their father, of the founder of Islam, had the Arabs been attached to the principle of strict hereditary right. At the death of Muhammad, Ali was not much more than thirty years of age; his unwillingness to press his claim to the headship of the Community was combined with an offended disappointment that he was not chosen, and he withheld for six months his recognition of Abu Bakr. Twice more was he passed over, a circumstance which suggests that his associates considered him unfit for the responsibilities of high office. In the revolt against Othman, he played an ambiguous part, and his natural irresolution proved fatal to his reputation. A strong stand by him might have saved the life of the aged Caliph, but Ali took no serious steps to protect his sovereign, and his inaction awakened the suspicion, in all probability unfounded, that he had connived at the murder in the hope of succeeding at last to the vacant throne. In an evil hour, he accepted it from the hands of rebels and assassins. By now a short, stout and aging man in his late fifties, he found himself beset with enemies, among them the acutest political genius of the time. Mu'awiya, now the head of the house of Omayya and by Arab custom obliged to avenge his kinsman's death, refused to recognize Ali as Caliph, and the bloodstained shirt of Othman and the severed fingers of his wife, which had been smuggled out of Medina, were exposed in the mosque at Damascus in order to stimulate public anger against the regicides. It soon became clear that Ali would have to fight for his throne.

He displayed little statesmanship. No attempt was made to punish Othman's murderers. A clean sweep was made of most of the late Caliph's officials, thereby raising against Ali a host of new enemies. Talha and Zubair quarrelled with him, renounced their allegiance, retired to Mecca, and joined forces with A'isha, who had been his bitter foe since in Muhammad's lifetime he had cast aspersions on her chastity when she had been left behind on a desert journey and had returned the next day with a youth. The three then proceeded to Basra, where they apparently planned to proclaim a new government. Ali collected an army and followed them, secured some reinforcements from Kufa, and after fruitless negotiations brought them to battle. A'isha, a vigorous and vivacious women of forty-five, was in the thick of the fight, seated on a camel and urging her men on with cries and gestures. 'The Battle of the Camel', as the Arabic chroniclers call it, was fought in December 656 and ended in victory for Ali; Talha and Zubair were killed, and A'isha was taken prisoner and escorted back to Mecca. Ten thousand Muslims are said to have died on this field, and aged believers mourned the death of Zubair, who had once helped destroy the idols of Mecca, and of Talha, who had saved the Prophet's life at Uhud. Ali's reputation was not enhanced by this domestic carnage: henceforth he was the prisoner of the regicides and of the turbulent Bedouin soldiery of Kufa and Basra.

Meanwhile in Syria Mu'awiya played a clever waiting game. He put forth no claim to the Caliphate himself, asserting only his right and duty to avenge his cousin's death; he made a truce with the Byzantines in order to be free to move his army into Iraq, and he remained strictly neutral in the conflict between Ali and the Talha-

Zubair alliance. He governed a quiet and orderly province, whose Christian inhabitants of every sect enjoyed full religious freedom and equality of treatment and where no camp-cities existed as centres of disaffection and tribal anarchy. By contrast, Ali's position was weak and unstable : his election was irregular, his relations with Othman's murders ambiguous, the urban classes feared the licence of his Bedouin levies, and the pious were inclined to blame him for the shedding of Muslim blood in the battle of the Camel. As Mu'-awiya continued to refuse him recognition, Ali was compelled to resort to force to vindicate his authority; he led his army northwards through Iraq, and encountered the Syrians at Siffin, a ruined Roman site on the swamps of the Euphrates near Rakka. Here, after vain attempts to reach a peaceful settlement, Muslims for the second time fought against Muslims (July 657). The Syrians got the worst of it, and the Omayyad cause might have been lost but for a wily stratagem on the part of Amr, the conqueror of Egypt, who had now thrown in his lot with Mu'awiya. At his suggestion, it is said, the Syrians fixed leaves of the Koran on the points of their lances and cried out along the line: 'The law of God, the law of God! Let that decide between us!' The story may be apocryphal: what is fairly certain is that in both armies there were a number of *kurra,* readers or reciters of the Koran, who were striving desperately to stop believers killing one another by appealing to arbitration. Public opinion was clearly on their side, and Ali, against his better judgment, was obliged to agree to the nomination of two umpires, one from each side, to determine on the basis of Koranic law to whom power in Islam legally belonged. The arbitration court was to meet at Adhruh, an old Roman camp near the ruins of Petra, and while it deliberated hostilities were suspended.

Ali had been caught in a trap. He claimed to be Caliph: Mu'awiya did not. If the verdict went against Ali, he lost more than his rival, since he would be compelled to confess himself a usurper. Mu'awiya selected Amr as his umpire, a man devoted to his cause, but Ali was forced by his supporters to appoint Abu Musa, a Kufan leader who was strictly neutral. What was debated and decided at Adhruh is obscure : it seems likely that the arbitrators first inquired into the legality of Othman's acts. If the dead Caliph had violated the sacred law, his death might be considered a just retribution: if not, it was a crime calling for vengeance. Apparently the court vindicated Othman and condemned the regicides, thereby invalidating the rule of Ali. Probably it recommended that a *shura* be convened to elect a new sovereign. Ali rejected the verdict and refused to abdicate, thereby putting himself technically in the wrong and strengthening the position of his rival. Dissension now broke out in his own camp. The murder of Othman had produced a crisis of conscience throughout the Muslim community: men anxiously consulted the Koran and the *sunna,* path or custom of the Prophet, gravely weighed conflicting claims and arguments, and sought to discover why God had allowed his people to succumb to the temptation (*al-Fitna,* by which the civil war is known to the Muslim historians) of deciding their disputes by force of arms. Extreme pietists raised the cry, 'The decision belongs to God alone!' and rejecting the role of human arbiters, declared that the divine judgment could be expressed only through the free choice of the whole community of believers. Some began to agitate for the replacement of the caliphal regime by a republican theocracy, a notion congenial to Bedouin tribesmen who detested anything in the way of monarchical rule. They left Ali's headquarters at Kufa and migrated to Nahrawan, on one of the Tigris canals, where they terrorized the locality by their fanatical excesses. Ali was forced to move against them, and they were crushed (July 658) in a bloody affray which was a massacre rather than a battle. They came to be known as Kharijites, 'those who go out,' the first but by no means the last of the sectaries of Islam who seceded from the main body of the faithful.

Taking advantage of these disturbances, Mu'awiya moved cautiously towards the throne. Amr occupied Egypt in his name, the country welcoming the return of its former conqueror. Persistent Syrian raids were made on Ali's positions in Iraq. An attempt to seize Mecca and Medina failed, but in July 660 Mu'awiya was formally proclaimed Caliph in Jerusalem, the third holiest city of Islam, and received the homage of the chiefs and notables of the western provinces. Thus four years after the murder of Othman was inaugurated the famous Omayyad dynasty, destined to reign for nearly a century over the greatest empire on earth. Unwittingly, the Kharijites consolidated Mu'awiya's throne. Beaten in the field, they took to terrorism, and resolved to rid Islam of Ali, Mu'awiya and Amr, but the plot achieved only partial success. Amr being sick, his deputy was murdered at Fustat in mistake for him; Mu'awiya was wounded by an assassin in the mosque at Damascus, but only slightly, while Ali, struck down as he was entering the mosque at Kufa, in January 661, died of his injuries, the third Caliph in seventeen years to meet a violent end. His partisans tried to continue the struggle with Mu'awiya, but his son Hasan had no stomach for fighting and resigned his claims to the Caliphate on promise of a substantial pension. The nation, tired of strife, accepted the rule of the Omayyads, and the First Civil War terminated in the celebration of the *jama'a,* or return to unity and concord.

Ali was over sixty at the time of his death; his portly and unwieldy figure excited the mirth and ridicule of poets and versifiers, but his moral qualities were respectfully recognized. He was a brave fighter, an eloquent orator, and a loyal friend; many sayings of his are quoted to prove his mastery of proverbial wisdom, a gift highly honoured among the Semites,[1] and he displayed towards his foes a patience and magnanimity expressive of a humane and generous disposition. His religion was founded on a genuine piety; he was shocked by the growing luxury and corruption of the age, and to his uneasy doubts whether Othman was an upholder or a violator of the law may be attributed the hesitating and ambiguous attitude he adopted towards the regicides, which proved so fatal to his rule and reputation. As his temper was indolent, he drifted rather than led; he was easily outmatched by the astute and the forceful, and he lacked the commanding personality to impose his will on a turbulent society. His authority was challenged by the politic shrewdness of Mu'awiya and the furious zealotry of the Kharijites; his inability to overcome either delivered Islam to schism and strife, and grave believers were driven to see in a reunion of the Empire under the Omayyads the only escape from tribal and sectarian anarchy. Yet this undistinguished and unsuccessful prince has been raised by a powerful sect to a level little below that of Muhammad himself; the

[1] Many anecdotes are also told of Ali: one may be quoted as a specimen of Arab humour. An Arab once recited his prayers in the mosque in so slovenly a manner as to rouse the indignation of Ali, who was punctilious in these matters; the Caliph, when the man had finished, severely rebuked him, and throwing his slippers at him, commanded him to repeat them with proper tone and emphasis. This being done, Ali said to him: 'Surely your last prayers were better than the first?' 'By no means,' answered the Arab, 'for the first I said out of devotion to God, but the last out of fear of your slippers!'

Shi'a or 'party' of Ali laid it down as an article of faith that he was
designated by God and the Prophet to be the lawful Caliph and
Imam of Islam, his three predecessors being treated as usurpers,
and that divine revelation continued to be interpreted by his descendants, and his supposed grave at Najaf, a sandhill on the edge
of the desert six miles west of Kufa, is annually visited by thousands
of devout pilgrims who curse his supplanters and revere him as the
friend of God and the first of the Imams.

With Ali ended the line of the so-called Orthodox or right-guided
Caliphs, whose reigns were later regretted as a lost age of pure theocracy; Arabia lost forever its political primacy in Islam, and the
capital of the Empire was moved to Damascus in Syria. For twenty
years that ancient city had been the centre of Omayyad power under
Mu'awiya as governor of Syria: for another twenty years he was to
reign as Caliph of Islam. The wisest and most fortunate of sovereigns, he rarely knew the bitterness of failure or even the vexation
of a setback; his enterprises were commonly successful; his enemies
were either humbled or transformed into friends, and his reign was
the longest age of peace and prosperity in the annals of the Caliphate. To persuade or to bribe was more natural to him than to com-
pel; to those counsellors who rebuked him for his lavish profusion
of gifts, he replied simply: 'War costs more!' On the loyalty of Syria
he could always count; Egypt was tranquil under Amr, but the disorderly province of Iraq needed a strong hand, and under the early
Omayyads it was kept in firm control by a series of ruthless and
competent viceroys, Mughira, Ziyad and Hajjaj, all natives of Ta'if
and members of the clan of Thakif. The cantonments of Kufa and
Basra were the sources of disaffection; the civil war had loosened the
bonds of society, and the Bedouin tribesmen were the enemies of
all civil government. Ziyad was particularly successful in curbing
their licence: he created a *shurta*, or picked bodyguard, to patrol
the streets, cultivated the friendship of the shaikhs, whom he made
responsible for the good conduct of their people, and he deported
the most truculent clans to distant Khurasan, where they were
settled as military colonists and employed in raids across the Oxus.

Having disposed of his rivals, Mu'awiya resumed the holy war as
the most efficacious means of solidifying his rule and preventing idle
garrisons from indulging in riot and rapine. In the East, the Arabs
crossed the Oxus in 667 and made a series of annual raids on Buk-

hara, Samarkand and other cities of Transoxiana then held by, or at least tributary to, the Turks, a people destined for a great future in Islam whom the Muslims now encountered for the first time. In the West, an excellent opportunity seemed to present itself on the death of the Emperor Constans in 668. Constans, the grandson of Heraclius, had reigned since 641; he had checked the Arab incursions into Asia Minor, and to supervise the defence of North Africa against a renewed Arab attack from Egypt, he had left Constantinople and taken up residence at Syracuse in Sicily. Here he was suddenly murdered in some obscure palace conspiracy, and in the ensuing confusion, Mu'awiya seized the chance to direct a naval assault on Constantinople itself and to authorize Amr's nephew Okba b.Nafi to lead a full scale expedition against Byzantine Africa. The siege of the imperial capital began in 668 and went on for eight or nine years, the Arabs using as their base the island of Cyzicus in the Sea of Marmora, but in the end it had to be abandoned owing to the damage inflicted on their ships by an inflammable liquid known as the 'Greek fire' which was discharged from the walls through tubes or cylinders and ignited as soon as it touched the decks and sails. Meanwhile Okba, at the head of ten thousand horse, cleared the Byzantines from southern Tunisia and in imitation of Amr at Fustat planted in 670 a military colony in an open plain not far from the sea near Susa, which he named Kairawan, 'the place of arms.' He soon ran into trouble, however, from the native Berbers, whom he despised with the hauteur of an aristocratic Arab, and the final conquest of North Africa was postponed for nearly thirty years.

In his last years Mu'awiya faced an uncertain future. No definite rules yet governed the succession to the Caliphate, which since Othman's murder had lost its early aura as a semi-religious institution but had not so far acquired the standing and trappings of a secular absolute monarchy. Mu'awiya ruled as a kind of super-shaikh: he was assisted by a *shura* or council of elders, and he enforced obedience to his wishes rather than his commands by making use of *wufud,* tribal delegations, who were persuaded or cajoled into pledging their loyalty to him. He resolved that his office should pass to his son Yazid, but hereditary succession was alien and distasteful to the Arabs, and he was obliged to proceed with the greatest circumspection. By exerting all his diplomatic arts, by warning the people that the only alternative was strife and disunity and the disruption of the Islamic community he secured from the *shura* and *wufud* recognition of Yazid as heir-apparent. Thus the dynastic principle was introduced into Islam, and the Arabs were henceforth governed (said an irate critic) after the fashion of the Greeks and Romans, where one Heraclius was followed by another.

Mu'awiya died in April 680, perhaps as old as eighty. Yazid succeeded peacefully enough, but in a few months the enemies of the house of Omayya raised their heads and re-kindled the flames of civil war. A number of circumstances combined to bring about a renewal of armed sedition. The new Caliph commanded none of the respect which had been accorded to his father: a man in his late thirties, he did not lack ability, but he preferred hunting to business, and he had recently retired without glory from the siege of Constantinople, where he had captained the Arab forces. In the twenty years which had passed since the *jama'a* of 661. Ali's sons had grown to manhood, and though the elder Hasan died before Mu'awiya (of poison, it was alleged), the younger Husain, the only surviving grandson of the Prophet, was now revered by the *Shi'a* as their Imam and future Caliph. He was living quietly in Mecca, and had no desire to plunge into the hurly-burly of politics, but the importunities of his party forced him out of his seclusion and drove him, a passive victim, to his fate. Another claimant to the throne emerged in the person of Abdallah b.Zubair, who after seeing his father killed at the Battle of the Camel, retired to Medina, where he built up a following among the Ansar and the Emigrants who resented the city's loss of status since the centre of government had been removed to Damascus. Husain and Abdallah both refused allegiance to Yazid; the former was invited to come to Kufa, where his father had reigned and died, and in the summer of 680 he set out for Iraq. The Second Civil War began.

What followed is as fresh in the memory of Muslims as if it had happened yesterday. Kufa was always anti-Omayyad, but the town had been thoroughly cowed by Ziyad, and at the first hint of trouble, Yazid despatched Ziyad's son Ubaid Allah to crush any attempt at an Alid rising. Husain was warned on his way across the desert that his cause was hopeless; the fickle Bedouins abandoned him, and he was left with a tiny force of seventy men, with whom he resolved to push on in the forlorn expectation that his appearance at the gates of Kufa would inspire a mass revolt. He reached the Euphrates at Karbala, some twenty-five miles north-east of Kufa, where he received envoys from Ubaid Allah demanding his submission. He tried to make conditions, was confronted with an ultimatum from the local commander, Omar b.Sa'd, a son of the victor of Kadisiya, and on his refusal to surrender, his camp at Karbala was attacked. Though the odds against him were overwhelming, Husain determined to die fighting; while his women and children crouched in terror in their tents, he drew out his little band and engaged the enemy. One by one his men fell; his nephew Kasim, a boy of ten, died in his arms; two of his sons and six of his brothers also perished, and he himself was at last struck down. The custom or humanity of the victors spared the woman and children, but the slain males were all decapitated, and their heads were brought to Ubaid Allah. As the head of the Prophet's grandson was cast at the feet of the viceroy, who turned it over with his stick, a shudder ran through the crowd, and a voice cried: 'Gently—on that face I have seen the lips of the Apostle of God!' Damascus was startled and disquieted by this bloody tragedy; Yazid hastened to disclaim responsibility for the death of Husain, but the memory of the tenth of the month Muharram of the year 61 (October 10, 680) has never fallen into oblivion, and a scene enacted nearly thirteen centuries ago is commemorated with grief to-day by millions of Shi'ite Muslims.

The ultimate result of Karbala was to provide the Shi'a with a martyr and Islam with a mediator between God and man: the immediate consequence was to benefit the second pretender Abdallah by removing a competitor from his path and rousing violent opposition to the Omayyads in the holy cities. In imitation of his father, Yazid tried conciliation, and received a deputation of notables from Medina, but the pious delegates returned home professing themselves scandalized by the godless luxury of the court of Damascus, and the city exploded into open rebellion. Yazid hesitated no longer and sent an army into Arabia; the insurgents were routed, the Syrian troops entered Medina (August, 683), the city of the Prophet was delivered to military punishment, and the Omayyads might seem to have avenged at last the blood of the murdered Othman. The army then moved on Mecca to deal with Abdallah. Fighting broke out, in the course of which, to the horror of pious believers, the Kaaba caught fire and the sacred black stone burst from its socket. Abdallah and Mecca were saved, however, by the death of Yazid (November 683), which threatened the total ruin of the Omayyad cause. Yazid's son Mu'awiya II, a sickly youth, was proclaimed Caliph, but died in a few months, and the line of Abu Sufyan became extinct. To a disputed succession was now added a new source of discord, the famous conflict between the Kalb and the Kais (Qays), the Arabs of the south and north.

Far back in pre-Islamic times the Arab tribes, as we have seen, traced their descent either from Adnan or from Kahtan. Adnan was the father of the northern branch of the race, the most noteworthy tribe of which was the Banu-Mudar, who settled along the Euphrates and one of whose clans, the Kais, often gave their name to the whole group. The southerners, the supposed progeny of Kahtan, were commonly called Yemenites; many had migrated to the north and settled in Syria, among them the Banu-Kalb, whose name was in time taken as a rallying cry for their party. Rivalry between the Kais and the Kalb was ancient and endemic; partly masked by the coming of Islam, which tried to substitute the bond of religion for that of race, it broke out afresh when Yazid, the son and husband of Kalbite women, was accused of favouring the southerners. Dahhak b.Kais, the head of the Kaisite clan, who had loyally served Mu'awiya and had been rewarded with the governorship of Damascus, deserted the Omayyad cause and acknowledged Abdallah as Caliph. The defence of the Omayyad fortunes had devolved on Marwan b.al-Hakam, a cousin of Mu'awiya and Yazid, and an elderly man of nearly seventy, who might have given up all claim to the Caliphate had not the tough Ubaid Allah urged him to make a stand, collect an army at Jabiya, and from that base march on Damascus. The Kalbites rallied to his support, and the Kaisites were beaten at Marj Rahit, a plain outside Damascus, in July 684, Dahhak being killed. Marwan was now accepted as Caliph in Syria, and as he established his authority over Egypt before his death after a brief reign in 685, he may be regarded as the second founder of the Omayyad dynasty. But the Kaisites remained sullen, discontented and unreconciled, and the re-opening of this ancient feud weakened the basis of Omayyad power and contributed to the eventual destruction of the Arab Empire.

Marwan was succeeded as Caliph by his shrewd and able son Abd al-Malik, a vigorous man of thirty-nine. The authority of the new sovereign was not, however, recognized outside Syria and Egypt:

Arabia and Iraq obeyed the anti-Caliph Abdallah, the Kharijites, who repudiated the rule of any human prince, fomented disorder in almost every province, and a formidable uprising in Kufa transformed the Shi'a from a political party into a religious sect, and endangered the supremacy of the Arabs over the conquered nations. Soon after the tragedy of Karbala, the Kufans were smitten with shame for their cowardly desertion of Husain; an 'Army of Penitents' was enrolled sworn to avenge the sufferings of the house of Ali, and its leadership was assumed by a man of genius. Mukhtar, a native of Ta'if, proclaimed himself the emissary of Muhammad b. al-Hanafiya, Ali's son by a women of the Banu-Hanifa. The choice of Ali's pretender was strange: Muhammad, not being Fatima's son, was not a direct descendant of the Prophet, but he was doubtless selected as the only available adult of Ali's line who survived after the massacre of Karbala. Mukhtar is a figure of revolutionary significance; his swift though ephemeral success may be ascribed to the skill with which he played on many deep desires and emotions, and though his movement was crushed, it revealed with alarming clarity the cracks and fissures in the structure of the Islamic Empire.

The claim of Ali and his descendants to the caliphal throne was originally based on a political legitimism, which held that the vicariate of the Prophet should be possessed as a natural right by the nearest of his kinsmen. But the martyrdom of Husain at Karbala elevated him and his family above the level of pretenders to worldly kingship, and in Iraq, where so many religious currents mingled, the Arab colonists might catch the infection of older faiths and view the progeny of Ali, the true Imams, as the manifestation of the divine in human form, an ancient notion endemic in eastern speculation. Even more prone to such beliefs were the non-Arab Muslims, the *mawali* or clients, who being largely of Persian origin, were familiar with the idea of sacred monarchy; they already resented their inferior status and the arrogant pride of their Arab lords, and they listened eagerly to the eloquent preaching of Mukhtar who assured them of the imminent coming of a Messiah, or *Mahdi* (literally, 'the right-guided one'), who would restore truth and virtue, obliterate all distinctions of class and race, and gather all believers into a community of equals. For the first time the *mawali* emerged as a political force and the privileged position of the Arab ruling class was seriously threatened.

73

The struggle for power among the various contestants was fought out chiefly in the key province of Iraq. Mukhtar prevailed against Abd al-Malik's first attempt to regain control of that region; the Omayyad troops were routed on the banks of the Zab (August 686), their leader Ubaid Allah was slain, and the head of that harsh and hated governor was thrown down before Mukhtar in the palace of Kufa on the same spot where three years before he had turned over with his cane the head of the Prophet's grandson. The two pretenders, Abdallah and Muhammad b.al-Hanafiya, remained strangely quiet and aloof in Arabia, while armies marched and fought in their names. Abdallah's brother Mus'ab undertook to secure Iraq; his general Muhallab roused the Bedouin warriors against Mukhtar, whose preaching of racial equality outraged all their pride of lineage; Kufa was besieged, and Mukhtar and his principal lieutenants were killed (March 687) in making a sortie from the citadel. The hand of the dead prophet was cut off and nailed to the wall of the mosque, and a brutal massacre of his party at Mus'ab's orders served only to inflame the anti-Arab feelings of the *mawali*. Mukhtar ruled Kufa for no more than eighteen months, but his brief career permanently modified the civil and religious history of the East. As the first to press the idea of the Mahdi, he ranks as a founder of theological Shi'ism: as the first to enrol the *mawali* in a movement of revolutionary egalitarianism, he struck the initial blow against Arab domination of Islam.

Meanwhile Abd al-Malik could watch with satisfaction his enemies fighting one another. Having made a necessary though humiliating peace with the Byzantines and suppressed a move to proclaim a rival Caliph in Damascus, he marched into Iraq in 691 and engaged Mus'ab near a Nestorian monastery on the Tigris known as Dair al-Jathalik. Iraq was weary of incessant strife, and the Kufans were weary of Mus'ab; they fought without spirit or conviction; their leader was killed; Kufa surrendered, and the Bedouin chiefs, still shaken by the uprising of the mawali under Mukhtar, swore allegiance to the Omayyad Caliph. Nothing remained but to deal with Abdallah, since Muhammad b.al-Hanafiya had never endorsed the claims of his supporters and was allowed to live out his life in peace. An able and ruthless soldier, Hajjaj, famous in after years as the greatest of eastern viceroys, led an army into Arabia and besieged Abdallah in Mecca. The pretender lost heart, and consulted his aged mother as to the propriety of capitulation. 'If you are conscious of your right,' replied the intrepid matron, who was a daughter of Abu Bakr, 'you will die like a hero!' Inspired by her courage, her son donned his armour, faced the besiegers, and fell sword in hand. The Syrians occupied Mecca; Abdallah's head, presented to Abd al-Malik in Damascus, assured the Caliph that he reigned at last without a rival, and the Muslim world thankfully celebrated in 692 a second *jama'a*, a year of peace and reunion.

The first domestic conflict which rent Islam had continued but five years, from the rising against Othman in 656 to the death of Ali in 661: the second dragged its length for twelve, from the accession of Yazid in 680 to the fall of Abdallah in 692, and inflicted more lasting wounds, since it was marked by the tragedy of Karbala, which provided Shi'ite Islam with a fanatical faith, nourished by the blood of martyrs, in place of a political programme, and by the first attempt of the client converts to vindicate their claim to equality with the Arabs in the Muslim *umma*, and these elements of discord were reinforced by the anarchical and irrepressible violence of Kharijite zealotry, the outbreak of the ferocious feud between the Kais and the Kalb, which dates, at least in its full intensity, from the battle of Marj Rahit in 684, and the unconquerable aversion of the Bedouin tribes to the controls of civilization. By dint of tremendous exertions and with the help of troops and administrators drawn from settled society, the Omayyad Caliphs put down these convulsions of barbarism and religion, but their success could not be lasting; the storm, quelled for a time, burst out afresh, and ultimately involved the dynasty and the domination of the Arabs in a common ruin.

BOOKS FOR FURTHER READING

ENC. OF ISLAM, Arts. ' 'Alī b.Abī Tālib,' 'Mu'āwiya I,' 'Othman b. 'Affan.'

LAMMENS, H., *Études sur le règne du calife omaiyade Mo'awia*, Beyrouth, 1908.

LAMMENS, H., *Le califat de Yazid Ier*, Beyrouth, 1921.

VAN VLOTEN, *Recherches sur la domination arabe. le chiitisme et les croyances messianiques*, Amsterdam, 1894

THE CIVIL WARS

WELLHAUSEN, J., *Das arabische Reich und sein Stürz*, Berlin, 1902; Eng. tr.
The Arab Kingdom and its Fall, Calcutta; 1927.
The standard work on the Civil Wars and the Omayyad period.

V

The Arab Empire

THE victory of Abd al-Malik over his rivals in the Second Civil War ensured the survival of the Caliphate as a political institution and permitted the resumption of imperialist expansion which within twenty years added North Africa, Spain and Transoxiana to the Arab Empire. Between 692 and the fall of the dynasty in 750 the Omayyads grappled with problems that might have baffled the wisest statesmanship. Many they failed to solve, and their failure ultimately brought their regime to ruin, but others they tackled with some degree of success, and they created the conditions in which a new Islamic civilization could be built up in the old urbanized lands of the Near East. Their services to Islam and to culture have been accorded full recognition only in recent times, for their history was written by their enemies (the oldest surviving Arabic chronicles were composed in the days of their Abbasid supplanters), and they were represented as godless tyrants, contemners of the Law, and scoffers at the Faith. A more discriminating and objective approach has enabled us to view the Omayyad age as formative and creative and the most glorious in the annals of the Arab race.

The first and not the least notable achievement of the Omayyads was to set up a stable and workable State. The very conception of a State was foreign to the Arab mind and no word for it existed in the Arabic language: a tribal society knows no citizens, but only kinsmen united by ties of blood. The Bedouins boasted of the freedom of the desert: they were ready to engage in and profit by wars of conquest, but they furiously resented being herded in garrison

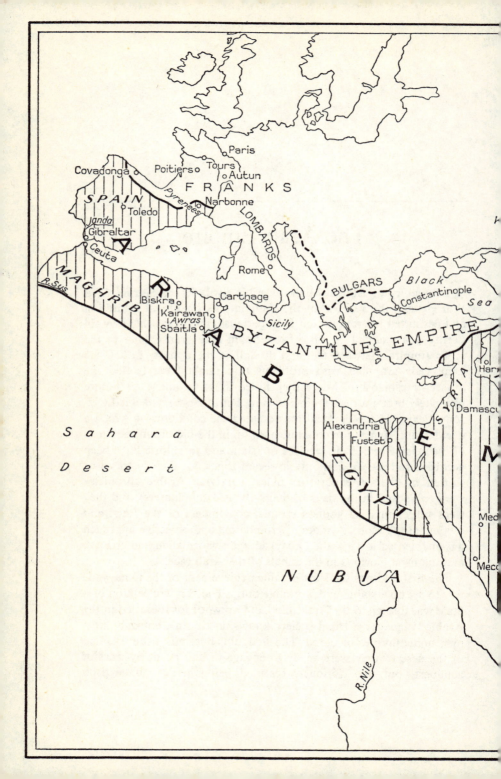

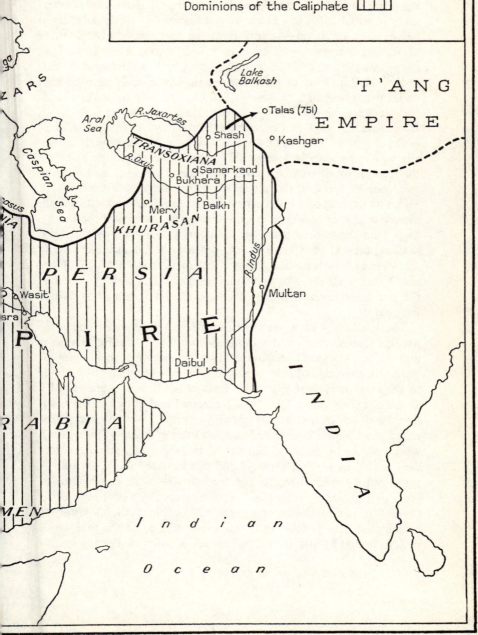

THE ARAB EMPIRE

AT THE FALL OF THE OMAYYADS 750

Dominions of the Caliphate ☐☐☐☐

XARS

ga

Caspian Sea

Aral Sea

R. Jaxartes

TRANSOXIANA

R. Oxus

Lake Balkash

o Talas (751)

T'ANG EMPIRE

o Shash

o Kashgar

o Samarkand

Bukhara

o Merv

o Balkh

KHURASAN

rosus

IA

PERSIA

o Wasit

sra

R. Indus

o Multan

PIRE

Daibul

INDIA

RABIA

MEN

I n d i a n

O c e a n

camps and subjected to centralized control. Their participation in the civil wars was motivated by the hope of escaping such subjection, and had Ali won in the first war or Abdallah in the second, the result must have been the collapse of the Caliphate and a reversion to tribal anarchy. From this disaster the Omayyads saved Islam: they recruited an army from the more sedentary Arabs of Syria, and stationed part of it in a new colony known as Wasit (='midway'), founded about 705 at a spot halfway between the disorderly cantonments of Kufa and Basra, which could thus be kept under better restraint. The early Caliphs were little more than glorified shaikhs, but the steady concentration of Omayyad power in Damascus impelled the Commander of the Faithful to assume more of the character of a king. Even Mu'awiya, accessible though he usually was to his people, segregated himself from the congregation in the mosque by sitting in a kind of box or compartment, and his long residence in Syria, in close contact with the Byzantine world, led him, almost unconsciously perhaps, to approximate his office more closely to that of the Christian Emperor. The enemies of the Omayyads later denounced them for abandoning the pure theocracy of Medina, turning the Caliphate into a *Mulk,* or kingdom, and aping the style of the Byzantine Caesars and the Persian Shahs. It is not easy to see what else Mu'awiya and his successors could have done. Only a centralized monarchy could control an expanding World Empire.

The machinery of government, crude and improvised under the Medina Caliphs, acquired a more elaborate and efficient character under the Omayyads. Administrative departments (*diwan*) multiplied: to the original *diwan al-jund* (war office), created by Omar to keep the records of pay and rations of the troops, were added a *diwan al-kharaj* (tax office), which assessed and collected the land-taxes, a *diwan al-rasa'il* (secretariat), which received, filed and answered the Caliph's correspondence, a *diwan al-khatam* (privy seal), where copies of State documents were kept and outgoing letters were sealed to prevent forgery, and a *diwan al-barid* (post office), organized by Abd al-Malik and used for the swift conveyance of news and orders by relays of horsemen over the vast Empire. No Chief Minister or Wazir as yet existed, but the Caliph's *katib,* or principal secretary, must often have contributed to the making of policy. Staffed at first largely by Greek-, Coptic- or Persian-speaking Christians, who continued the administrative practices of the Byzantine and Sassanid regimes, the *diwans* passed gradually under Muslim control, Arabs and *mawali* alike entering the public service, and under Abd al-Malik Arabic became the official language of the government. The administration of Iraq was arabized in 697, of Syria in 700, and of Egypt in 705. Coins bearing Greek and Persian inscriptions, with effigies of Byzantine and Sassanid rulers, which had continued in circulation since the conquests, were withdrawn in 696 and replaced by Arabic coins stamped with phrases or quotations from the Koran. The structure of the Caliphal State was taking shape.

The second service rendered by the Omayyads was the consolidation of Islam in the lands of the first conquests. The mere passage of time and the fading hopes of a Byzantine-Christian restoration worked in favour of the new religion: by 700 almost all who had known the Prophet were dead, but the new generation of Muslims, who had been born into Islam, displayed, as is common in such cases, a zeal and sincerity often wanting in their fathers, who had not infrequently embraced the faith for purely selfish and material motives. It was these younger Muslims who were the most effective missionaries and who enabled Islam to put down deep roots in the lands which had been the cradle of Christianity. No coercion was applied: the Omayyads followed the Prophet's injunction to tolerate 'the peoples of the Book'; Christian worship and monastic life was not interfered with; churches were built even in new Muslim cities like Fustat; Christian pilgrims from overseas like the Saxon bishop Arculf continued to visit the holy places in Palestine, and a distinguished theologian like St. John of Damascus, the last of the Greek Fathers, was allowed in his learned works to criticize Islam itself from the standpoint of Christian orthodoxy as a species of Arian heresy. The Government was indeed unwilling actively to encourage conversion, because the treasury suffered from the diminution of the *jizya*, or poll-tax payable by non-Muslims, and at the end of the Omayyad age the majority of the population of Syria, Egypt and Iraq was still Christian. But though numerically in the minority, the Muslims were politically and socially the dominant class, and the growing strength, solidity and prestige of Islam owed not a little to the policy of the Caliphs of Damascus. They promoted the construction of mosques in the principal cities of the Empire, Abd al-Malik raising the magnificent Dome of the Rock in Jerusalem on the site of the older and simpler Mosque of Omar; they introduced the minaret, from which the faithful were called to prayer and which was imitated from the church tower of the Christians, and the *mihrab*, or niche indicating the direction of Mecca, which from the sacredness of its character became the nearest approach in the mosque to the Christian altar. They sponsored, or at least presided over, the beginnings of the systematization of the sacred law, the study of the Arabic language, and the collection of *hadith*, or traditions of the Prophet, inquiries pursued mainly at Kufa and Basra. Abu Hanifa, the founder of one of the four great schools of law whose teachings are canonical in Islam, flourished in the last years of Omayyad rule.

Finally, the most spectacular feat of the Omayyads was to inaugurate a second age of conquest and to double the size of the Arab Empire by carrying the holy war simultaneously into Western Europe and the heart of Asia. The new advance was a much more surprising affair than the first. The lands occupied under Abu Bakr and Omar were racially and to some extent culturally merely extensions of Arabia itself, and the invaders of Syria, Egypt and Iraq did not feel themselves fully in a foreign country. The new conquests were achieved thousands of miles from the homeland, at the end of long lines of communication, and in regions whose people had no bonds of race, language or sympathy with the assailants. The Arabs had overrun the Semitic world and subjugated the greater part of the Iranian: they were now to break into two new culture-areas, the Latin and the Turkish. The motives for this fresh outburst of conquering zeal are fairly clear. As after the Ridda, and at the end of the first Civil War of 656-661, so now at the end of the Second Civil War in 692, the victors felt the need of mobilizing the Arab armies, which had been fighting one another, in a common enterprise against external foes, in the hope that domestic enmities would be forgotten in foreign triumphs. There was the desire to tap new sources of wealth. There was also a shrewd and accurate assessment of the weaknesses of Byzantine Africa and Turkish Transoxiana.

Once in possession of Egypt, the attention of the Arabs was naturally drawn to the lands between the Nile and the Atlantic which they named the *Maghrib*, or the West. Since the dawn of history,

the vast area north of the Sahara has been peopled by a race[1] known
to the Greeks as Libyans, to the Romans as Moors, and to the
Arabs as Berbers, who through the revolutions of three thousand
years have tenaciously preserved their identity, their language and
their manners, and stolidly resisted the enticements of civilization
which have been successively and variously presented to them by
the Carthaginians and Romans, the Arabs and Turks, the French
and Italians. This persistent and untamable barbarism, commemorated in their very name, is doubtless to be ascribed to their proximity to the greatest desert in the world; a clan, a tribe, a whole confederacy, might be drawn within the circle of civilization and induced to settle as peasants in the villages or craftsmen in the towns,
but their abandoned pastures and hunting-grounds were, it is con-
jectured, speedily replenished by fresh hordes of nomads from the
recesses of the Sahara, and the strongest imperial authority was unable to police a wilderness of such a magnitude. In North Africa the
tide of barbarism has often flowed northwards and threatened to en-
gulf the settled communities clinging precariously to the coastal
fringe. The struggle has been endemic: the Berbers have never been
tamed, but since the days of Carthage the merchant and the farmer
have never been wholly expelled from the southern shores of the
Mediterranean.

The Phoenicians were the first to plant towns in North Africa:
under the Romans the frontier of civilization was pushed towards
the foothills of the Awras mountains; the olive was introduced on
the high plateaus, which though stony are rendered fertile by irrigation, and the *limes* or defensive works, forts, walls and ditches, protected the fields and groves of the farmer from the raids of the nomads who lurked in the oases of the south. The ruins of Timgad and
Lambesa attest the depth and extent of the urbanized culture of
Rome in North Africa, but the more westerly regions were never
occupied, and the ancient geographers appear to have been ignorant
of the very existence of the rich plain between the high and middle
Atlas, in which the city of Marrakesh now stands. Christianity entered the land in the second century; an African Church rose and
flourished, and acquired lustre from such men as Tertullian, Cyprian

---

[1]Ethnologists might cavil at the term 'race', since 'Berber' is properly
applied to those who speak Berber dialects, irrespective of their racial descent. See G. Bousquet, *Les Berbères,* Paris, 1956.

and Augustine, but in the age of Diocletian and Constantine its unity was broken by the heresy of the Donatists, and the province, plagued by religious dissension and persecution, fell an easy victim to the Vandal invaders, who crossed from Spain in 429. The overthrow of Roman rule disrupted the entire social and economic system of the country; the peasants rose against their landlords, the heretics against the Catholics: the wealthy provincials fled, and the *limes* and irrigation works alike fell into neglect. The Vandal kingdom survived barely a century, but the imperial reconquest under Justinian in 533 could not restore the old prosperity. Byzantine authority scarcely extended beyond the limits of modern Tunisia; the Vandal interlude had afforded the Berbers opportunity to encroach on the regions Rome had reclaimed from barbarism, and the camel, introduced into North Africa in early imperial times, increased the mobility of the nomads and the destructiveness of their raids.

The state of North Africa on the eve of the Arab conquest was far from secure or satisfactory. The Latin-speaking provincials were now governed from Constantinople; the ecclesiastical policy of the house of Heraclius favoured the Christology known as Monothelitism, or doctrine of the single will, which was repudiated as heretical by the Popes, in whose sphere of jurisdiction the African Church lay; religious dissension produced political disloyalty, and at the time of the first Arab raid in 647 the Exarch Gregory had apparently renounced allegiance to Constantinople and proclaimed himself Emperor. The land was parcelled out in large estates, on which corn and oil were raised for export, and an oppressed peasantry felt small inclination to fight for its masters. The native Berbers were turbulent, disorderly and disunited. Their tribal organization was loose, and they acknowledged no common leader; some clans had abandoned their ancient nomadism and settled as cultivators, which brought them to some extent under Byzantine influence, but the majority of the tribes remained beyond the reach of civilization. They also remained beyond the reach of Christianity, for though some missionary work had been done among the Berbers (the modern Tuaregs are believed to have once been a Christian people), the gospel was never translated into their language, and their primitive paganism was successfully challenged only by the coming of Islam.

The first serious attempt at Arab colonization, as distinct from mere raiding, was made by Okba, who is revered by his co-religionists to this day as the founder of Muslim Africa. By planting a permanent camp at Kairawan in 670, he threatened alike the Byzantines and the Berbers: by undertaking his famous march to the West more than ten years later, he boldly claimed the whole continent for Islam and brought the Arabs to the verge of Europe. How much is truth and how much legend in the story of this grand razzia, is impossible to say. Starting from Kairawan, and avoiding the Byzantine towns and forts north of the Awras, he struck across the central plateau, pushed beyond the Atlas, reached the coast at Tangier, turned south into Morocco, and followed the course of the river Sus to the point where it discharges into the Atlantic. Spurring his horse into the waves (so runs the tale), and raising his lance aloft, he cried, like a new Alexander, 'Great God, if my advance were not stopped by this sea, I would still go on, to the unknown kingdoms of the West, preaching the unity of thy holy name, and putting to the sword the unbelieving nations who worship other gods than thee!' His ruthless treatment of the Berbers provoked a rising of the tribes under one Kusaila, and on his return journey he fell into an ambush on the edge of the Sahara near the modern Biskra, and perished with all his men (683). Kusaila occupied Kairawan, with some help from the Byzantines, and though the place was recovered and the Berber leader killed three years later, the Arabs were faced by a new native revolt, this time among the more nomadic tribes led by a woman, a *kahina* or prophetess, a Berber Deborah. No further progress was made until Abd al-Malik had restored peace at home and a new series of revolutions in Constantinople paralysed Byzantine resistance in North Africa.

In 695 the Emperor Justinian II, a crazy tyrant and the last of the line of Heraclius, was deposed and exiled, and for more than twenty years *coup* succeeded *coup* in Constantinople, until order was restored by Leo III the Isaurian in 717. It was during this interval that the last and most startling of the Arab conquests were made in the West, and North Africa and Spain were torn away from Christendom. The Caliph sent a new army under Hassan b.al-Nu'man, who by a bold surprise attack seized Carthage, but was obliged to retire in face of strong pressure from the *kahina* and her tribes. Receiving reinforcements, he came back; Carthage fell finally into

Arab hands in 698, and a year or two later the Berbers were driven into the Awrasian hills and compelled to surrender. Carthage, less fortunate than Alexandria, was abandoned to ruin and decay, and a new city a few miles to the south was founded on an isthmus joining two salt lakes and named Tunis. Most of the Byzantine officials and landowners withdrew to Sicily or Greece, and North Africa, which had been since the Punic Wars a province or annex of Europe, was severed from the Latin-Christian world and reoriented towards the Hamitic and negro south.

The fall of Byzantine power in North Africa confronted the Christian kingdoms of the West with a grave peril. So long as the ports and harbours of the southern Mediterranean were filled with Byzantine shipping, the Goths, the Franks and the Lombards were guarded from Islamic aggression, but this shield was now withdrawn, the imperial fleet had retired to its bases in Sicily, and Muslim naval power, spreading westwards, might easily cover an Arab descent on Europe. These fears were speedily realised. The Arabs, who in the course of a long struggle, had learnt to respect their Berber foes, shrewdly sought their alliance and enlisted them in a daring new enterprise, the invasion of Spain. No swifter conquest is recorded even in the astonishing annals of early Islam; a single campaign was sufficient to overturn the Visigothic monarchy and to carry the invaders towards the Pyrenees. Only the inherent rottenness of the Gothic State could account for so signal a triumph.

Since the days of the Phoenicians, the wealth of the Iberian peninsula had attracted the cupidity of foreigners: the silver mines of the south were exploited by the Carthaginians, the tin and copper of the north by the Romans, but the latter at least gave Spain in return four centuries of peace. The German invasions of the fifth century delivered the country to the misrule of coarse and ignorant barbarians, and it would be difficult to point to a single service or benefit which they conferred on Spain during the three hundred years (406-711) of Gothic domination. The land stagnated in misery and disorder; the standards of education and public administration fell; the elective monarchy became the sport of aristocratic factions; a series of rebellions, murders and palace revolutions undermined the structure of the State, and a feeble government lacked the strength and will to protect the mass of serfs and slaves against the rapacity of the great landlords, Goth and Roman, whose vast estates perhaps covered two-thirds of the kingdom. Driven to seek the backing of the Church against the lay nobles, the kings were often the prisoners of the clergy and displayed most vigour, not in reforming society, but in persecuting the Jews, who constituted a large, alien and industrious minority. King Witiza or Witiges, who ascended the throne in 702, did indeed venture on some measures of reform, being possibly alarmed at the growing Arab threat from Africa, but he only provoked armed opposition and was supplanted by Duke Roderick or Rodrigo, a shadowy and ill-starred figure better known to romance than history. The story was told that Roderick seduced the daughter of Count Julian, the governor of Ceuta, the last remaining Byzantine stronghold on the African coast, and that in revenge her father invited the Arabs into Spain and placed a squadron of ships at their disposal. He may have done so, but is is more likely that reports of the disorders and unrest in Spain reached Kairawan and prompted the decision to intervene, strengthened possibly by the urgings of the persecuted Spanish Jews.

In Africa Hassan b.al-Nu'man, the conqueror of Carthage, had been succeeded by Musa b.Nusair, who pacified Morocco and induced many of the Berber tribes to accept Islam. Apprised of the situation in Spain, he consulted the court of Damascus, but the Caliph Walid, who had followed his father Abd al-Malik on the throne in 705, warned him not to risk a full-scale invasion. A reconnoitring raid was made on the Spanish coast in 710, and the results were so encouraging that Musa decided to organize a joint Arab-Berber expedition under the command of his Berber freedman Tarik. In the spring of 711 the troops disembarked at the foot of the mighty rock whose familiar modern name of Gibraltar distorts and abbreviates its Arabic designation Jabal Tarik, the mountain of Tarik. Striking westwards towards the lake or lagoon of Janda, Tarik took up a strong defensive position on the river Barbate, which flows into it, and there awaited the march of the Gothic army from the north, which arrived, like Harold's at Hastings, fatigued by a long and exhausting trek across the length of the kingdom. On a single July day the fate of Spain was decided for many centuries: the wings of the Gothic forces were commanded by partisans of Witiza who deserted at the critical moment, and though Roderick in the centre maintained for a time a desperate defence the weight and fury of the Arab-Berber attack finally carried the day. The king disappeared in the mêlée, most probably being drowned in the river and swept out to sea; the most loyal of his adherents were demoralized by the loss of their leader and the revelation of widespread treachery, and Tarik was presented on the morrow of victory, like Napoleon after Jena, with the gratifying though astonishing prospect of a kingdom in dissolution.

Nothing like so complete a collapse had been seen since the conquest of Egypt seventy years before. Tarik marched rapidly on Toledo, the capital, which is said to have been delivered into his hands by the Jews. Musa, jealous that a victory of this magnitude should be won by a Berber freedman, landed in Spain with an army of veteran Arabs; he struck across the central uplands to the valley of the Ebro; a city or two held out here and there, but the peasantry remained passive; each class or group tried to make the best terms it could with the invader, and by 714 all organized resistance was over, and the scattered remnants of the Goths had been driven into the wild glens of the Asturias. Pursuant to their usual policy, the Arabs permitted the Spanish Christians to be judged by their own laws, and though in every big town a few churches were seized and transformed into mosques, freedom of worship was respected, and the Jews especially blessed the tolerance which the Muslims had brought into the land.

The sudden ruin of the Gothic power in Spain is sufficiently surprising, but even more amazing is the fact that the Arab Empire was at the same moment being expanded in the east by the conquest of Transoxiana and the Indus Valley. Their initial probings beyond the Oxus had revealed to the Arabs the confused disunity of the Turkish tribes and the wealth to be harvested from the silk trade with China, which passed along the highways and oases of Central Asia. When Hajjaj b.Yusuf, the great viceroy of Iraq, had firmly established Omayyad power in that province, he gave the governorship of Khurasan to Kutaiba b.Muslim in 705 with instructions to carry the holy war eastwards into the heart of Asia. The nucleus of his force was the Arab tribal element which had been removed to this distant frontier from Kufa and Basra, but many recruits were obtained from the native Iranian population under their *dihkans*, or village headmen, a large number of whom had adopted Islam, who were willing to fight under Arab leadership against their hereditary enemies, the nomads of Turan. In this way the Caliphs took over the functions of the Sassanid Shahs as defenders of the Iranian world against the Turkish barbarians. Kutaiba was a soldier and diplomat of outstanding ability: he exploited the quarrels of the Turkish chiefs and left those who submitted in possession of their thrones, and he was careful to assure the merchant class that their commercial interests would be adequately safeguarded. After clearing the enemy from Transoxiana, he crossed the Jaxartes in 712 and exacted the submission of Shash and Khujand; two years later, he pushed forward into eastern Turkestan, a land which even Alexander had never seen, and he entered, if he did not hold, the town of Kashgar, on the frontier of China. The domains of the Caliph touched those of the T'ang Emperor, and we may reflect on the curious circumstance that Islam has never penetrated much farther east than the Arab-Persian forces were led by Kutaiba less than a century after the Hijra.

Farther to the south, the Arabs achieved in a single campaign the conquest of much of the Indus Valley, which has never since abandoned its allegiance to Islam and forms to-day the core of the Muslim State of Pakistan. Except for brief periods, the Indian sub-continent has never enjoyed political unity: the short-lived Empire of Harsha, who reigned over the north from Kathiawar to Assam, had dissolved at his death in 646; the Rajput clans were scattered over the western plains, and the Tamil kingdoms of the south belonged to a different world. The coast of western India had long been familiar to the Persians and Arabs; as early as 636 Omar had launched a naval raid against the port of Daibul, but nothing more was done till Persia was securely in Arab hands. In 711, while Tarik was defeating the Goths in Spain, Hajjaj despatched his son-in-law, Muhammad b.Kasim, across the hills and deserts of southern Persia; Daibul was captured with help of powerful siege-engines; the local rajah was pursued up the Indus, and in 713 Multan surrendered, the spoils of the rich Buddhist shrine there paying twice over the cost of the expedition.

As the first century of the Hijra drew to its close, the whole civilized globe appeared about to fall into Arab grasp. Everywhere the Muslim armies were advancing, with kingdom after kingdom falling before them. Dreams of universal empire filled the minds of their leaders. Hajjaj is said to have promised the governorship of China to either Kutaiba or Muhammad b.Kasim, whichever of the two first set foot in the country, while Musa b.Nusair is credited with a plan for the total subversion of Christian Europe, involving the overthrow of the Byzantine Empire and the kingdoms of the Franks and Lombards. Neither Alexander nor the Romans had conceived of world conquest on such a scale. Yet in fact the end of Arab imperial expansion was in sight. Every advance of this nature must at last outrun the resources of the conquering Power and encounter mounting resistance, and internal quarrels and accidental or unpredictable circumstances will contribute to slow down and disorganize the machinery of war and conquest.

The first check came with the death of the mighty viceroy Hajjaj in 714, followed by that of the Caliph Walid in 715. Walid, an indolent, good-natured man, had little to do with the amazing victories which rendered his reign illustrious; he was more concerned with building than war, and his most enduring memorial is the great Omayyad mosque in Damascus. Dying at the early age of forty-five, when his sons were still young, he was succeeded by his brother Sulaiman, a harsh and unforgiving man, whom Hajjaj had tried to get excluded from the throne. Hajjaj being dead, Sulaiman's vengeance fell on his protégées Kutaiba and Muhammad b.Kasim. Kutaiba withdrew from Turkestan to his headquarters at Merv in Khurasan, tried to start a revolt against the new Caliph, failed and perished. Muhammad was deprived of his command, accused of various offences, and executed. The Muslim offensive in Asia came to a halt. In Europe, Musa, who had acted like a sovereign prince and coined money in his own name, was summoned back from Spain and dismissed in disgrace. The almost simultaneous disappearance from the scene of the three conquerors gave the ambitious Caliph the chance to win for the house of Omayya a personal triumph that would overshadow all else—the capture of Constantinople.

For twenty years the Byzantine Empire had been a victim to misgovernment, disorder and palace revolutions, and the killing in 711 of the brutal Justinian II (who had been restored to the throne in 705) plunged it into fresh confusion. Walid commissioned his brother Maslama, an able soldier who commanded in Armenia, to cross the Taurus and attempt to break Byzantine power in Asia Minor. When Sulaiman became Caliph the Arabs were wintering on the Anatolian plateau, and plans for a concerted sea and land attack

90

on the imperial capital were pushed forward. In the summer of 717 Maslama's advance guards reached Abydos on the Hellespont, and a vast armada of 1800 vessels from the ports of Syria and Egypt steered through the Aegean and conveyed the troops to the European shore. A few months before the imperial throne had been seized by Leo the Isaurian, a masterful general who put the defences of Constantinople in order and infused the people with a fearless and determined spirit, the Church seconding his efforts with exhortations to fight for Christ and beat off the infidel enemy. The besiegers ran into difficulties; their ships were harassed by the Greek fire; their foraging parties were attacked by Bulgarians, and a winter of exceptional rigour reduced them to pitiable straits, huddled in their frozen camps, their supplies running out, their horses and camels dying in the unfamiliar snow. Sulaiman died in the previous autumn, without seeing the realisation of his hopes: his successor Omar II in 718 ordered Maslama to withdraw. The failure of the second and last siege of Constantinople by the Arabs was decisive: had the city fallen, the Balkan peninsula would have been overrun, the Arabs would have sailed up the Danube into the heart of Europe, and Christianity might have lingered, an obscure sect, in the forests of Germany. As it was, the Byzantine Empire was galvanized into new vigour by the Isaurians; the Arabs were forced to evacuate Asia Minor, and so long as the imperial government retained possession of Sicily, Italy was safe from Arab invasion.

Nonetheless, the Byzantines, though they had saved their capital, could do nothing to recover Spain, and from this European base the Arabs proceeded to a land assault on Western Christendom. Their first detachments appeared north of the Pyrenees as early as 718; the next year they descended on Narbonne, and though repulsed from Toulouse in 721, they launched a grand razzia in 725 up the Rhone valley, captured Nimes, plundered Vienne and Lyons, and passing into Burgundy, pillaged and burnt the city of Autun. Frankish Gaul seemed likely to go the way of Gothic Spain, and similar elements of weakness and decadence could be detected. The royal house was degenerate; society was barbarous; the power of the crown had passed into the hands of the great landowners, by race a fusion of Frank and Gallo-Roman; the Church was corrupt; the once free peasants were sinking into serfdom, and the unity of the realm was imperilled by the mutual jealousies of the northern provinces of Austrasia and Neustria, which were largely Germanized, and by the semi-independent status of the great duchy of Aquitaine, between the Loire and the Pyrenees, where few Franks had settled and which therefore preserved in considerable measure the laws, language and civilization of Rome. Yet the Franks enjoyed certain advantages which had been denied to the Goths. They remained in direct contact with the Germany from which they sprang and could draw on fresh reserves from beyond the Rhine; political power was now exercised by the remarkably able Carolingian family, who governed the land under the modest title of Mayors of the Palace, and the Gothic catastrophe in Spain was a warning which no Frank could ignore.

In 732 a new governor of Spain (or Andalus, as the Arabs called the country), Abd al-Rahman al-Ghafiki, led a strong Arab-Berber force across the Pyrenees and struck northwards along the old Roman road to the Loire, his immediate objective being the wealthy shrine of St. Martin at Tours. Between that town and Poitiers, at a spot still known as Moussais la Bataille, he was intercepted by the main Frankish army under the command of Charles Martel, the Mayor of the Palace of Austrasia: after a week's fighting, the Muslims were routed and retreated towards Narbonne. Abd al-Rahman and many of his officers were killed, and so heavy were the Muslim casualties that the Arabic historians style this fatal battle *Balat al-Shuhada,* the way or path of martyrs. Frankish losses were, however, not light; Martel was unable to follow up his victory, and not for twenty years were the Arabs ejected from Narbonne, their last remaining base in Gaul.

The repulse of the Arabs in Gaul paralleled their failure at the walls of Constantinople. Gibbon amused himself by conjecturing that, had the battle gone the other way, the Arabs would have reached the Rhine and the Channel, and sailed up the Thames, with the result that 'the Koran would now be taught in the schools of Oxford.' The consequences of Abd al-Rahman's defeat were indeed momentous. The Franks were hailed as the saviours of Latin Christendom, and Martel's success ultimately gained for his house the throne and for his grandson Charlemagne the splendid title of Emperor of the West. Spanish Christianity was saved from annihilation: in the Asturian hills around Covadonga a resistance movement was born, whose leaders were encouraged by the proximity of a strong Christian Power on the other side of the Pyrenees, and the first halting steps were taken towards the Reconquista, the recovery of Spain from Islam. Yet it still remains to be asked, why the Arabs never renewed the attempt on Gaul in contrast to the persistence with which they returned again and again to the attack in Transoxiana and Turkestan, where they finally won ascendancy by a victory over the Chinese at Talas in 751. In the latter case, the profits of the silk trade were, no doubt, a strong inducement, whereas Gaul was a poor and backward land. But what really put a stop to the Arab advance in Western Europe was the great Berber revolt which broke out in Africa in 739 and spread to Spain, where the Berbers bitterly complained that the finest lands had been appropriated by the Bedouin chiefs. Arab racial arrogance was the root cause of the trouble, Berber resentment being fanned by the preaching of Kharijite missionaries, whose revolutionary egalitarianism accorded well with the anarchical democracy of the tribes. After a bloody struggle, the revolt was crushed by 742, but at the cost of the suspension of military operations against the Christian Powers.

By the close of the Omayyad age the Caliphate had reached the limits of its political expansion. A huge segment of the globe, roughly between the 25th and 43rd parallels of latitude, obeyed the mandates of the Prophet's Vicar, an area which remains to this day the solid core of Islam. The resistance of the Franks and the revolt of the Berbers confined Islam to the south of the Pyrenees and soon of the Ebro; Constantinople was never again menaced by the Arabs, and the Byzantine Empire, its unity strengthened by the loss of the Monophysite East and the firm rule of the Isaurians, retained its grip on Asia Minor, which was to stay Greek and Christian for another 350 years, and its continued possession of Sicily challenged Arab naval control of the Mediterranean. Arab attempts to press northwards from Armenia through the Caucasus into the Russian steppes had run into the opposition of the Khazars, a semi-civilized Turkish people who inhabited the lower Volga region, and who shielded Eastern Europe and the future State of Kievan Russia from Muslim aggression. No progress was made beyond the Indus for three hundred years after Muhammad b.Kasim, but in Central Asia the disunited tribes of Western Turkestan were subjugated and Arab authority established as far east as Farghana. No conquests were made at the expense of the T'ang Empire of China. Within these limits the Caliphs ruled a vaster domain than the Caesars. Experience was to show that it was easier to conquer than to administer and retain it.

BOOKS FOR FURTHER READING

BARTHOLD, W., *Turkestan down to the Mongol Invasion*, Eng. tr. 2nd. ed. 1958. Standard work, first published in Russian in 1900.

D. C. DENNETT, *Conversion and the Poll-Tax in Early Islam*, Camb. Mass., 1950.

GAUTIER, E., *Le Passé de l'Afrique du Nord*, Paris, 1952. Brilliant and stimulating, marred in places by risky theorizing.

GIBB, H. A. R., *The Arab Conquests in Central Asia*, London, 1923.

JULIEN, C. A., *Histoire de l'Afrique du Nord*, 2 vols. Paris, 1951-52. Summarizes well the results of modern French scholarship.

LÉVY-PROVENÇAL, E., *Histoire de l'Espagne musulmane*, vol. 1, Cairo, 1944. Standard account of Muslim Spain.

MERCIER, M. & SEGUIN, A., *Charles Martel et la Bataille de Poitiers*, Paris, 1944.

PERIER, J., *Vie d'al-Hadjdjadj ibn Yousof*, Paris 1904. A rather uncritical life of the famous viceroy taken from the Arabic chronicles which are mostly hostile to him.

PIRENNE, H., *Mohammed and Charlemagne*, 1935; Eng. tr. 1939. Argues the controversial thesis that the Arab conquests 'closed the Mediterranean' to Christian shipping and caused the economic backwardness of Frankish Europe.

REINAUD, J., *Les Invasions des Sarrazins en France*, Paris, 1836. Still useful, despite its age.

TERRASSE, H., *Histoire du Maroc*, vol. 1, Casablanca, 1949.

TRANSLATED SOURCES

Baladhuri, as before.

IBN ABD AL-HAKAM, *La conquête de l'Afrique du Nord et de l'Espagne*, ed. & tr. A. Gateau, Algiers, 1942. The author of this chronicle, in which a good deal of romance is mixed, died at Fustat in 870.

NARSHAKHI, *History of Bukhara*, tr. R. N. Frye, Cambridge, Mass., 1954. Written about 943, later abridged and continued by other hands. One of the earliest accounts of the Arab conquests in Central Asia.

VI

The Abbasid Revolution

OMAYYAD rule had been accepted by the Muslim community less because of its virtues and merits than because of the lack of a satisfactory alternative, and it was never universally popular. The pious never ceased to be scandalized at the profane and secular atmosphere surrounding the court of Damascus; luxurious living, a growing staff of eunuchs and concubines, and the extravagant retreats and hunting-lodges built on the edge of the Syrian desert, contrasted unfavourably with the puritan simplicity of the first Caliphs. The partisans of Ali, who never forgave the Omayyads for the tragedy of Karbala, remained irreconcilable enemies of the dynasty, though their inability to agree upon a candidate for the throne long weakened their influence. Upholders of the ancient Arab traditions, who hated the government of kings, felt small loyalty to sovereigns who seemed to be aping the despotism of foreign infidels. The Kharijites no longer appeared in arms, but they propagated their republican and theocratic ideas through underground channels, and their scornful assertion that a negro slave had as good a right to the Caliphate as the members of the aristocratic Kuraish awoke a favourable response among many of those who resented the arrogance and pretensions of the Arab ruling class.

Yet none of these critics of the reigning house would have seriously endangered it had they not been able to enlist the support of the *mawali*, the non-Arab converts to Islam. By 700 the religion of the Prophet had ceased to be a monopoly of his people, and the Arab Muslims were at last outnumbered by those of the subject races, notably the Persians and Berbers. In theory, all believers were equal within the brotherhood of Islam: in practice, the *mawali* were treated as lowborn inferiors. Racial segregation was common: in Kufa Arabs and non-Arabs used separate mosques; intermarriage was strongly discouraged; and in some towns an Arab risked social ostracism if he walked down the street in company with a *mawla*. The *mawali* paid taxes from which the Arab Muslims were exempt; and though they were permitted to serve in the army, they were excluded from the cavalry, and as foot-soldiers, drew lower rates of pay. So long as the converts were a small minority, they could be kept in their place, but as their number rose, their complaints and grievances grew louder, and the Mukhtar revolt of 685 had shown the alarming political dangers latent in this situation. It was natural that the *mawali* should tend to be anti-Omayyad, since the government was associated in their minds with the maintenance of Arab domination, and equally natural that the enemies of the dynasty should seek to win them as allies. When the regime was at last driven to seek means of conciliating the *mawali*, it found the position complicated by economic difficulties almost impossible to overcome.

The economic history of the Omayyad age is very imperfectly known. There seems to have been a considerable though patchy prosperity; big fortunes were made and invested principally in land, and enormous sums were expended in buildings, from mosques to the Omayyad desert palaces which have been excavated from the sand in recent years. The disappearance of the Euphrates frontier, which for seven centuries had separated the Roman from the Persian world, created a huge free trade area in which goods could circulate and from which customs barriers were absent; the Arab navy protected the commerce of the Indian Ocean; the conquest of North Africa and Spain flooded the East with treasure, goods and slaves, and it is possible that gold from the mines of the Wadi al-Allaki, near Aswan in Nubia, was already reaching the Caliphate. On the other hand, any sudden increase in the circulation of the precious metals must have raised prices and brought about a financial crisis; the defeat of the expedition against Constantinople and the cessation of conquests in the West must have seriously depleted the Treasury, and the vast inequalities of personal wealth, which were now becoming obvious, fostered social discontent and often led the 'poor

Arabs' to throw in their lot with the *mawali* against the dominant aristocracy.

The first attempt to tackle the *mawali* problem was made by Omar II, who succeeded his cousin Sulaiman in 717. This man, a grandson of the first Omar, made an extraordinary impression on his age, despite the brevity of his reign. Of austere morals and deep piety, he recognized no distinction of race or party: he stopped the public cursing of Ali, relieved the Berbers of the harsh tribute of children which had been imposed on them, discouraged raids and wars against peaceful nations, and boldly set out to remove the economic grievances of the *mawali*. This involved something like a fiscal revolution: hitherto Muslim landowners had paid only *ushr* or tithe on their estates, and non-Muslims a much heavier impost, at first indifferently called *kharaj* or *jizya*, both words signifying tribute. If the owner of tribute-paying land turned Muslim, he was in future liable only for *ushr*. To prevent a diminution of State revenue, the Omayyads had discouraged conversion and often continued to exact payment of *kharaj* and *jizya* from the *mawali*, notwithstanding that as Muslims they should have been exempt from taxation. In Khurasan *mawali* who had fought against the unbelievers were placed on the pension-list as well as being freed from these imposts. Omar decreed that after the hundredth year of the Hijra (718-719) no *kharaj*-paying land should be purchased by a Muslim, though he could rent it and continue paying the tax, and that should a non-Arab embrace Islam, his land was to revert to the village community, he himself staying on, if he desired, as the tenant. To complaints from his advisers that conversions would reduce the Treasury's receipts, the Caliph replied scornfully: 'The Prophet was sent by God as a missionary not a tax-gatherer!'.

The pious Omar was not destined to live to see the result of his experiment: he died in 720, at the age of thirty-nine, leaving behind him a reputation as the best of the Omayyads, so that the chroniclers of the Abbasid age specifically exempt him from the general censure they pass on his house, and regret that the reformer of the world was snatched away before his time. The Caliphate passed to his cousin Yazid II, a brother of Walid, a frivolous drone who had none of his predecessor's devotion to religion and who by favouring the Kaisites, re-opened a slumbering feud. Fortunately, his reign was short, and on his death in 724, his younger brother Hisham was chosen Caliph, the fourth of the sons of Abd al-Malik to mount the throne. The long reign of Hisham (724-743) was the Indian summer of the Omayyads. An able and moderate man, he preserved the outward decorum of the correct Muslim without displaying the ardent piety of Omar; of reserved disposition, he hated the noise and bustle of cities, and passed most of his time at his hunting-lodges far out in the Syrian desert, while the financial straits in which the State was involved in consequence of Omar's reforms obliged him to restrict expenditure and exposed him to charges of meanness and avarice.

He faced a highly critical situation. The war against the Byzantines was pursued with some success, and a brilliant Muslim commander nicknamed 'al-Battal', the hero, who was killed in the fighting in Asia Minor in 740, acquired legendary fame as a valorous champion of the faith and figured in later ages in a Turkish romance of chivalry. But the disastrous defeat in Gaul in 732, followed by the great Berber revolt of 739-742, which at one time threatened the loss of the entire Maghrib and was marked by an Arab reverse involving the death of so many leaders of distinguished lineage as to be called 'the battle of the nobles,' clouded the scene and added to the unpopularity of the regime. Hisham's energetic measures restored order in North Africa, but Berber unrest, fomented by Kharijite propaganda, could never be completely quelled. After a long period of quiescence, Shi'ism raised its head again, though 'the party of Ali' had ceased to be a unity, one group supporting the claims of the descendants of Ali and Fatima, another those of the descendants of Ali and Khawla the Hanafite woman, and a third those of the descendants of Ali's brother Ja'far. All these factions recruited the bulk of their following in southern Iraq, and strange messianic and millenarian ideas were now entering and transforming what had been originally a protest of political legitimism. In 737 the Omayyad police caught and executed a number of Shi'ite agents in Kufa, and in 740 Husain's grandson Zaid led an abortive rising in the same city. Hisham's response was to cultivate the religious leaders and institute proceedings against heresy, in the hope of convincing the faithful that the Omayyads were loyal defenders of Islamic orthodoxy and to strengthen the State by introducing Persian administrative methods into the Caliphal secretariat.

Had the house of Omayya remained united and resolute in face of these mounting troubles, they might have divided their enemies and kept their throne. But the reigning family was becoming riddled with feuds and jealousies, and the successors of Hisham came to blows over his inheritance. His son Mu'awiya, the ancestor of the Spanish Omayyads, was killed in the hunting-field in his father's lifetime, and Hisham reluctantly recognized as his heir his nephew Walid, a son of Yazid II, a handsome and dissolute rake, whose blasphemies and drunken debaucheries are detailed by the chroniclers with shocked horror. While Walid neglected his duties and amused himself in his desert retreats, a conspiracy was set on foot by Yazid, a son of Walid I, who received the backing of the Marwanid clan; Damascus was seized by a sudden *coup,* and the Caliph was slain near Palmyra (April 744), the first of his house since Othman to meet a violent death. In the capital his rival was invested with the caliphal insignia of ring and staff as Yazid III, but he failed to win the acceptance of the Empire; Marwan, the governor of Armenia and a grandson of the first Caliph of that name, espoused the cause of the sons of the murdered Walid II, and set his army in motion for Syria. Before any fighting took place, Yazid III died suddenly in November 744 after a reign of only six months; his brother Ibrahim was proclaimed Caliph, but was recognized nowhere outside southern Syria; Marwan crossed the Euphrates and occupied Damascus, and on finding that Walid II's children had been put to death, himself took possession of the throne.

If the Omayyad regime could have been rescued by courage and energy, Marwan II would have been its saviour. An able soldier, he had distinguished himself in campaigns against the Byzantines and the Khazars, and he had improved the quality of the army by breaking up the old tribal framework and forming regular regiments under the command of trained professional officers. But he came too late, for the troubles that followed the death of Hisham had irretrievably wrecked the unity of the Omayyad house. Marwan's title was irregular, his mother was a Kurdish slave; the family of Hisham treated him as a usurper; he had the support of the Kais and therefore the enmity of the Kalb, and his impolitic move in transferring the government to Harran, the ancient Carrhae in northern Mesopotamia, was bitterly resented in Damascus, which was thus robbed of its status as the seat of empire. He was forced from the beginning to fight for his throne. A son of Hisham's, Sulaiman, rebelled against him; the Kharijites rose in Mosul under one Dahhak, while a Shi'ite revolt broke out in Kufa led by Abdallah b.Mu'awiya, a great-grandson of Ali's brother Ja'far. After a three years' struggle, the disturbances were put down, and by 747 Marwan could congratulate himself on the apparent restoration of peace and order. At this point, however, a new peril arose in an unexpected quarter, not in anti-Omayyad Iraq, but in the distant and hitherto loyal province of Khurasan.

A new element had entered into the situation: the Persians were reassuming a decisive role in the politics of Western Asia. By the mid-eighth century no Persian alive could recall the days of Sassanid rule: any political restoration could obviously take place only within the framework of Islam. Of the process and speed of Islamization we are ill-informed. Despite the fact that the Prophet almost certainly contemplated toleration only for Jews and Christians, the Arabs had been forced to recognize the Persian Zoroastrians as 'People of the Book', liable to tribute but not extermination. The Magian faith survived, though deprived of the support of the State: as late as the tenth century there were still fire-temples in every big Persian city, and in the hill country of Tabaristan and Dailam, Islam did not gain an entrance till the age of the Buyids. But over the greater part of Persia conversions to Islam may have begun soon after the conquest, when the coercive power of the Magian priesthood was destroyed; exemption from the payment of the tribute was doubtless a strong inducement, and if Hisham decreed the fiscal equality of Arab and non-Arab Muslims, as is likely, the trend must have been greatly hastened. In some regions like Khurasan the new religion was embraced by large numbers of *dihkans,* hereditary small proprietors who under both the Sassanids and the Caliphs acted as tax-collectors for the central government, and whose conversion was often followed by that of the villages in which they resided. These *mawali* were frequently exposed to the scorn of race-conscious Arabs, Bedouin tribesmen from Kufa and Basra, who garrisoned the towns and forts along the eastern border. Yet some Arabs married Persian wives and adopted Persian customs such as the wearing of trousers and observance of the old Iranian New Year festival, and the children of these unions tended to be Persian rather than Arab in spirit and education.

This situation was turned to the advantage of a new enemy of the reigning dynasty, the descendants of the Prophet's uncle Abbas, whence they obtained the name Abbasids. According to tradition, Abu Hashim, the son of the Alid claimant Muhammad b.al-Hanafiya (Ali's descendant through the Hanafite wife) was poisoned by the Caliph Sulaiman, but before he died in Palestine in 716 he bequeathed his claims to Muhammad b.Ali, a great-grandson of Abbas, in whose dwelling he had found shelter. The Abbasid party thereby took over the organization of one of the principal Alid sects, and from its headquarters in Kufa it started a vigorous propaganda campaign in Khurasan. Though its earliest missionary Khidash was caught and executed in 736, his work was continued more circumspectly by Sulaiman b.Kathir, who on the death of Muhammad b.Ali in 743 espoused the cause of his son Ibrahim. The latter, anxious to turn to account the troubles which followed the death of Hisham, entrusted the management of his affairs to Abu Muslim, a Persian slave of obscure origin, who was recommended to him as a man of extraordinary capacity. A leader of genius who changed the history of the East, Abu Muslim (his Arabic name was a privilege sometimes granted to non-Arab *mawali*) combined the hard and sombre ruthlessness of the fanatic with the skill and adroitness of the politician; he succeeded in being all things to all men, and he inspired in his followers a passionate attachment. The disaffected *mawali* were eager to enlist under the standard of one of their own race, but though the Persians were his chief hope, his designs could be accomplished only by splitting the Arab colonists and fomenting the endemic quarrel between the Kais and the Kalb. As soon as he had won over the bulk of the Kalb, he struck the blow he had long been maturing. In June 747 two black flags, emblems it seems of messianic significance, sent by the Imam Ibrahim were unfurled at a village near Merv, in the presence of two thousand armed rebels, and at the Friday service the name of the Abbasid chief was publicly inserted in place of the reigning Caliph.

The Omayyad Government was slow to grasp the gravity of this event. The suppression of the Kharijite and Shi'ite revolts had given it a false sense of security, nor did it realise that this had simply removed two dangerous rivals from the path of the Abbasids. Nasr b. Sayyar, the veteran governor of Khurasan, saw the danger, but he misinterpreted the affair as an anti-Arab rising, and sent alarmist reports to Harran warning Marwan that a general massacre of Arabs in the province was intended. This was not so: Abu Muslim's movement was directed, not against the Arabs as such, but against Arab political and social domination as represented by the Omayyad officials and ruling class, and his army was commanded by Kahtaba b. Shabib, an Arab of the Tayyi tribe. Unable to conciliate the Kalb, who either went over to the enemy or stood sullenly aside, Nasr was driven out of Merv and fled westwards, while Kahtaba made a brilliant and rapid march across Persia from Khurasan to Iraq. Here the Omayyad governor was shut up in Wasit, and though Basra was held for the government, Kufa opened its gates without resistance, and in its mosque, in November 749, Abu'l-Abbas, the brother of Ibrahim (who had died in an Omayyad prison), was enthroned as Commander of the Faithful. Thus the political centre of Islam swung back from Syria to Iraq, and the new dynasty arose in the city where Ali had ruled and died nearly a century before.

The last hope of the falling regime reposed on the Syrian army, now a small and demoralized force. Too late, Marwan led these troops across the Tigris, and in January 750 they encountered the victorious Khurasanians on the banks of the Great Zab. The last Omayyad field army was routed; Marwan retreated on Harran, but the pursuers were at his heels, in the cities of Syria, once so loyal to his house, not a hand was raised in his support, and he fled through Palestine into Egypt, where at Busir he was overtaken and killed by a Kalbite Arab who gave orders to his men in Persian. His head was cut off, and despatched with the caliphal staff and ring to Abu'l-Abbas, who ascended the throne in an atmosphere of cowardice, treachery and bloody terror almost unsurpassed even in the history of Asia. The towns and fortresses of Syria, including Damascus, surrendered with scarcely a struggle; Wasit, protected by the Tigris marshes, held out until the news of Marwan's death and then capitulated on terms which were promptly and brutally violated; the graves of the Omayyad Caliphs, with the single exception of that of the pious Omar, were broken open and the corpses torn out and burnt, and the new Caliph's uncle Abdallah b.Ali perpetrated a deed of outstanding infamy. Trusting to his solemn promises, eighty princes of the fallen house accepted his invitation to a banquet; at a given signal a band of executioners entered the room and clubbed them all to death; leathern covers were spread over the bodies, and the host and his friends feasted upon them to the sound of their victims' dying groans. From this savage holocaust, which may be compared with the extermination by Jehu of the line of Omri, few escaped save Abd al-Rahman, the young grandson of the Caliph Hisham, who after being hunted through the deserts of Egypt and Barbary, found refuge in Spain, where the writ of the Abbasids did not yet run and where he became the father of a new dynasty of Omayyads, who reigned in the peninsula for upwards of three hundred years.

The Abbasid Revolution, like the displacement of the Merovingians in Gaul by the Carolingians about the same time, was something more than a change of dynasty. The Abbasids themselves proclaimed that they had brought to Islam a *dawla,* a turn or change, a new order; their government, they averred, would, unlike that of their godless predecessors, be based on the true principles of Muslim piety; religion not race was to be the foundation of the State, and the Caliphs henceforth styled themselves 'Shadows of God on earth' and added to their personal names titles expressive of moral or religious qualities such as 'al-Mahdi', the guided one, and 'al-Rashid', the orthodox. The revolution preserved the Caliphate as an institution, but altered its character and spirit. The removal of the seat of government from Syria to Iraq accentuated the trend towards monarchical despotism which was already noticeable under the Omayyads. The political tradition of Persia had long been exerting an influence on Arab governmental practice. Under Hisham the secretariat became increasingly Persianized, and Marwan had foreshadowed the downgrading of Syria by moving the capital to Harran. With the coming of the Abbasids, Persians streamed into the public services; a new office, that of Wazir or Vizier, was created whose holder exercised the authority of a Vice-Caliph, the sovereign himself retreating, like the old Sassanid Shahs, into the depths of his palace, hidden from his people behind a crowd of officials, ministers and eunuchs, and when al-Mansur, the second Abbasid, resolved to build himself a new capital, he selected a site near the ruins of ancient Ctesiphon which bore the old Persian name of Baghdad, signifying probably 'gift of God'. If some trace of Arab tribal democracy survived among the Omayyads, it was totally eliminated under the Abbasids, who seemed to have inherited the sacred absolutism of the kings of Nineveh, Babylon and Persia. The executioner with his leathern carpet stood beside the throne as the symbol of his royal master's power of life and death over his subjects, whose rights were unprotected by any law or senate or constitution.

Yet it would be highly misleading to interpret the revolution of 750, as some have done, as a simple triumph of Persian over Arab. The supremacy of the Arab race in the East was indeed destroyed; the *mawali* were raised to a status of equality with the Arab Muslims; the army ceased to be dominated by Bedouin tribesmen and became largely Persianized; the founding of Baghdad reduced the power and influence of the camp-cities of Kufa and Basra, and the Bedouin warriors who had conquered half the civilized world tended to withdraw back into the Arabian deserts from which their fathers had emerged more than a century before. Yet in the powerful sphere of religion, the Arab maintained his primacy; *his* was the nation to whom Allah had first vouchsafed his revelation, *his* was the tongue in which Gabriel had delivered the divine oracles to the Prophet, nor could Arabic, the holy language of the Koran, ever be displaced by the profane idioms of the convert peoples. Whatever success the Persians could claim had been won within the framework of Islam; a national Iranian revival implied no return to Magianism; the mosque had supplanted the fire-temple; Abu Muslim and his henchmen professed the fervour of pious Muslims eager to restore the purity of the faith, and for three centuries the scholars of Persia, who founded the literature and science of Islam, published their works in Arabic, as though their native speech were unworthy of the study and attention of the true believer. Moreover, the dynasty was still Arab, the Abbasids being as proud as the Omayyads of their membership of the Kuraish; they were unable to appeal to Persian race-feeling, and unlike the Sassanids, they could not rely on the loyalty of a native priesthood and feudal class. The Abbasids were driven to seek a delicate balance between Arab and Persian, which was difficult to attain; the pride and superiority felt by Muslims of Arab descent provoked, in early Abbasid times, the movement known as the Shu'ubiyya, which stressed the brotherhood and equality of all races, (*shu'ub*, peoples, nations), and racial jealousy and disharmony may be accounted one of the principal causes of the disintegration of the Caliphate which followed swiftly on the overthrow of the Omayyads.

BOOKS FOR FURTHER READING

GABRIELI, F., *Il Califfato di Hisham*, Alexandria, 1935. The only detailed study of the crucial reign of Hisham (724-743).

LEWIS, B., Art. 'Abbāsids', in the new *Enc. of Islam*.

VAN VLOTEN, G., *Recherches sur la domination arabe*, Amsterdam, 1894. The first critical account of the events leading to the 750 revolution.

WELLHAUSEN, J., *The Arab Kingdom and its Fall*, Eng. tr. Calcutta, 1927. The German original of this standard work was published in 1902. The last three chapters contain the fullest and acutest analysis of the overthrow of the Omayyads.

VII

The Breakup of the Caliphate

THE Abbasids proved to be one of the longest-lived dynasties of Islam. Their rule lasted for half a millennium, from the overthrow of the Omayyads in 750 till the destruction of Baghdad by the Mongols in 1258, and even then a line of shadow-Caliphs was prolonged in Cairo, under the protection of the Mamluk Sultans, from 1261 till the Ottoman conquest of Egypt in 1517. Their effective government came to an end, however, as early as 945, when their political authority passed into the hands of the Buyid amirs and later of the Turkish sultans: henceforth they exercised only spiritual power as the successors of the Prophet and Imams of the Muslim world. Their history is much better known to us than that of the Omayyads, owing to the rapid growth of Arabic historiography from the late eighth century onwards. Contemporary chronicles provide us with a mass of information, much of it not yet adequately sifted: of these the fullest is the great *Annals of Apostles and Kings* by the learned Persian Tabari, who as his name implies was a native of the province of Tabaristan on the shores of the Caspian and who died at Baghdad in 923, after a lifetime devoted to historical and theological scholarship. On the other hand, archival material (charters, official decrees, legislative enactments) is almost wholly wanting, as Islam never had a clergy, a feudal aristocracy, urban communes, or representative assemblies, and the social and economic history of the Abbasid age has to be pieced together with such meagre evidence as is afforded by coins, business documents, geographical handbooks, and archaeological finds.

106

Our knowledge and understanding of the early Abbasid period is therefore still woefully defective, but the main political trends are clear enough. The dynasty owed its consolidation to the able and ruthless Mansur (754-775), the founder of Baghdad, and reached the peak of its fame under Harun al-Rashid (786-809), though signs of disintegration were already evident, and North Africa became autonomous as early as 800. On Harun's death, the Empire was thrown into confusion by a civil war between his two sons Amin and Ma'mun: the latter's victory in 813 was a further blow to Arab ascendancy and strengthened Persian influence in the central government. Ma'mun (813-833) was a munificent patron of the arts and sciences, but he seems to have been politically inept, and he allowed the great eastern province of Khurasan to slip from his grasp, an independent Persian principality establishing itself there in 820. Under his successor Mu'tasim (833-842) the Caliph surrounded himself with a Turkish bodyguard, whose excesses provoked so much popular discontent in Baghdad that the court removed to Samarra, farther up the Tigris, in 836. This 'Avignon Captivity' of the Caliphate lasted for more than fifty years, until the government returned to Baghdad in 889. Attempts by Mutawakkil (846-861) to control the Turkish soldiery produced a mutiny in which he was killed, followed by ten years of anarchy, in which one Caliph after another was put up and pulled down by the turbulent praetorians. During this unhappy period the greater part of Persia fell away from the Caliphate; a Turkish soldier of fortune, Ahmad b.Tulun, made himself master of Egypt and Syria, and a terrible slave revolt broke out in Basra and spread up lower Iraq. Under Mu'tamid (870-892), recovery set in, thanks mainly to the energy of his brother Muwaffak; the Turks were curbed, the slave rising was crushed, and the authority of the central government restored over a large part of the Empire. The last able Abbasid ruler for many years was Muktafi (902-908), who recovered Egypt from the Tulunids; after him decline proceeded apace; the Fatimid anti-Caliphate was set up in North Africa in 909 to challenge even the spiritual supremacy of the Abbasids; and in 945 the Buyids, a clan from Dailam in north-west Persia, seized power in Baghdad and finally extinguished the political authority of the Caliphs.

Behind these political changes a more fundamental transformation of the Near East on the religious, economic and cultural level

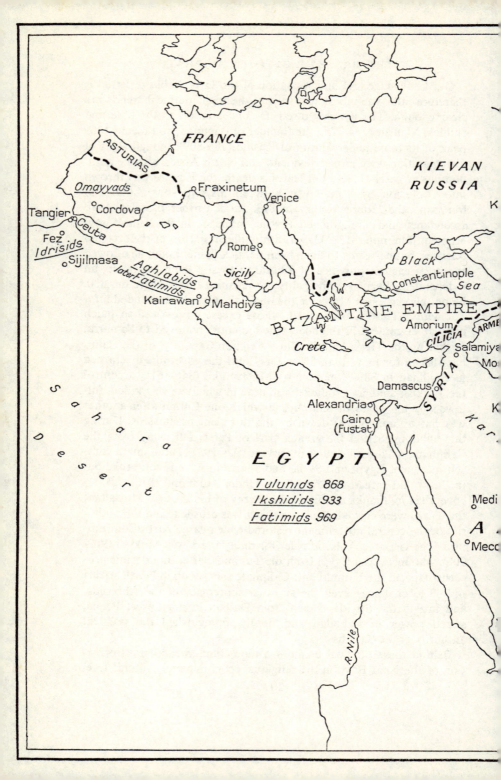

THE BREAKUP OF
THE CALIPHATE
Showing the independent
dynasties

BULGHARS

Volga

ZARS

KARA-KHANIDS

Aral
Sea

R. Jaxartes

R. Oxus

Caspian Sea

Bukhara° °Samarkand

Samanids

Nishapur° °Balkh

KHURASAN

Ghazna°

SIJISTAN

Ghaznavids

AZER-
BAIJAN

TABARISTAN

harra

ghdad

uyids

KHUZISTAN

R. Indus

°Delhi

ians

BAHRAIN

BIAN

Somnath

INDIA

EN

Indian

Ocean

Ceylon

was taking place. We may first consider the attitude of the new dynasty towards the theological ferment that was boiling up throughout the Empire, but especially in Persia and Iraq.

1. When Abu'l-Abbas was proclaimed Caliph at Kufa in 749, he delivered a famous speech in which he promised that the accession to power of his house meant the coming of a new era (*dawla*) of concord, happiness and just rule. The godless Omayyads had been cast down: the Abbasids would govern in strict accordance with God's law, and henceforth every Caliph, on assuming power, adopted a pious 'reign-name', such as *al-Rashid*, 'the right-guided,' *al-Mutawakkil ala'llah*, 'he who trusts in God,' *al-Mu'tamid ala'llah*, 'he whose support is in God.' By a curious coincidence their Christian contemporaries were also seeking a stronger religious basis for their rule. In Byzantium the new Isaurian dynasty had launched in 726 the Iconoclast movement, designed to purify the Church of superstitious regard for images, and in Frankish Gaul in 752 the old Merovingian line of kings was supplanted with papal support by the Carolingian house, which added to its titles the formula *Dei gratia*, by the grace of God. In Islam, where there was no distinction of Church and State, the Caliph was obliged to defend the Faith against heresy and schism as well as protect the temporal interests of the Muslim community. The Abbasids found that Islam was itself facing a moral and theological crisis in consequence of its contacts with older cults, sects and philosophical schools which abounded in the regions where the Semitic and Iranian worlds met and overlapped.

In the first place, there was the Orthodox Greek Church, which still had many adherents in the Caliph's domain and whose imposing system of theology was being expounded in the late Omayyad age by St. John of Damascus, often called the last of the Fathers. His lucid summary of Christian dogmatics was accompanied by tracts refuting Islam as an anti-Trinitarian heresy rather than as a new religion. Muslim teachers, faced by this intellectual challenge, felt obliged to deepen and systematize their own theology and to employ, like the Christians before them, Greek logic and philosophical concepts in which to express it. Hence vast fields of speculation were opened up to them, and they were compelled to grapple with problems concerning the nature and attributes of God, the meaning and scope of revelation, and the perennial question of free will and predestination. Then there were curious baptist or gnostic sects found there, and the pagan community at Harran, in northern Mesopo-tamia, who professed neo-Platonism and were close students of Hellenic thought. These people did not seek converts and kept to themselves, but their strange beliefs and rites attracted Muslim attention. Very different were the Manichaeans, followers of the third century Persian prophet Mani, who propagated their teachings over a large part of Asia; their dualistic tenets were obnoxious to all their monotheistic neighbours, and their missionaries were often put to death as dangerous infidels. In Persia, though Islam had little to fear from the Zoroastrians, discredited by their close association with the defunct Sassanid regime, it was gravely disturbed by con-stant outbreaks of social-revolutionary religious fanaticism, which seemed to follow in the tradition of the sixth-century communist prophet Mazdak, who was alleged to have taught community of goods and women and who had been executed by Khusrau Nus-hirvan in 529. Out of this medley of creeds arose widespread popu-lar faith in divine incarnations, metempsychosis, and the messianic return of a God-sent leader. Islam could hardly fail to be affected to some degree by these age-old manifestations of the Semitic-Iranian religious spirit, and they had a marked influence on Shi'ism.

The Abbasids during the first century of their rule had to cope with a double problem of a religious nature: first, the growth of theological dissension within Islam, and secondly the threat of poli-tical religious revolutionary movements without.

As early as the reign of Hisham a group of teachers appeared known as Kadarites, who championed the freedom of the will against the upholders of predestination. They merged in a larger body, the Mu'tazilites, "those who separated" from other Muslims on this question, or rather on the position of the sinner in the *umma*. The Mu'tazilites were the real founders of speculative dogmatics in Islam, and they were strongly supported by the early Abbasid Caliphs, who accorded their theology a sort of official recognition. Some acquaintance with Greek philosophy induced them to seek a more rational basis for religion and to deny the opinion commonly held in Islam that the Koran, being, so to speak, the reflection of the mind of God, was co-eternal with him and therefore uncreated. The Caliph Ma'mun, who delighted in intellectual debate (he is said to have presided over discussions between Christian and Muslim divines), pronounced in favour of the doctrine of the created Koran, and imposed a test (*mihna*) in 827 on all judges (*kadis*) and teachers requiring them to subscribe to it on pain of death. This ruthless inquisition was maintained during the reigns of his two immediate successors, Mu'tasim and Wathik, but was abolished by Mutawakkil in 842, when the Koran was finally declared to be uncreated. The Mu'tazilites never had much popular support; they had a doughty opponent in Ahmad b.Hanbal, the Athanasius of Islam and founder of one of its four canonical schools of law, and persecution conferred on their enemies the prestige of martyrdom. To this episode is to be traced in part the failure of the Caliphate to develop into a Papacy. Islam has never known ecclesiastical councils or a hierarchy of priests and bishops: the task of interpreting the sacred law has devolved on the *ulama,* learned canonists, who voice the *ijma,* or consensus of the Muslim community, and the inability of the Caliphs to impose the Mu'tazilite doctrine, despite their use of the power of the State, restricted them in future to the defence of a Faith which they were never again minded to define or modify.

A more serious threat to the throne of the Abbasids came from the partisans of Ali, who had been cleverly used to overthrow the Omayyads and had then been cast aside. The Alids, divided as always, could only express their fury by a series of futile and unsuccessful risings. Muhammad b.Abdallah, a great-grandson of Ali's elder son Hasan, headed a revolt in Medina in 762, but the city was captured by Mansur's troops and the pretender was killed. His brother Idris fled to North Africa and later founded an independent Alid principality in Morocco. Another revolt broke out in Mecca in 786. In 791 descendants of Hasan's son Zaid sought refuge in Dailam, a pagan kingdom on the south-west shores of the Caspian, where a Zaidite dynasty was founded about 864. Harun al-Rashid had to suppress another Alid insurrection: his son Ma'mun had to put down two attempts, one in Iraq and the other in Mecca. Ma'mun, who had much sympathy with the Shi'a, endeavoured to win over the Alids by recognizing Ali al-Rida, a descendant of the martyred Husain, as his heir but the opposition to this plan was so violent that he was obliged to abandon it. Mutawakkil, a dour bigot, was bitterly hostile to Alid pretensions, and in 851 the shrine of Husain at Karbala was destroyed at his orders, the site ploughed up, and pilgrimages to the place forbidden. For a time the Alid movement died down, only to burst afresh in a more furious form in the

Isma'ilian uprising at the close of the century. The Alids failed to displace the Abbasids, but they kept the Empire in a state of constant disturbance and contributed not a little to its ultimate disintegration.

A third religious danger was represented by the Manichaean and millenarian sects of Persia and Iraq. A Manichaean preacher was put to death as early as 742, in Omayyad times: a generation later the Caliph Mahdi (775-785) instituted a rigorous inquisition designed to extirpate the *zindiks,* infidels or heretics, as the dualists had come to be known, as a result of which they were driven eastwards into the Turkish lands of Central Asia. The revival of Persian national sentiment in the eighth century was accompanied by a series of fanatical outbreaks, some harking back to the Mazdak affair of Sassanid days, some inspired by the career and memory of Abu Muslim, who after putting the Abbasids on the throne, had been treacherously slain by Mansur in 754 for fear of his growing power. Abu Muslim had himself put to death in 749 an agitator named Bih-afaridh who claimed to have received divine revelations and commanded his followers to worship the sun, but after his own murder it was widely believed that he had merely disappeared and would return to punish his foes. Among those who looked for his second coming were the Rawandis (so-called from Rawand, a village near Isfahan), who taught the transmigration of souls. In the reign of Mahdi, Khurasan was thrown into disorder by the appearance of Mukanna, the 'Veiled Prophet' celebrated in Moore's *Lalla Rookh.* Masked in green silk, to hide the brightness of his face according to his followers, to conceal his deformities according to his enemies, he claimed to be the manifestation of God, revived the doctrines of Mazdak, and beat back the armies sent against him until 780, when he was besieged in a castle where he had taken refuge, and burnt himself to avoid falling into the hands of the Caliph's troops. In 817, under Ma'mun, another prophet named Babak or Papak rose up in Azerbaijan, leading a sect named after Mazdak's wife Khurram, and terrorized the countryside for twenty years until he was captured and executed in 838, in the reign of Mu'tasim. These popular disturbances sapped the strength of the regime, and foreshadowed the falling away of the Persian lands from the direct jurisdiction of the Caliphs.

2. The Abbasids, as the self-styled exponents of Muslim piety, felt

impelled to fulfil the duty laid upon the Caliphs by law and tradition of conducting the *jihad*, or holy war against the unbelievers, but the character of this unending conflict had completely changed from what it had been in Omayyad times. The era of conquest was over; the Caliph's armies, once filled with Bedouin tribesmen, were now recruited from Persians, chiefly Khurasanians, and soon from Turks from beyond the Oxus, and instead of fighting six or seven nations at once, the Muslims concentrated their attacks on the Byzantine Empire. Even here the theatre of operations had narrowed: the capital of the Caliphate having been removed far inland from Syria to Iraq, the naval arm was neglected; no more attacks were launched against Constantinople, and fighting was confined to the frontier districts of Asia Minor. The early Abbasids were mostly experienced soldiers, and until the reign of Mu'tasim, the Caliph marched almost every year against the Christian Empire. The Byzantines, hard pressed by the Slavs and Bulgars in the Balkans, and distracted by the iconoclast quarrel at home, were often obliged to purchase a humiliating truce by the payment of tribute. Harun al-Rashid distinguished himself in these wars; he organized the defences of northeastern Syria, and created stronger bases from which to invade Anatolia. When in 802 the Emperor Nicephorus announced in a letter to the Caliph that the tribute payments were being stopped, Harun is said to have dictated a brief but vigorous answer: 'From Harun al-Rashid. Commander of the Faithful, to Nicephorus, the Roman dog. I have received your letter, son of an unbelieving mother. You will see, not hear, my reply!' and to have forthwith crossed the border and laid waste a large part of Asia Minor. His son Ma'mun encouraged the revolt of Thomas the Slav, which threw the Byzantine world into confusion between 821 and 823 in the hope, unfulfilled, that it would break down the Empire completely. In 838 Mu'tasim led the last major Arab invasion of Anatolia and captured the strong fortress of Amorium in Phrygia. Thereafter the struggle languished. It achieved curiously meagre results. The Arabs never made any permanent settlement in Asia Minor; the native peasantry, attached to the Greek Church and imperial rule and protected by the Emperors against the big landlords, valiantly resisted Muslim incursions, and not until the political and social character of the country had been wholly changed for the worse did it pass from Christendom to Islam.

In the West a situation of much greater flexibility developed. The advance into Europe had been stopped by the Arab defeat at Poitiers in 732, the Berber revolt of 739, and the revolution of 750, which last brought an Omayyad refugee, Abd al-Rahman, to Spain, where he set up in 756 an independent amirate owning no allegiance to the Abbasid Caliphs. This event, the first breach in the unity of the Muslim Empire, encouraged the Spanish Christian princes in the north to fight for the enlargement of the small areas under their control; the Franks were impelled to come to the assistance of their co-religionists, and in 778 Charlemagne erected the wide strip of territory between the Pyrenees and the Ebro into a province known as the Spanish March. Meanwhile every Abbasid attempt to recover Spain failed, and the Franks and the Caliphs tended to draw together in common enmity to the Spanish Omayyads. Diplomatic missions were exchanged between Charlemagne and Harun al-Rashid, in the course of which the Caliph sent, among other gifts, an elephant to the Frankish Emperor, and granted special facilities to Frankish pilgrims visiting the Holy Places in Palestine.

So far as the West was concerned, the *jihad* seemed a thing of the past, except for sporadic fighting in the Spanish March. But Muslim aggression against Christendom was shortly revived in a new form, and was in fact directly related to the disappearance of Abbasid authority in the Maghrib. In 788 an Alid kingdom was set up in Morocco under Idris, a great-grandson of Hasan, who won over a number of Berber tribes, and planted a new settlement at Fas or Fez in a valley of the middle Atlas. In 800 Harun al-Rashid granted to Ibrahim b.al-Aghlab the province of Ifrikiya (roughly, modern Algeria and Tunisia) as an hereditary fief: on payment of an annual subsidy of 40,000 dinars to the Caliph's treasury, the governor received the right to rule as an autonomous prince and to bequeath his powers to his heir. From this time onwards the Abbasids exercised no authority west of Egypt. The Aghlabid regime rested, however, on very shaky foundations. The Berbers were, as usual, difficult to control; the Arab colonists in Kairawan, who lorded it over the natives, displayed the unruly and anarchic traits of their forbears, and the religious teachers and canon lawyers were quick to denounce the slightest deviation from the path of orthodoxy on the part of the *amirs*. To win popularity and recall Arab and Berber to their common Islamic faith, the Aghlabids resolved to resume the *jihad,* and selected Byzantine Sicily as their chief target. The rising of Thomas the Slav in 821 paralysed the imperial government and forced it to withdraw military and naval forces from its island possessions in the central Mediterranean. About 823 Crete was seized by a group of Arab refugees from Spain. Sicily was thus left isolated, and in 827 Aghlabid forces began to disembark on the island. A number of strong points were secured, from which the coasts of Italy could be menaced, and in 846 a raid was made up the Tiber and the outskirts of Rome were plundered. No strong Power now existed in Western Europe to deal with this renewed Muslim assault, for the Carolingian Empire had broken in pieces soon after Charlemagne's death in 814, and his heirs had to face the piratical ravages of the pagan Vikings from the north and had little to spare for the defence of the Mediterranean front. Naval control of the Mediterranean passed into Muslim hands; as an Arabic historian put it, 'the Christians could not float a plank' on that sea; the trade and commerce of the Western nations fell off; in 888 a Muslim base was established at Fraxinetum on the coast of Provence, which interrupted traffic across the Alps, and in 902 the Aghlabids completed the conquest of Sicily. But for the discords within the Islamic world (conflicts between the Aghlabids and the Spanish Omayyads, and the rise of the Isma'ilian movement which led to the emergence of the Fatimid Anti-Caliphate in North Africa in 909), Europe would have been in much greater peril.

3. A third feature of the early Abbasid age was the revival of Persian national life and culture. The wholesale destruction of records at the time of the Arab conquest has left us ignorant of the manner in which the Persian people reacted to the fall of their ancient monarchy, but it was natural that a gifted and civilized nation should in time rise from its defeat and impose its customs and values and traditions on its conquerors. On one plane, indeed, that of religion, the Arabs were bound to retain their superiority: as the vehicle of divine revelation, no tongue could compete with Arabic; an educated Persian, on embracing Islam, took to using the language of the Koran, and for several generations no Persian writer on law or theology, history or grammar, philosophy or medicine, employed any other medium than Arabic. But the political and social domination of the Arabs was broken early: the Persian *mawali* rallied behind their countryman Abu Muslim in the drive

to overthrow the rule of the Omayyads, centered in Arab Syria, and after 750 the nation found itself faced with a choice of means to express its newfound sense of liberation. It could seek to control and Persianize the new Caliphal regime; it could repudiate Islam by reverting to a pre-Muslim cult of Mazdakism or the like; it could take up with some form of Shi'ism, thereby adopting a solution within the framework of Islam, or it could strive for political independence of the Caliphate under native though Muslim princes. All these means were tried with success, save the second; after the collapse of the Mukanna and Babak movements, a return to the pre-Islamic past was effectively ruled out, and the Persians set to work to mould and colour Islam according to their Iranian conceptions and traditions.

The Caliphate, from being a magnified Arab Shaikhdom, took on the aspect of a resurrected Sassanid monarchy. Baghdad, the new imperial capital, was built by Mansur only a few miles from Ctesiphon; the civil service was filled with Persian clerks; a new official, the *wazir* or vizier, headed the Caliph's chancery, his duties and functions seemingly modelled on those of Buzurgmihr, the semi-legendary minister of Khusrau Nushirvan, and the subjects of the Commander of the Faithful, when received in audience, prostrated themselves at his feet, a homage unknown in Medina or even in Damascus. The tall, conical Persian hat was adopted by Mansur and his court as part of their official dress, and Persian festivals, such as that of the New Year, were widely observed. For nearly fifty years, from the reign of Mansur to that of Harun, the government of the Empire was in the hands of the Persian Barmakids or Barmecides, a remarkable family who had been hereditary guardians of a Buddhist shrine at Balkh, in Khurasan, and had been converted to Islam around 670. Khalid b.Barmak held high office under Mansur; his son Yahya was made *wazir* by Harun, and Yahya's sons Fadl and Ja'far were promoted to provincial governorships. The sudden ruin of the family in 803, when Jafar was executed and Yahya and Fadl imprisoned, was due probably to Harun's jealousy of their growing power, but it was a severe blow to the loyalty of the Persian administrative class to the Abbasids, and prepared the way for the breakdown of the Caliph's rule in the Persian lands.

The Abbasids were in a difficult position. Dependent though they might be on Persian support, they were themselves Arabs and were the chiefs of an *umma* or community which in theory was universal. The parallel between the Caliphate and the Sassanid Empire here fails. The Abbasids could not appeal to a sentiment of *national* loyalty nor had they the backing of a national clergy. They could try and balance Arab and Persian, and stress the principle of fidelity to a common faith, but this was not always possible. In the civil war which broke out in 810 between Amin and Ma'mun, the sons of Harun, Ma'mun, whose mother was Persian and whose armed support came mainly from Khurasan, was almost forced into the position of champion of Iranian Islam. His general Tahir, who commanded the Khurasanian army, took Baghdad for him, and he seriously considered moving the capital to Merv. So violent was the opposition aroused that Ma'mun abandoned the scheme, and in fact the Abbasids never moved the seat of the Caliphate out of Iraq. But Ma'mun's ultimate resolve to stay in Baghdad may have hastened the trend towards political separatism in the eastern provinces. Tahir, rewarded for his services with the governorship of Khurasan and all the lands east of Iraq in 820, omitted the Caliph's name in the Friday prayers in 822, an act equivalent to the renunciation of allegiance. He died soon after, possibly poisoned, but Ma'mun felt compelled to follow the example his father had set in the case of the Aghlabids and to grant Khurasan to Tahir's heirs as an hereditary fief, in return for a recognition of his theoretical suzerainty. Thus arose the first independent Persian dynasty of Muslim times. About forty years later, Ya'kub al-Saffar (the coppersmith), a brigand turned general, seized the province of Sijistan in 867, extended his power to Balkh and Kabul, and in 873 drove the Tahirids out of Nishapur. When the Caliph refused to accept him as governor of Khurasan, Ya'kub repudiated his authority and led his armies against Baghdad itself. His attack on Iraq was beaten off, but the Saffarids kept possession of a good deal of south-eastern Persia till the end of the century.

Yet a third dynasty arose in Khurasan, that of the Samanids, who hailed from Saman, a village near Balkh, and claimed descent from the Sassanids. A family of *dihkans,* they were employed as local governors by the Tahirids and fought for them when they were attacked by Ya'kub the Coppersmith. The Tahirid regime disintegrated, and the Samanids, using as a base their estates in Transoxiana, were able in 900 to bring Khurasan under their control, and to rule from Bukhara nominally as the viceroys of the Caliph but in reality as independent Persian princes. Ardent admirers of Iranian culture, they encouraged the revival of Persian art and letters, and poets and historians at their court began to write in their mother tongue instead of in the hitherto dominant Arabic.

4. The political dissolution of the Caliphate was accelerated also by the transformation of the military system of the Empire. The first conquests were achieved by armies almost wholly Arab in composition: the prospect of booty and glory hitherto undreamed of attracted a steady flow of recruits from Bedouin tribesmen. As the sphere of military operations widened, it was deemed desirable to enlist Berbers in the West for the conquest of Spain and Khurasanians in the East for the subjugation of Transoxiana, but these alien soldiers were treated as inferiors and permitted to serve only in the infantry. The revolution of 750 abolished these distinctions; under the early Abbasids, three equal corps are recognized in the Caliph's forces, the northern and southern Arabs and the Khurasanians; the influence of the great Arab cantonments of Kufa and Basra declined, and the Bedouin element in the army was rapidly diluted by the admission of *mawali* of all ranks into the military establishment. The conquests were over; the State treasury was no longer enriched by the plunder of foreign lands; the army had to be maintained by the taxpayer; when distant provinces became virtually independent, their garrisons passed from the Caliph's control to that of the local *amir*, and the court of Baghdad thus found itself with a diminishing defence force at a time when Alid and religious revolts were of frequent occurrence. The Caliphs did not possess a standing army of modern type: their regular troops consisted of household guards, and every season they purchased the services of volunteers from many different nations and localities, who made their own terms and dispersed to their homes when the main campaign was over. Until the reign of Mu'tasim, the Khurasanians continued to form the core of the regular army, and it was they who enabled Ma'mun to seize the throne from his brother Amin in the civil war of 810-813. On Ma'mun's death in 833, some of the troops came out in support of his son Abbas as Caliph instead of his brother Mu'tasim whom he had nominated. Abbas disclaimed any political ambitions, and Mu'tasim succeeded, but the latter's suspicions of the fidelity of the

Khurasanians induced him to remodel the army and to fill it with slave soldiers recruited from Berbers, Sudanese negroes, and above all, Turks from Central Asia.

Slavery is sanctioned by the Koran, though emancipation is declared a meritorious act, and the institution, which existed in pre-Islamic Arabia as elsewhere in the ancient world, received a tremendous stimulus from the conquests, when the slave-markets were crowded with thousands of prisoners of war. The conquests coming to an end, this source of supply dwindled, and was made good by the purchase of slaves on a commercial basis from the chiefs of barbarian tribes in Europe, Africa and Asia. By the ninth century an international traffic had developed in this human merchandise, in which Christian, Jewish and Muslim dealers all participated. Slaves were in special demand as soldiers, in the belief that, cut off from all ties of clan or race or country, they would be more loyal to their masters than free warriors. As early as the reign of Harun, companies of Turks appeared in the Caliph's armies, and from this time onward large numbers of hardy Turkish youths were bought and given military training. Under Mu'tasim Turkish slave troops came to outnumber the free Khurasanians, and the campaign of 838 in Asia Minor was led by Turkish generals. The experiment by no means answered to the Caliph's hopes. The Turkish regiments, commanded by men of their own race, grew more truculent and disorderly than the old Bedouin levies, especially when their pay fell in arrears; street riots between them and the citizens of Baghdad forced Mu'tasim to quit the capital in 836 and betake himself to Samarra, and one of their leaders, Afshin, suspected of instigating a revolt in Tabaristan, was tried in 841 for treason and apostasy and was starved to death in prison. Yet the Turks had by now become indispensable, and Mu'tasim's son Wathik (842-846), an undistinguished prince known to fame only from Beckford's romance *Vathek,* bestowed provincial governorships upon their chiefs.

The next Caliph, Mutawakkil (846-861), made a serious effort to deal with this menace by resuming the recruitment of Arab troops, but he was a narrow bigot, who made enemies everywhere by his persecution of Christians, Jews, Shi'ites and the defenders of the doctrine of the created Koran, and quarrels among his sons gave the Turks an excuse to mutiny and kill him. His son Muntasir, who supplanted him, died in six months; the Turkish generals put his cousin Musta'in on the throne, but his position was challenged by Mu'tazz, another son of Mutawakkil's, and in 865 he was forced to abdicate. Mu'tazz got rid of two of the most obnoxious Turkish chiefs, but he failed to pay the troops what they demanded, was deposed and tortured to death in prison. The Turks then made Muhtadi, a son of Wathik's, Caliph; his attempts to restore order were equally fruitless, and he also perished in 870. By this time new and more responsible Turkish commanders had appeared on the scene; the unrest subsided, and Muhtadi's successor Mu'tamid was allowed to reign in peace for twenty-two years (870-892). But the damage done by a decade of military coups could not be repaired. The Caliphate had been shorn of its dignity and prestige; the administration had been reduced to near anarchy: the independence of the provinces had been confirmed, and a Turkish chief, Ahmad b.Tulun, had seized control of Egypt in 868, the first of his race to carve out rich principalities from the once united Empire of the Caliphs, the forerunner of the Seljuks and the Ottomans.

5. Despite the political disruption of the Caliphate, the Muslim world enjoyed a rapidly expanding economic prosperity in this age. With the cessation of the conquests and the creation of a vast area of relative internal peace, international trade received a powerful stimulus. The Arabs of the towns had always been commercially-minded; the Prophet himself had been a merchant and had thus, so to speak, sanctified that calling; the sweeping away of so many State frontiers, particularly of the Euphrates barrier which Rome and Persia had maintained for seven centuries, facilitated travel and business; the Arabic language, spreading from Spain to Transoxiana, provided a common medium of communication, and supplies of gold and silver, obtained from sources as far apart as the Sudan and the Hindu Kush, assured the trading classes of a plentiful currency of dinars and dirhams. By the mid-ninth century, thanks mainly to the Aghlabids, Muslim naval control had been established over the Mediterranean, the Byzantine fleet rarely venturing far from its home bases, while in the Indian Ocean Arab ships could sail the seas without challenge from a foreign Power. Nothing inhibited the Muslim from trading with infidels; he sought business and profit where he could find it. The absorption of the Berber lands into Islam opened up regular caravan routes across the Sahara to the negro kingdoms of the Niger: gold and ivory, slaves and ostrich

feathers, came from the regions known to the Arabs as Bilad al-Sudan, the country of the blacks. From the ports of Arabia, the Red Sea and the Persian Gulf, Arab vessels crossed the Indian Ocean to Ceylon, Malaya and even distant China, where a Muslim colony was installed at Canton, as we learn from the narrative of Sulaiman the Merchant, a shipowner or captain whose account of a voyage to the Far East was written up and published by an anonymous author in 851 and became the source of the travel romances associated with the name of Sindbad the Sailor. When the Samanids came to power in Khurasan and Transoxiana, in the late ninth century, they entered into commercial relations with the Khazars of the lower Volga, through whom a brisk traffic developed with the Vikings of Scandinavia, who exchanged the furs and amber of the Baltic lands for the textiles and metal-work of Persia. Trade was now conducted on a scope and over an area unsurpassed since the days of the Roman Empire.

This material wellbeing was productive of consequences good and bad. Increased wealth meant more leisure for the upper classes, and hence the intensive cultivation of the arts and sciences and the creation of the Muslim or rather Arabic civilization which led the world for some four centuries between 800 and 1200 and which is analysed in a later chapter. Socially, the Abbasid age may have marked a retrogression. The conquests had lifted from the backs of the peasantry a heavy burden of taxes and services, but this was in time reimposed, as a new class of landowners emerged whose demands on the cultivators were as exacting as the old. Evidence of peasant discontent is not wanting: the religious revolts in Persia between 750 and 850 appear to have been partly social-revolutionary in character. Yet the peasant in Muslim lands was technically a free man and not a serf, though if he were a Christian or Magian he had the inferior status of a *dhimmi;* plantation slavery was rare in Islam, slaves being mostly soldiers or domestics. Occasionally slaves were employed on public works, as in the salt marshes round Basra, where thousands of negroes (*zanj*) toiled in appalling conditions clearing the nitrous top soil to lay bare the arable ground beneath. Roused to rebellion by an Alid pretender in 869, they drove out their masters and set up a strange communistic State which subsisted for fourteen years until it was finally suppressed by the Caliph Mu'tamid's brother Muwaffak in 883. The Zanj revolt, which may be compared with that of Spartacus in ancient Rome, was an isolated episode, but in the towns, where the growth of commerce and manufactures had brought a large working-class into existence, social dissatisfaction and economic exploitation drove the artisans to organize themselves for mutual protection in gilds or religious associations. It was this situation which was turned to advantage by the Isma'ilians, the revolutionary wing of the Alid movement, who in the tenth century made a bold attempt to capture Islam and whose schism broke for generations the unity of the Muslim *umma*.

BOOKS FOR FURTHER READING

ABBOT, N., *Two Queens of Baghdad*, Chicago, 1937. A picture of court life under the early Abbasids. The queens are the wife and mother of Harun al-Rashid.

BARTHOLD, W., *Turkestan down to the Mongol Invasion*. Includes a critical account of the dynasties which arose in the East out of the ruins of the Caliph's Empire.

BOUVAT, L., *Les Barmécides*, Paris, 1912. The only monograph on this famous family of viziers.

BUCKLER, F., *Harunu'l-Rashid and Charles the Great*, Cambridge, Mass., 1931. A discussion of the diplomatic exchanges between the two rulers.

HASSAN, Z. M., *Les Tulunides*, Paris, 1933. A history of the first independent Muslim dynasty of Egypt.

HERZFELD, E., *Geschichte der Stadt Samarra*, Hamburg, 1948. Good historical and archaeological account of the city which was the seat of the 'Avignon Captivity' of the Abbasid Caliphs from 836 to 889.

LANE-POOLE, S., *A History of Egypt in the Middle Ages*, London, 1901; 3rd ed. 1924.

LE STRANGE, G., *Baghdad under the Abbasid Caliphs*, London, 1900. Now somewhat antiquated. Cf. the art. 'Baghdād' in the new *Enc. of Islam*.

MARCAIS, G., *La Berbérie musulmane et l'Orient au moyen âge, Paris*, 1946. Shows how North Africa became detached from the Caliphate.

NÖLDEKE, T., *Sketches from Eastern History*, Eng. tr. 1892. Contains essays on the Caliph Mansur, the Saffarid dynasty and the Zanj revolt.

PHILBY, H. ST. J., *Harun ar-Rashid*, London, 1933.

SADIGHI, G. H., *Les mouvements religieux iraniens*, Paris, 1938. Analyses the religious revolts in Persia of the early Abbasid era.

SOURDEL, D., *Le vizirat 'abbaside de 749 à 936*, 2 vols. Damascus, 1959-60. Now the standard work on the origin and growth of the office of wazir.

SPULER, B., *Iran* (as before).

WIET, G., *L'Égypte arabe* (as before).

TRANSLATED SOURCES

MAS'UDI, *Les Prairies d'Or,* 9 vols. Paris, 1861-77. Mas'udi was a great scholar and traveller who was born at Baghdad and died at Cairo about 957. His *Muraj al-Dhahab,* Meadows (or perhaps, Washings) of Gold, is a big, rambling encyclopedia somewhat resembling Pliny's *Natural History*: it contains a good deal of miscellaneous historical information, especially about the early Abbasid period.

TABARI, *The Reign of Mu'tasim,* Eng. tr. E. Marin, New Haven, 1951. Very little of Tabari's great chronicle from the Creation to 915 has been translated into European languages. This is the only substantial portion of it available in English: it covers the nine years of Mu'tasim's Caliphate (833-842).

VIII

The Isma'ilian Schism

EVERY great movement splits into sects and schisms. Rival interpretations of its aims and beliefs and disputes concerning the best
way to implement them destroy the original unity of the church or
party or community. Islam was no exception to this rule. The murder of Othman in 656, only twenty-four years after the Prophet's
death, first disrupted the young Muslim *umma* and led to a bloody
civil war. Around his successor Ali there gathered the *Shi'a*, the
'party' destined to live in eternal opposition to Sunni or orthodox
Islam. In the fourth century of the Hijra, corresponding roughly to
the tenth century of the Christian era, this quarrel erupted into a
violent and widespread revolutionary movement which tore whole
provinces away from orthodoxy, shook the Muslim world to its
foundations, and presented Christendom with its first serious chance
to recover some of its lost ground and regain partial control of the
Mediterranean. The literature of the Isma'ilians, Karmathians, Fatimids and Assassins, the principal off-shoots of the 'Sevener' *Shi'a*,
has perished, save for some late documents which have come to light
in recent times in India; we see these sects only through the eyes of
their enemies, and we are as yet ignorant of the social forces which
set in motion what seems to have been an organized challenge to the
whole existing order.

The Shi'a passed through three fairly defined stages. It began as a
political protest against the conferring of the Imamate or leadership
of Islam on men like Abu Bakr, Omar and Othman, who were not

125

kinsmen of the Prophet.[1] The civil authority of Muhammad should have been inherited, it was argued, by the *Ahl al-Bait*, 'the family of the house' of the Apostle of God, and therefore in the first place by Ali. The exponents of this view were mostly Yemenite Arabs, who were perhaps influenced by the memory of the hereditary succession of the kings of ancient Saba and Himyar. This first stage may be said to have ended with the tragic death of Ali's son Husain at Karbala in 683, after which the Shi'a acquired a strong racial and religious tinge. From the time of Mukhtar's revolt in 685 it was joined by many *mawali*, chiefly Persians, who hated the Omayyad regime as a symbol of Arab domination and used the Alid movement as a means of fighting for social and racial equality. Husain provided the party with a martyr and (what had hitherto been lacking in Islam) a mediator between God and man. Not only did the government of Islam belong lawfully to Ali and his descendants, but they were more than Caliphs or civil magistrates; they were divinely-guided and infallible Imams, charged by God with expounding the true faith. Mukhtar espoused the cause of Muhammad b.al-Hanafiya, Ali's son by the Hanafite woman, and apparently hailed him as the *Mahdi*, 'the guided one' who would usher in the millennium, and after Muhammad's death it was widely believed that he had been hidden by God and would return in the last days. Such was the origin of the belief in the Hidden Imam, which was henceforth incorporated in the Shi'ite system and which has produced a variety of pretenders and impostors from the Fatimid Caliphs to the fanatic by whose followers Gordon was killed and who ruled the Sudan at the close of the last century.

The source of these ideas, which turned the Shi'a from a political party into an eschatological sect, is obscure. The soil of Syria and Iraq was saturated with ancient legends and superstitions: no region in the world has been more prolific in religions. Gnostic and Manichaean cosmology may have contributed something. The Mahdi-idea has obvious affinities with the Jewish-Christian Messiah. Some features of the Shi'ite faith may have been genuine developments within Islam itself, indeed it has been claimed that the Shi'a were initially more Sunni than the Sunnis themselves are to-day. Be that

[1] But see M. G. S. Hodgson's article, 'When did the early Shi'a become sectarian?' *Journal of the American Oriental Society*, vol. 75, 1955, for a different view.

as it may, the peculiar position of the Imam in the Shi'a carried the party into factionalism and farther away from Islamic orthodoxy. Since God spoke through the Imam, the latter tended to replace the Koran, Tradition and consensus of the community as the source of truth and to be elevated to a status not much short of divine: among some Shi'ite sectaries Ali was virtually deified. Furthermore, as the contact of God and man was not at one point but in a continuous series of 'manifestations', it became uncertain which particular line of descent from Ali was to be followed. Did the Imamate come down through the children of Ali by Fatima or by the Hanafite wife? When this issue was in effect settled by the action of the son of Muhammad b.al-Hanafiya in bequeathing his claims to the Abbasids, and so helping them to seize the throne in 750, there still remained the question whether the true Imams were to be looked for among the progeny of Hasan or Husain, the sons of Fatima.

The Alid revolts against the early Abbasids were led mostly by the followers of Hasan, and were all quenched in blood. The Husainids remained quiet, and yet it was from this branch of the family that the most vigorous and violent assertion of Shi'ite claims was to come, and oddly enough, through a rift in their ranks. Ja'far, the sixth in descent from Ali through Husain, disinherited his elder son Isma'il, owing, it is said, to his addiction to drink, in favour of a younger son Musa. Isma'il predeceased his father, who died in Medina in 765. Some denied the right of Ja'far to alter the succession; some declared Isma'il to be not dead but hidden, and recognized him as the Seventh Imam, being in consequence known as Seveners or Isma'ilians. The majority accepted Musa and his descendants, the last of whom, Muhammad al-Mahdi, the twelfth Imam, 'disappeared' at Samarra in 873 or 874. The champions of this succession, styled Twelvers, expected the return of the vanished Imam in the last days; they therefore ceased from political action, and were prepared to tolerate Abbasid rule as a thing indifferent. Not so the Seveners: to them the line of 'visible' Imams ended with Isma'il (or as some said, his son Muhammad b.Isma'il), but a series of 'concealed' Imams continued, who taught the faithful through their agents and who would reappear in the fullness of time to inaugurate the reign of justice and truth. Like many revolutionary bodies they did not wait passively for the millennium, but worked feverishly to hasten its coming. It was they who hurried the Shi'a into its third phase of social-revolutionary violence.

The author of this extraordinary development was Abdallah b. Maimun, one of the strangest and most enigmatic figures in the history of Islam. He and his father were disciples of Abu'l-Khattab, a *da'i* or missionary agent of the Imam Ja'far who taught that the Koran was to be understood in an 'inward' (*batin*) or symbolical rather than in a literal sense, that concealment (*takiya,* literally 'caution') or denial of the faith was permissible in case of threatened death or injury, and that the divine 'Light' had been manifested in successive incarnations. Ja'far repudiated these extravagant doctrines, and Abu'l-Khattab was executed in 755 by the Caliph Mansur as a dangerous heretic. According to the stories later spread by the orthodox anti-Isma'ilian writers, Abdallah b.Maimun took up these teachings, hid himself at Salamiya, a small town in northern Syria, and from there organized a vast conspiracy which had as its aim nothing less than the destruction of Islam and the universal triumph of atheism and libertinism. His *da'is* or propagandists formed a trained hierarchy; each *da'i,* who commonly disguised himself as a merchant or artisan, was assigned a particular territory, where he sought to interest likely converts and initiated those who joined the movement step by step into its secret doctrines and ritual. Of the propagandist skill of the Isma'ilians there is no doubt; of the reality of Abdallah b.Maimun's plot to blow up Islam from within, there is the greatest doubt. Some writers have dismissed him as a legend, a product of fevered orthodox imagination. He was probably a historical character, but when he lived and what he taught we have no certain means of knowing.

The origins and early history of Isma'ilism are indeed veiled in obscurity. Its leaders work in the shadows and flit about from place to place. We get the impression of a vast network of 'cells' extending to the remotest corners of the Muslim world, of an 'underground' constantly striving to evade the police, of spies and traitors and internal feuds and schisms. The identity of the 'hidden Imams' who were the nominal chiefs of the sect from the death of Ja'far in 765 to the emergence of the Fatimids in North Africa in 909, is not clearly made out. After flowing in concealment for many years like a subterraneous stream, Isma'ilism suddenly burst out in a number of widely separated regions in the closing decades of the ninth century. About 875 one Hamdan Karmat, converted by a *da'i* from Khuzistan, set up his headquarters at Kalwadha near Baghdad. In 879 a mission under Ibn Hawshab was despatched to the Yemen and brought a large part of that province under its control. In 891 the Karmathians, Hamdan Karmat's followers, are first reported in arms. In 893 Abu Abdallah al-Shi'i, a native of the Yemen, after helping to convert his countrymen, went off to North Africa to work among the Berbers and rouse them against the Aghlabids in Tunisia and the Idrisids in Morocco. In 902-3 Karmathian bands, recruited mainly from the Bedouins, raided Syria, took Damascus and sacked Salamiya. In 909 Abu Abdallah, having overturned the kingdom of the Aghlabids, produced the 'hidden Imam' and proclaimed him Mahdi and Caliph at Rakkada near Kairawan, thus inaugurating the Fatimid anti-Caliphate, which was to survive down to the time of Saladin.

This astonishing series of events points not only to a highly efficient organization but to deep-rooted social ills which the agitators offered to cure. In every age the promised coming of a millennium of justice and happiness has attracted the downtrodden and the oppressed, but conditions in the Islamic world at the turn of the ninth and tenth centuries must have been peculiarly favourable to the preaching of the Isma'ili *da'is*. The workers and artisans of the craft-guilds of the big cities are said to have been specially receptive to Isma'ili propaganda: one theory has it that the Islamic *sinf* or guild was the creation of the Karmathians. There may have been some connection between the Karmathian outbreak and the Zanj revolt in Basra: refugees from the latter probably helped to found the strange, communistic Karmathian republic in Bahrain. Tabari says the Karmathians were peasants and tillers: the name Karmat may be an Aramaic word meaning 'villager'. The city population of Syria, Iraq and Persia often provided converts resentful of the depredations of the turbulent Turkish slave soldiery. In North Africa the Berbers of the great Katama confederacy hated the racial arrogance of the Arabs of the towns. Like the Abbasids in their drive against the Omayyads just before 750, the Isma'ilis made skilful use of all the prevailing discontents to challenge the existing order.

The most sensational blows against that order were struck by the Karmathians, whose sacrilegious brutality shocked and horrified Islam. Much about these sectaries is unclear: they may not have been Isma'ilis at all at the outset, and their conduct and customs gave plausibility to the belief that they were not merely heretics but bitter enemies of Islam. About 899 Hamdan Karmat apparently broke with the movement he had launched, and it passed under the control of one Zakruya and his three sons, who raised troops among the Bedouin tribesmen, invaded Syria and Iraq, routed in 903 an army sent against them by the Caliph Muktafi, captured Damascus, and taking possession of Salamiya, killed all the Abbasid princes they found there and the family of the Imam, who had left the town and was on his way to Egypt and the Maghrib. This looks as though the new Karmathian chiefs were claiming the Imamate for themselves or else the Imam had repudiated their destructive ravages and the massacre of his relatives was an act of revenge. The Abbasid Government bestirred itself; the invaders were expelled from Syria, and in 905 Muktafi's forces regained Egypt from the Tulunids, who had held it since 868. The Karmathians retired to Bahrain, where under new leaders (Abu Sa'id al-Jannabi and his son Abu Tahir) they started a reign of terror along the pilgrim routes crossing Arabia. In 906 they ambushed the pilgrim caravan returning from Mecca and killed 20,000 persons. During the Caliphate of Muktafi's successor Muktadir (908-932), the waste, corruption and incompetence of the Abbasid court left Iraq as well as Arabia exposed to Karmathian attack: Basra was plundered in 923, a second pilgrim caravan was destroyed in 924, Kufa was sacked in 925, Baghdad itself was threatened in 927, and in 928 the Muslim world learnt with horror that Karmathian bands had broken into Mecca, torn the sacred Black Stone from the wall of the Kaaba and carried it off to Bahrain.

The Karmathians remain a good deal of a puzzle. They created in Bahrain a sort of oligarchic republic, governed by a council of six, with a chief who was first among equals; no taxes were levied (revenue presumably derived from loot and plunder), 30,000 negro slaves performed the labour of the community, and an army of 20,000 men defended it from attack. Stories that the Karmathians practised community of goods and women are probably false: such accusations have been made against all social radicals from the Mazdakians to the Bolsheviks. More difficult to refute is the charge of rejecting the law and rites of Islam: travellers who visited Bahrain in the eleventh century reported that there were no mosques or prayers or Friday services. Though the Karmathians later acknowledged the Fatimid Caliph as their Imam (at his order the Black Stone was returned to Mecca in 950), they seem always to have followed a line of their own, and the sect possibly had an extremist antinomian left-wing. Politically, their attempt to overthrow the Abbasid Caliphate failed with their ejection from Syria in 903: henceforth they were a small but irritating minority movement, and the real challenge to Sunni orthodoxy came from the Fatimids in North Africa.

Here the ancient enmity between Arab and Berber still persisted. The Aghlabids, nominally viceroys of the Abbasids, drew their support from the Arabs of the towns. As a mark of independence and dislike of Arab racial pretensions, the Berbers tended to join dissident sects. In Morocco the Idrisids, claiming descent from Hasan, had erected a Shi'ite kingdom with Berber backing. A Persian adventurer named Rustam founded a Kharijite principality among the Zenata Berbers of the Awras. The Berbers never formed a united nation: their two great confederacies, the Zenata and the Sanhaja, were traditional foes. Isma'ili propaganda was started by Abu Abdallah al-Shi'i in 893 among the Sanhaja in favourable circumstances, for both the Rustamid and Aghlabid regimes were by now weak and decadent. Within fifteen years he had built up a powerful connection and mobilized a formidable army of Berber warriors. The Imam, invited to join him, secretly left Salamiya, and made his way via Egypt to the Maghrib. The local authorities, suspecting his identity, had him arrested and imprisoned in Sijilmasa. Abu Abdallah took the field, seized the Rustamid capital Tahert in 908, and marched on Kairawan. The last Aghlabid amir fled the country; the Imam was freed from captivity, and in 909 Abu Abdallah proclaimed at Rakkada, outside Kairawan, the coming of the Mahdi.

Ubaid Allah al-Mahdi, as he is commonly known, is a mysterious figure: no one has satisfactorily traced his pedigree. To his followers he was the descendant, through Isma'il and Husain, of Ali and Fatima: his enemies pronounced him an impostor, and some alleged that he was the grandson of the notorious Abdallah b.Maimun. He strikes us as a cool, cautious man, who did not take seriously the semi-divine status accorded him by his enthusiastic devotees. He was clearly a shrewd statesman: to balance Arab against Berber, to overcome the suspicion and hostility of the Sunni party, to found a durable Isma'ili State, required abilities of a high order. He found it necessary quickly to get rid of Abu Abdallah, whose fall and execution in 910 reminds us of the fate of Abu Muslim at the hands of the Caliph Mansur. Probably the man who had put him in power was disillusioned with him, or else he had begun to alienate the Sunnite Arabs by trying to force Shi'ite rites and beliefs on them, and Ubaid-Allah intervened to halt a policy which would have endangered his throne. As it was, a section of his Berber supporters revolted and hailed a new Mahdi, so that it would have been madness to antagonize the Arab townsmen. Kairawan was so strongly Sunnite that Ubaid Allah moved his government to a new capital Mahdiya, which he began to build in 916 on a small peninsula between Susa and Sfax. He never displayed the fanaticism of a zealot, and the toleration he practised was, with one or two exceptions, characteristic of Fatimid rule to the end.

The emergence of the Fatimid Caliphate is a major event in Islamic history. For the first time a large part of Dar al-Islam had passed under the control of a sect which not only rejected the spiritual claims of the Abbasids, but declared its resolve to replace them by a new universalist Imamate. The progeny of Ali were to govern the whole Muslim world, not as civil magistrates but as the sinless and infallible spokesmen of God. To the Fatimids North Africa was only a base of operations from which to conquer all Islam, as the Abbasids had started out from Khurasan in 747, and they proceeded to put their plans in action with all convenient speed. They took over Sicily, which the Aghlabids had captured, they launched two expeditions against Egypt, and they overthrew the Idrisid kingdom in 922. Their incursions into Morocco provoked a reaction from the Spanish Omayyads, whose chief Abd al-Rahman III made a bid for the support of the Sunnites of Western Islam by assuming in 929 the title of Caliph. Three Commanders of the Faithful, reigning respectively at Baghdad, Mahdiya and Cordova, now competed for the allegiance of Muslims.

Ubaid Allah died in 934: his son and successor, Abu'l-Kasim, a far more fanatical Isma'ili than his father, assumed as his reign-name al-Ka'im, 'he who arises', a title employed in the literature of the sect for the real Mahdi, who will arise at the Last Day. The Sunnite chroniclers denounce him as a cruel atheist, a persecutor of true Muslims, a more bitter enemy of Islam than the *Rumi,* or Byzantines, and relate that devout believers were unable to attend the mosques on Friday lest they be obliged to listen to prayers for impious tyrants. A man of vigour, he made Fatimid power feared all over the Mediterranean: his fleets raided the coasts of France and Italy and plundered Genoa, and a third attack was made on Egypt. The cost of this aggressive policy fell heavily on the people: merchants, peasants and even nomads were taxed severely, and economic grievances were added to orthodox resentment at heretic rule. Discontent flared up in the rebellion of Abu Yazid, nicknamed 'the man on the donkey', which broke out in 943 in the old Kharijite lands of the former Rustamid kingdom, and spread all over North Africa. After some hesitation, the Sunnite jurists of Kairawan decided that the Kharijites were less odious than the Ismaʿilis and gave their blessing to the rebels. Kaʾim was shut up in Mahdiya, where he died in 946. His son Mansur, who followed him, appealed successfully to the loyalty of the Sanhajas, who relieved Mahdiya, routed the insurgents, and hunted down Abu Yazid in the mountains of Morocco. The failure of this rising greatly strengthened the Fatimid regime, and Mansur, after a brief reign of seven years (946-953), left a tranquil and prosperous realm to his son Muʿizz, the ablest of the Shiʿite Caliphs.

Under Muʿizz (953-975) the Fatimids reached the height of their glory, and the universal triumph of Ismaʿilism appeared not far distant. The fourth Fatimid Caliph is an attractive character: humane and generous, simple and just, he was a good administrator, tolerant and conciliatory. Served by one of the greatest generals of the age, Jawhar al-Rumi, a former Greek slave, he took fullest advantage of the growing confusion in the Sunnite world. A Persian dynasty of Shiʿite connection, the Buyids, had seized Baghdad in 945 and reduced the Abbasid Caliphate to nullity; Egypt had fallen into the hands of a Turkish family, the Ikhshidids, whose Sudanese troops were terrorizing the population; an Arab dynasty, the Hamdanids, centred in Mosul, challenged the Ikhshidids for the possession of Syria, while the Byzantines, under two vigorous Emperors, Nicephorus Phocas and John Tzimisces, had taken the offensive against the Muslims on sea and land, were threatening Crete and pressing down south of the Taurus. Egypt, a rich and easily governed country, was still the principal goal of Fatimid endeavour, but Muʿizz resolved first to make sure of the West and teach a lesson to the Omayyads of Spain, who had backed the rising of Abu Yazid.

A naval attack was made against Almeria in 955, and Jawhar led a grand razzia, reminiscent of Okba's, which carried him through Tahert, Sijilmasa and Fez to the stores of the Atlantic. By 959 the Shi'ite Caliph was being prayed for throughout the Maghrib, save for Ceuta and Tangier, which were still held by the Omayyad Caliph Abd al-Rahman III.

The way was clear for the conquest of Egypt. Early in 969 Jawhar marched out of Kairawan at the head of an army of 100,000 men, routed the Ikhshidid forces outside Fustat, and on a sandy waste north-east of the capital he marked out the boundaries of a new city to be called al-Kahira, 'the victorious,' which Western speech has corrupted to Cairo. By a judicious distribution of food and gold, he won the loyalty of a people habituated to foreign rule; the name of Mu'izz supplanted that of his Abbasid rival in the public prayers, and a mosque-college, the Azhar, was erected for the instruction of Muslim youth in the precepts of Isma'ilism. Fatimid power spread into Arabia and Syria: the heretic Caliph was acknowledged in the holy cities of Mecca and Medina; the Hamdanids submitted, and Jawhar's troops entered Damascus, one of the main citadels of Sunnite orthodoxy. In 973 Mu'izz made his solemn entry into Cairo, the coffins of his ancestors being borne before him. The story goes that he received a deputation of notables, who invited him to prove his descent from Ali. He drew his sword, exclaiming: 'Here is my pedigree!' and scattering gold among the crowds, he cried: 'Here is my proof!' The evidence was found convincing.

Half Islam was now at the feet of the Isma'ilis. A swift advance eastwards might enable them to seize Baghdad, extinguish the line of the Abbasids, and recreate a Muslim world empire under Alid sovereignty. But the Fatimids were destined not to imitate the success of the Abbasids in 750. They had conquered Muslim Africa: they failed to capture Muslim Asia. Three obstacles stood in their path. One was the resistance of the Buyids, who were masters of Persia and Iraq; the second was the breach between the Fatimids and the Karmathians, and the third was the revival of Byzantine power in Syria and the eastern Mediterranean.

The Buyids were a clan of freebooters who sprang from the hill country of Dailam, where Alid missionaries had long been active. Three sons of their chief Buwayh or Buyeh set out around 932 to carve out a kingdom for themselves in Persia and Iraq, the Caliphate having fallen into final decay under the incompetent Muktadir (908-932). The Buyids were Shi'ites of some sort, probably Twelvers, but their precise religious affiliations are unknown. The military anarchy in the Caliph's realm, or what was left of it, grew worse: the Caliph Radi (934-940), whom the chroniclers describe as the last Abbasid to exercise a semblance of authority, the last to show himself to the people and preach the Friday sermon, sought to restore order in 936 by investing Ibn Ra'ik, an army chief, with the title of Amir al-Umara, Commander of Commanders, and giving him the power of a Mayor of the Palace. Matters were not thereby mended: a host of generals and princes continued to struggle for place, until in 945 Ahmad, the youngest of the Buyid brothers, seized Baghdad and compelled the Caliph Mustakfi (944-946) to grant him supreme control under the title Mu'izz al-Dawla, 'strengthener of the State.' Buyid power spread over the East from the Caspian Sea to the Persian Gulf and from the Oxus to Iraq.

The Abbasids had sunk to the lowest depths of humiliation. Not only was their real authority at an end, but they had been forced to yield it to a Shi'ite dynasty, whose leaders placed their names on the coins and inserted them in the public prayers after that of the Caliph. Surprise has been expressed that the Buyids did not get rid of the house of Abbas altogether and replace it by an Alid line. But they were not Isma'ilis and had no Imam to produce; the bulk of their subjects were Sunnites, whom they were unwilling to antagonize, and they had no desire to create a new dynasty of Caliphs who might prove stronger than they, the fate of Abu Abdallah at the hands of the Fatimids having no doubt been noted. Hence the Abbasids were kept on the throne and contemptuously allotted a pension and a secretariat, and the Buyids prepared to resist a Fatimid advance from Egypt.

Their task was rendered easier by a violent clash between the Fatimids and the Karmathians. Not long before, the latter had on orders from Mahdiya restored the Black Stone to the Kaaba, but the Karmathian leadership had since changed its attitude for reasons which are obscure, but which may be connected with the failure of the Fatimids to play the part of radical revolutionaries. Apart from Ka'im, the Fatimid Caliphs were shrewd enough to avoid pursuing extremist policies, and the fanatics of Bahrain were possibly disgusted by what they regarded as cowardice and a betrayal of Isma'-

ili ideals. With help from the Buyids and Hamdanids, they attacked the Fatimid positions in Syria, and twice (in 971 and 974) invaded Egypt. Though repulsed, they effectively checked a Fatimid drive towards Iraq, since they lay athwart the desert roads along which an army from Egypt must pass on its way to Baghdad.

A further complication was introduced by the Byzantine threat to Muslim Syria. The reconquest of Crete in 961 had strengthened the Byzantine position in the eastern Mediterranean, and was followed by the occupation of Cilicia in 965 and the capture of Antioch in 969. For the first time since the days of Heraclius, imperial armies reappeared in Syria and advanced as far south as Palestine. The Fatimids were obliged, not only to ward off assaults from the Karmathians, but to protect Dar al-Islam from Byzantine aggression. Not until 988 did they regain Damascus, and not until 998 was the Byzantine menace removed by a naval victory off Tyre and the raising of the imperialist siege of Tripoli.

Despite these setbacks, the power of the heretic Caliphate was a sufficiently alarming threat to Sunni Islam. Under the Fatimids, Egypt became an independent sovereign State for the first time since the days of the Ptolemies, the centre of a great Mediterranean Empire, its wealth no longer drained off to some distant imperial capital. Its economy was put on a sound basis by a brilliant finance minister, Ya'kub b.Killis, a converted Jew, made wazir by the Caliph Aziz (975-996). Special attention was paid to the navy, not only to ward off Byzantine attacks, but to protect Egypt's growing share of international commerce. Trade with India and the Far East was lured away from the Persian Gulf towards the Red Sea, with the result that Egypt flourished and Iraq languished. Alexandria became, as William of Tyre was to call it later, 'the market of two worlds', and the Italian commercial republics, led by Amalfi and soon followed by Venice and Pisa, began to purchase silks and spices and precious stones in Egypt and to re-sell them to a Europe emerging at last from the Dark Ages. The prosperity of the land was the wonder of eleventh century travellers, who describe the splendour of the mosques and palaces rising in the new capital and the crowded shops and warehouses of the admirably policed cities.

Notwithstanding its material wellbeing, the regime faced peculiar difficulties as a millenarian theocracy. Like many revolutionaries, the Fatimids in power grew conservative; their Shi'ite tenets acquired but a slight hold on the people of Egypt and the Maghrib, who remained fundamentally Sunnite, and impatient Isma'ili radicals were puzzled and disgusted by the failure of their Caliph-Imams to conquer the world and inaugurate the promised reign of justice and bliss. The tall, red-haired Aziz was the best of his race, but his liberal policy was scarcely calculated to please his Muslim subjects. Married to a Christian wife, a sister of the patriarchs of Alexandria and Jerusalem, he raised several of her coreligionists to high office, and refused even to punish a Muslim who turned Christian. To check the licence of the Berber troops whom Mu'izz had brought to Egypt, he recruited regiments of Turkish slave soldiers, as the Abbasids had done in the previous century, but the only result was to provoke a bitter race-conflict between Berbers and Turks, and weaken the unity and discipline of the army. Dying in 996, at the age of forty-one, he left the throne to his son Hakim, then a boy of eleven, who has attained an unenviable notoriety as the Caligula or Nero of Islam.

Until Hakim came of age, the government was in the hands of Barjawan, a slave-eunuch, who broke the power of the Berber soldiery and concluded a ten years' truce with the Byzantines. He slighted the young Caliph, and called him a lizard. Bitterly resentful, Hakim awaited his chance: in 1000, though only fifteen, he seized control and put Barjawan to death. The lizard, he remarked, had become a dragon. To the chroniclers, a dragon he certainly was: they represent him as a freakish savage, who oppressed his people by crazy laws and tortured and slew all who stood in his path. No business was to be done save at night; drinking and gambling were banned; dogs were to be killed wherever found, and women were forbidden to appear in the streets. The Caliph roamed the town at night to see that his orders were obeyed: offenders were scourged or beheaded. He launched a vicious persecution of Jews and Christians; they were made to wear a distinctive dress, and subjected to the most humiliating annoyances and restrictions. In 1009 he began the demolition of churches and synagogues, and ordered the destruction of the Church of the Resurrection at Jerusalem. A reign of terror raged for years: wazirs, generals, officials of all kinds were executed at the whim of a mad despot. As a sample of the atrocity stories told of Hakim, it is recorded that a general once accidentally came upon him cutting up a child: the horrified intruder hurried home and had barely time to put his affairs in order before the executioner arrived.

How much truth there is in these tales and how far Hakim's character has been blackened by his enemies, is impossible to tell. A cruel eccentric he undoubtedly was, yet there was perhaps method in his madness. His anti-Christian policy was designed to nullify the discontent aroused by his father's ultra-liberal attitude to non-Muslims, and to bring pressure to bear on the Byzantines, who were a constant threat to Fatimid Syria and who may well have had spies among the Christian population of Egypt. His moral and sumptuary regulations bear the imprint of a narrow puritan, anxious possibly to clear the Fatimids from the charge of laxity and contempt for the sacred law brought against them by their orthodox foes. He strove to reassure those Isma'ilis who were disturbed by the growing secularism of the regime by stressing the religious basis of the State and sponsoring a new propaganda drive in Sunni Islam. A 'House of Wisdom' was founded in Cairo in 1004 for the training of Isma'ili missionaries, and the renewed activity of the *da'is* impelled the Abbasid Caliph Kadir (991-1031) to issue in 1011 a manifesto ridiculing the Fatimid claim of descent from Ali and denouncing his rival as an atheist, infidel, materialist and enemy of Islam. Hakim foolishly gave plausibility to these charges. About 1017 two Isma'ili *da'is* from Persia, Hamza and Darazi, arrived in Cairo, preaching that the divine spirit, transmitted through Ali and the imams, had become incarnated in Hakim, who was thus virtually deified. An attempt to proclaim this doctrine in the principal mosque of Cairo led to a riot, and Darazi retired into Syria. Hakim never publicly endorsed this teaching, though he must have secretly encouraged it, and this last extravagance proved fatal to him. In 1021 he went off on one of his frequent nocturnal rambles in the Mukattam Hills, and did not return. He was almost certainly murdered, though his body was never found. In Egypt nothing more was heard of his divinity, but Darazi met with a favourable response from the primitive hillmen of Lebanon and Hawran, and the Druzes, the strange sect which bears his name, revere to this day the half-demented Hakim as the incarnation of God and expect his return in the last age of the world.

Under Hakim's son Zahir (1021-1036), Egypt recovered from this nightmare, though the repression of Jews and Christians continued in a modified form. During the fifty-eight years' reign of Mustansir (1036-1094), the longest in Muslim history, the Fatimid regime began to go the way of the Abbasids: the authority of the Caliph declined, generals and wazirs struggled for power, and the outlying provinces, starting with the Maghrib in 1051, fell away from their allegiance to Cairo. Yet Isma'ili propaganda continued as vigorously as ever in Asia, as far afield as Transoxiana, and in 1058 Basasiri, a Turkish commander who had been won over by the *da'is*, took possession of Baghdad, and for forty Fridays the *khutba* was read in the Abbasid capital in the name of the Fatimid Imam. This was, however, but a fleeting triumph. As internal troubles multiplied in Egypt, the Fatimids' control of their agents abroad slackened, and revolutionary extremists, of whom the Assassins are the best known, tended to fight for domination in the movement. Isma'ili dreams of universal empire were finally dissipated by the coming of the Seljuk Turks, who entered Islam with all the zeal of converts, were recruited in the service of orthodoxy, and without abolishing the Caliphate, in effect replaced it by a new institution—the Sultanate.

BOOKS FOR FURTHER READING

DONALDSON, D. M., *The Shi'ite Religion*, London, 1933. A general history of the Shi'a, rather uncritical.

GOEJE, M. J. DE, *Mémoire sur les Carmathes du Bahraïn et les Fatimides*, Leyden, 1886. The first scholarly inquiry into the difficult question of Karmathian origins.

HODGSON, M. G. S., 'When did the early Shi'a become sectarian?' *Journal of the American Oriental Society*, vol. 75, 1955.

IVANOW, W., *A Guide to Isma'ili Literature*, London, 1933.

IVANOW, W., *The Rise of the Fatimids*, London, 1942. Two of the many works by this scholar on the history of Isma'ilism based on Indian documents.

LANE-POOLE, S., *History of Egypt*, (as before).

LEWIS, B., *The Origins of Ismā'īlism*. Cambridge, 1940. Standard authority.

MANN, J., *The Jews in Egypt and Palestine during the Fatimid Caliphate*, 2 vols. Oxford, 1920. Useful for the social and economic life of Fatimid Egypt.

MINORSKY, V., *La Domination des Daylamites*, Paris 1932. Brief account of the Buwayhids or Buyids and Persian Shi'ism.

O'LEARY, DE L., *A Short History of the Fatimid Caliphate,* London, 1923. The only monograph in English.

SACY, S. DE, *Exposé de la Religion des Druzes,* 2 vols. Paris, 1838. Despite its age, this study by the great French Arabist is still of value for the whole Isma'ili movement and not only the Druze sect.

WIET, G., *L'Égypte arabe,* (as above).

IX

The Turkish Irruption

THE entry of the Seljuk Turks into Western Asia in the second half of the eleventh century forms one of the great epochs of world history. It added a third nation, after the Arabs and Persians, to the dominant races of Islam; it prolonged the life of the moribund Caliphate for another two hundred years; it tore Asia Minor away from Christendom and opened the path to the later Ottoman invasion of Europe; it allowed the orthodox Muslims to crush the Isma'ilian heresy, and provoked in reprisal the murderous activities of the Assassins; it put an end to the political domination of the Arabs in the Near East, it spread the language and culture of Persia over a wide area from Anatolia to Northern India, and by posing a grave threat to the Christian Powers, it impelled the Latin West to undertake the remarkable counter-offensive of the Crusades.

The Turkish family of nations first emerged into the light of history in the mid-sixth century, when they built up a short-lived nomad empire in the heart of Asia, the steppes which have ever since borne the name Turkestan, the land of the Turks. When it broke in pieces, in the manner of such confederacies, fragments of the Turkish race, under a bewildering variety of names, were scattered over a vast area, from the Uighurs, who once dwelt in Mongolia, to the Polovtsians of the Russian steppes, familiar to us from Borodin's opera *Prince Igor*. Despite the wide differences between them—some came under Chinese, others under Persian influence; some were pure nomads, others were settled agriculturists—they all spoke dialects of the same tongue; they possessed common folk memories and legends; in religion they were shamanists, and they reckoned time according to a twelve-year cycle named after animals, events being placed in the Year of the Panther, the Year of the Hare, the Year of the Horse, and so on.

The Oxus was the traditional boundary between civilization and barbarism in Western Asia, between Iran and Turan, and Persian legend, versified in Firdawsi's great epic, the *Shah-namah*, told of the heroic battles of the Iranians against the Turanian king Afrasiyab, who was at last hunted down and killed in Azerbaijan. When the Arabs crossed the Oxus after the fall of the Sassanids, they took over the defence of Iran against the barbarian nomads and pushed them back beyond the Jaxartes. The Turkish tribes were in political disarray, and were never able to oppose a unified resistance to the Arabs, who carried their advance as far as the Talas river. For nearly three centuries Transoxiana, or as the Arabs called it, Ma Wara al-Nahr, 'that which is beyond the river', was a flourishing land, free from serious nomadic incursions, and cities like Samarkand and Bukhara rose to fame and wealth.

From the ninth century onwards the Turks began to enter the Caliphate, not in mass, but as slaves or adventurers serving as soldiers. They thus infiltrated the world of Islam as the Germans did the Roman Empire. The Caliph Mu'tasim (833-842) was the first Muslim ruler to surround himself with a Turkish guard. Turkish officers rose to high rank, commanding armies, governing provinces, sometimes ruling as independent princes: thus Ahmad b.Tulun seized power in Egypt in 868, and a second Turkish family, that of the Ikhshidids (from an Iranian title *ikhshid*, meaning 'prince'), ran the same country from 933 until the Fatimid conquest in 969. The disintegration of the Abbasid Empire afforded ample scope for such political adventurism, but so long as Transoxiana was held for civilization, the heart of Islam was safe from a massive barbarian break-through. When the Caliphs ceased to exercise authority on the distant eastern frontier, the task was shouldered by the Samanids, perhaps the most brilliant of the dynasties which took over from the enfeebled Abbasids. In the end it proved too heavy a burden, and the Samanid collapse at the end of the tenth century opened the floodgates to Turkish nomad tribes, who poured across both Jaxartes and Oxus into the lands of the Persians and Arabs.

Despite their brief rule of little more than a hundred years, the Samanids had much to their credit. Of Persian origin, they set up a strong centralized government in Khurasan and Transoxiana, with its capital at Bukhara; they encouraged trade and manufactures; they patronized learning, and they sponsored the spread of Islam by peaceful conversion among the barbarians to the north and east of their realm. It was during their time that the vigorous and commercially-minded Vikings gained possession of Russia, and traded their furs and wax and slaves in the markets of the south in exchange for textiles and metal goods, evidence of this traffic being provided by the hoards of Arabic coins dug up in Sweden, Finland and North Russia. One of the main international trade routes of the age ran through the territory of the Bulghars, a Turkish race living in the region of the middle Volga, who accepted Islam before 921, in which year a mission from the Caliph Muktadir visited them and reported on life among this most northerly of Muslim peoples. The Bulghars in turn tried to convert the Russians, but Vladimir of Kiev decided in 988 in favour of Christianity, thereby barring Islam's advance into Eastern Europe. Most probably the Bulghars were converted by merchants from the Samanid kingdom, who also brought the faith to the Turks beyond the Jaxartes, nomads who did a brisk trade in sheep and cattle with the frontier towns. About 956 the Seljuks, destined to so glorious a future, embraced Islam, and in 960 the conversion of a Turkish tribe of 200,000 tents is recorded: their precise identity is unspecified. Thus the tenth century witnessed the islamization, under Samanid auspices, of a large section of the Western Turks, an event of great significance.

Notwithstanding the prosperity of their kingdom, the Samanids failed to keep the loyalty of their subjects. Their heavily bureaucratized despotism was expensive to maintain, and the burden of taxation alienated the *dihkans,* on whose support the regime depended. One of their rulers, Nasr al-Sa'id, who reigned from 914 to 943, favoured the Isma'ilis and corresponded with the Fatimid Caliph Ka'im, thereby forfeiting the sympathy of the orthodox. Following the example of the Abbasids, they surrounded themselves with Turkish guards, whose fidelity was far from assured. In 962 one of their Turkish officers, Alp-tagin ('hero prince'), seized the town and fortress of Ghazna, in what is now Afghanistan, a wealthy commercial centre whose inhabitants had grown rich on the Indian trade, and set up a semi-independent principality. He died in the following year, and after an interval another Turkish general, Sabuktagin, won control of Ghazna in 977 and founded a dynasty which gained immortal lustre from his son Mahmud. The Samanid kingdom fell into anarchy; the Kara-Khanids, a Turkish people of unknown antecedents (they may have been the tribe converted to Islam in 960), crossed the Jaxartes and captured Bukhara in 999, while Mahmud of Ghazna, who had succeeded his father Sabuktagin two years earlier, annexed the large and flourishing province of Khurasan. Thus Persian rule disappeared along the eastern marches of Islam, and Turkish princes reigned in Khurasan and Transoxiana. Barbarians though they might be, they found a certain favour with their subjects: they stood for order, they allowed Persian officials to run the government, they protected trade, they were orthodox Sunnite Muslims, and they professed themselves ardent champions of the faith against heretics and unbelievers.

The fame of Mahmud of Ghazna rests upon his expeditions into India. In the thirty years between 1000 and his death in 1030 he led some seventeen massive raids into the Indus valley and the Punjab. Ghazna was an admirable base for such attacks; the vast Indian sub-continent was a mosaic of principalities great and small; no strong State existed capable of throwing back the invader, and there was no trace of national consciousness. Mahmud's motives were a mixture of cupidity and religious zeal: when he was looting Hindu shrines he could claim to be destroying idolatry in the name of God and his Prophet, and he received congratulations and honours from the Caliph for his services to the faith. He fought not only against the unbelievers of Hindustan but against the Isma'ili heretics, among them the Muslim ruler of Multan. His most celebrated exploit was the capture of Somnath in Gujarat in 1025, where he stormed the temple of Shiva, one of the most richly endowed in India, and levelled it to the ground amid frightful carnage. Ghazna was flooded with Indian plunder, and the multitude of prisoners was such that they were sold as slaves for two or three dirhams apiece. Some of the wealth was used to promote art and learning, and the court of Mahmud was adorned by such notabilities as Firdawsi, Persia's greatest epic poet, Biruni, the most distinguished scientist of the age, and Utbi, the historian of the reign.

Two consequences of immense importance flowed from Mahmud's repeated incursions into India. First, the collapse of Hindu resistance in the Punjab turned this province into an area of Muslim settlement and exposed the whole Gangetic plain to invasion from the north-west. The early raids up and down the Indus in the days of Muhammad b.Kasim had only touched the fringe of a vast country, but Mahmud's expeditions penetrated deep into Hindustan, disorganized its defences, and opened the way to later Muslim invaders, from the Ghurids to the Moguls, who gradually brought all northern and central India within the domain of Islam. Secondly, the preoccupation of Mahmud and his son and successor Mas'ud with their Indian campaigns left them little time or opportunity to observe and check the steadily mounting pressure of Turkish nomads along the Oxus. While their backs were turned, so to speak, the Seljuks rose to prominence and power in their rear and bcame the masters of all Western Asia.

The pasture-lands to the north of the Caspian and Aral Seas had long been the home of a group of Turkish tribes known as the Ghuzz or Oghuz, later styled Turkomans. About 950 a number of clans withdrew from the Ghuzz confederacy, and settled in and around Jand, along the lower reaches of the Jaxartes, under a chief named Seljuk. A few years later they abandoned their ancestral shamanism for Islam, a change of faith as momentous for the future of Asia as the conversion of Clovis and his Franks to Catholicism in 496 was to Christian Europe. Seljuk is a semi-legendary figure who is said to have lived to the patriarchal age of 107, but he seems to have been an able leader, who welded his people into a first-class fighting force and by adroit diplomacy played off one neighbouring prince against another. He supported the Samanids against the Kara-Khanids; his son Arslan ran into trouble with Mahmud of Ghazna, to whom he boasted that he had 100,000 bowmen under his command, whereupon Mahmud's minister advised his master to have these men's thumbs cut off, so that they could no longer draw the bow! However, Mahmud contented himself with holding Arslan as a hostage for the good behaviour of his people, some of whom he brought into Khurasan and settled in widely-separated areas in the hope that they could thus be kept under control. The hope was vain: the tribesmen began raiding all over northern Persia and holding towns to ransom. After Mahmud's death in 1030, the rest of the tribe, led by Arslan's nephews Tughril-Beg and Chaghri-Beg, after encamping for a time in Khwarazm, along the lower Oxus, pushed their way into Khurasan and in 1036 seized Merv and Nishapur. Mahmud's son Mas'ud, attempting to bar their path, was routed with heavy loss at Dandankan near Merv in 1040, and retreated on Ghazna. From this battle dates the foundation of the Seljuk Empire.

The Seljuks now moved westwards into the disintegrating realm of the Buyids. Conditions in Persia and Iraq favoured their intervention. Political power had been split up among the various members of the Buyid family. The semi-feudal practice had grown up of paying high officials out of the taxes of certain fiscal districts: hence there was a serious loss of control by the central government. The Fatimid policy of diverting trade with the East from the Persian Gulf to the Red Sea had impoverished the Buyid State. Isma'ilian propaganda helped to undermine its authority. It had no outlet to the Mediterranean since the Byzantines and the Fatimids had divided Syria between them. The urban merchant class resented the loss of trade and the arrogance of the military aristocracy. Local dynasties, some Arab, some Kurdish, sprang up and drained the strength of the regime. Orthodox Muslims chafed under the rule of Shi'ites, especially those unable to maintain peace and order. The Abbasids, humiliated by their impotence, yearned for deliverance from their heretic masters, and entered into negotiations with Tughril. One by one the towns of Persia fell into Seljuk hands. In Iraq power was held by the Buyid general Basasiri, who asked for help from Cairo in order to stop the advance of the Seljuks by declaring for the Fatimids. An extraordinary struggle ensued, with Tughril defending the Abbasid Caliph Ka'im and Basasiri striving to get the Fatimid Caliph Mustansir recognized in Baghdad. The Seljuks occupied Baghdad in 1055, but the excesses and indiscipline of the tribesmen provoked a reaction among the populace, and Wasit, Mosul and other places went over to the Fatimids. Tughril recaptured Mosul, and returning to Baghdad in 1058 was solemnly received by Ka'im and given the title of 'King of the East and West'. Called away by a rebellion of his younger brother Ibrahim, he was unable to prevent Basasiri recovering control of Iraq and proclaiming the Fatimid Imam in Baghdad itself. For forty Fridays the *khutba* was recited in the Abbasid capital in the name of Mustansir of Cairo. Finally in 1060 the Seljuks fought their way back into Baghdad; Basasiri was killed, and Tughril replaced the Abbasid on his throne.

Many things were decided by this episode. First, the Fatimids lost their last chance of repeating the success of the Abbasids in 750: the failure of Basasiri's *coup* in Baghdad meant that the Alid Caliph would be restricted to Egypt and the neighbouring lands and would never acquire universal dominion in Islam. Secondly, the fall of the Buyids and the coming of the Seljuks registered a great triumph for Sunnite orthodoxy: the power of the State could now be employed to put down Shi'ism of all kinds and Isma'ilism in particular. Thirdly, the Abbasid Caliphate was restored to some sort of life and independence, but its character was changed, and a new institution—the Sultanate—was created in an endeavour to re-establish the political unity of Islam. For the Caliphate, as a centralized monarchy ruling all Muslim peoples, had woefully failed. It could not even preserve the religious and spiritual unity of the *umma*: half Islam had fallen to the Fatimids. It never developed into a Papacy, for the interpretation of the law and the faith had long passed to the *ulama,* the canonists and judges. Yet even in its weakness it was still revered by the new Turkish converts as the symbol of religious legitimacy: the Vicar of the Prophet alone could confer lawful authority on Muslim kings and princes to whom in theory he delegated his powers. Mahmud of Ghazna had been glad to win recognition from the Caliph, and his court poets had hailed him as 'Sultan', a word meaning originally 'governmental power' but henceforth used as a personal title. The Seljuks were even more anxious to have their rule legitimized: as aliens and barbarians they were unpopular with the civilized townsfolk of Persia and Iraq, and Tughril's investiture by the Caliph in 1058, in a magnificent ceremony during which two crowns were held over his head as symbols of his regal authority over East and West, informed the people that the Commander of the Faithful had delegated his *sultanate* to his Turkish lieutenant. It was now the Sultan's duty to act as the early Caliphs had done, to defend the *umma,* to extirpate schism and heresy, and to resume the *jihad* against the nations who rejected God and his Prophet. Politically, the Seljuks were to play Shoguns to the Caliph's Mikado.

Two enemies were obviously marked out for attack by the new protectors of Sunnite Islam: the Byzantines and the Fatimids. In the previous age the former had thrust deep into the heart of Islam, had conquered a good deal of Syria and annexed Armenia to the

Empire. But the Byzantine revival had now spent itself: the vigorous Macedonian dynasty was no more; the central government was in conflict with the great landed families of Asia Minor, and in order to reduce their power, had cut down the military establishment, thereby rendering the Empire defensively weak against the new assault from the East. The Turks drove towards the Byzantine frontiers, partly by design, partly by accident. Their coming had produced something of a social crisis in the Persian and Arab lands. In a society where the fundamental distinction was between believer and unbeliever, the fact that the Turks were Muslims counted for much; but even so, the educated city-dweller could scarcely avoid a feeling of disgust at the presence of these coarse and uncouth sons of the steppes. The chroniclers of the time draw a sharp contrast between the Sultans and their people: 'Their princes are warlike, provident, firm, just and distinguished by excellent qualities: the nation is cruel, wild, coarse and ignorant.' To make matters worse, once the barrier of the Oxus was down, the regular Seljuk forces, cavalrymen of slave origin, were followed by swarms of 'Turkomans', free and undisciplined nomads seeking pasture and plunder, who raided estates, destroyed crops, robbed merchant caravans, and fought other nomads, such as Kurds and Bedouin Arabs, for the possession of wells and grazing-lands. Many of them poured into Azerbaijan, a fertile province of orchards and pastures which in a few generations became mainly Turkish-speaking, and from there began raiding Byzantine territory. When Tughril died childless in 1063, the Sultanate passed to his nephew Alp Arslan ('hero lion'), Chagri's son, who was probably anxious to divert the stream of nomadic violence away from the lands of Islam towards Christendom and at the same time to win glory as a *ghazi,* or champion of the faith. His armies pushed into the valleys of Armenia and Georgia, while the Turkomans plunged deeper and deeper into Anatolia. An appeal from the enemies of the Fatimids then diverted him into southern Syria, but his plans for an invasion of Egypt were abandoned at the news of an impending massive Byzantine counter-stroke.

The Emperor Romanus Diogenes had resolved on a desperate effort to clear the Turkish raiders out of his dominions, and at the head of a motley army of mercenaries, including Normans from the west and Pechenegs and Uzes (Turkish tribes) from southern Russia, he marched eastwards into Armenia. Alp Arslan, hurriedly returning, met him at Manzikert, near the shores of Lake Van. The Normans started a quarrel and refused to fight for the Emperor; his Turkish mercenaries, perhaps unwilling to face their kinsmen, deserted, and this, combined with Romanus's bad generalship, produced (August 1071) a catastrophic Byzantine defeat. For the first time in history, a Christian Emperor fell a prisoner into Muslim hands.

Alp Arslan stands out a not unattractive figure, his name indissolubly connected with the momentous battle which turned Asia Minor into a Turkish land. We picture him as an impressive soldier in his thirties, his long moustaches tied over his tall Persian cap to prevent them interfering with his shooting. In his humanity and generosity he anticipates Saladin. He treated the captive Emperor with courtesy, and when the ransom money was paid sent him home with a Turkish escort. Perhaps he hardly grasped the significance of his victory. He had no plans to conquer Asia Minor and destroy the Byzantine State; he was soon called away to deal with a Kara-Khanid invasion from Transoxiana, and in 1073, while interrogating a rebel chief, the man suddenly sprang at him and stabbed him dead. In fact, Manzikert struck a fatal blow at Christian and imperial power in Anatolia. With the Byzantine field-army gone, the Turks spread over the central plateau, so well adapted for pastoral settlement; in the struggles for the throne which now ensued, rival pretenders hired Turkish troops, and in this way the nomads got possession of towns and fortresses they could never have taken otherwise. The Greek landlords and officials fled; the peasants, deprived of their natural leaders, in time adopted the religion of their new masters, and the faith of Muhammad was taught in the lands where St. Paul had proclaimed the gospel of Christ. With Asia Minor, its principal source of soldiers and revenue, lost, menaced by the aggression of the Normans from Italy and the Pechenegs from across the Danube, the Byzantine Empire faced total ruin, and appeals for help to the Pope and the Latin world went out from Constantinople which produced twenty-five years after Manzikert the preaching of the First Crusade.

On the murder of Alp Arslan, he was succeeded as Sultan by his son Malik-Shah, a youth of eighteen whose twenty years' reign (1073-1092) marked the fullest expansion of Seljuk power. Malik-Shah was a more cultivated man than his father and great-uncle, who were essentially rough tribal chiefs, and he wisely entrusted the civil administration to the great Persian minister usually known by his title Nizam al-Mulk, 'order of the kingdom'. A just and humane ruler, he received the praise of Christian and Muslim historians alike. His suzerainty was recognized from Kashgar to the Yemen, but risings and disturbances were not uncommon in his vast dominions, and he was obliged to leave to others the conduct of operations against the Byzantines and the Fatimids. A cadet of the Seljuk family, Sulaiman b.Kutulmish, founded a durable State in Asia Minor, the so-called Sultanate of Rum; he captured Nicaea in 1081 and threatened Constantinople itself. The war on the Fatimids was inaugurated, not by the Seljuks, but by a Turkoman chief named Atsiz, who in 1070 marched into Palestine and drove the Egyptians out of Jerusalem. Malik-Shah could not tolerate this, and gave his brother Tutush charge of the Syrian front. The Fatimids proved tougher opponents than might have been expected: the Seljuks were not destined to heal the schism that had rent the Muslim world for nearly two centuries.

The Fatimid regime had, in fact made a surprising recovery from what had seemed certain ruin. A dreadful six years' famine had paralysed Egypt from 1067 to 1072; the civil government virtually broke down; thousands fled from the country, and the misery of those who remained was heightened by the brutal lawlessness of the Turkish, Berber and Sudanese slave soldiery who killed and robbed in quest of food and plunder. The Fatimid Empire all but vanished. The Maghrib had long been lost; Sicily was conquered by the Normans from South Italy, Atsiz seized Palestine, and the Abbasid Caliph was once more prayed for in the Holy Cities. But in 1073 Mustansir called in the governor of Acre, Badr al-Jamali, a brilliant general of Armenian birth, to restore order; the mutinous troops were disciplined, the defences of Cairo were strengthened, trade revived, the revenues rose, and prosperity returned. The price paid was the creation of a military dictatorship, Badr, with the title of *Amir al-Juyush*, 'Commander of the Armies,' replacing the civilian wazir, and the Caliph being reduced almost to the level of the Abbasids under Buyid rule. Badr then set out to recover Syria, and though he failed to regain Damascus, which fell to the Seljuks in 1076, he succeeded in checking Tutush's advance to the Egyptian frontier and in re-establishing Fatimid authority along the Levantine coast as far as Tyre and Sidon. The Alid Caliphate, though shorn of much of its glory, was put on its feet again and enabled to survive for another century. When Badr died in 1094, a few months before the aged Caliph, Seljuk hopes of restoring Egypt to orthodoxy had been frustrated, and the rival parties were still struggling for the control of Syria, a situation highly advantageous to the Latin Crusaders who broke into the Levant three or four years later.

The Seljuks rendered notable service to Islam, but their successes were balanced by many failures. They brought a new vigour and unity into Western Asia and put an end to the decadent regime of the Buyids. They dealt a staggering blow to Byzantine power by winning Asia Minor for Islam, a feat the Arabs had never been able to achieve, thereby breaking down the last defences of Christendom on the Asiatic continent, and opening up this ancient land to Turkish colonial settlement. Their vehement orthodoxy checked the spread of Isma'ilism, which in future was able to operate only as an underground terrorist movement whose agents became notorious as the Assassins. Under Seljuk protection the champions of Sunnite Islam launched a strong propaganda drive against heretics and deviators from the true faith: *madrasas* or 'college-mosques' were founded in the principal cities for the instruction of students in *fikh* (Islamic jurisprudence), according to the teaching of the four orthodox schools. The best known of these institutions was the Nizamiya Madrasa in Baghdad, named after Nizam al-Mulk and dedicated by him in 1067. Orthodoxy produced at this time its ablest defender in al-Ghazali, who died in 1111, and whose massive and comprehensive system of theology has won him the title of 'the Aquinas of Islam'.

On the other hand, the Seljuks proved unable to create a strong, durable and centralized Empire or to destroy the Fatimid Anti-Caliphate in Egypt. Their conceptions of government were primitive, and despite the efforts of Nizam al-Mulk to instruct them in the principles of ancient Persian despotism, which he regarded as the only satisfactory form of rule, they treated their realm as family property to be divided up among sons and nephews, who if minors were entrusted to the care of *atabegs* ('father-chiefs'), usually generals of servile origin who governed their appanages until their wards came of age and who often became hereditary princes in their own right. Until the death of Malik-Shah in 1092 some degree of unity was preserved, but under the fourth Seljuk Sultan Berkyaruk (1095-1114) the Empire was changed into a kind of federation of autonomous princes, not all of them Turks, for in certain localities Buyid and Kurdish chiefs held sway while admitting only a vague Seljuk suzerainty. Incessant struggles for the succession further weakened the Empire and gave the Abbasid Caliphs a chance to recover some of their power by playing off one candidate for the Sultanate against another. Political disintegration was hastened by the spread of the *ikta* system, by which military officers were paid out of the revenues of certain landed estates, *ikta* meaning literally a 'section' or portion of land 'cut off' for that purpose, and in some respects resembling the knight's fee of Western feudalism. *Ikta*-holding tended to become hereditary and the 'fief' thus escaped from the jurisdiction of the central government. By 1100 the best days of the Seljuks were over, and it was precisely at this juncture that the Franks chose to launch against Islam the strange Christian counter-offensive which we know as the Crusades.

BOOKS FOR FURTHER READING

BARTHOLD, W., *Histoire des Turcs d'Asie Centrale*, Paris, 1945.

BOSWORTH, C. E., *The Ghaznavids*, Edinburgh, 1963.

CAHEN, C., 'The Turkish Invasions: the Selchükids', in the Pennsylvania *History of the Crusades*, vol. 1, 1955. The best recent account of the Seljuks, by a leading French scholar.

NĀZIM, MUHAMMAD, *The Life and Times of Sultān Mahmūd of Ghazna*, Cambridge, 1931. The only full modern biography of the famous conqueror.

SANAULLAH, M., *The Decline of the Saljūqid Empire*, Calcutta, 1938. The first part of this work contains a survey of the little that is known of Seljuk institutions.

TALBOT RICE (MRS.), *The Seljuks in Asia Minor*, London, 1961. Good account, especially valuable on the archaeological side.

VASILIEV, A. A., *History of the Byzantine Empire*, Madison, 1952, chap. vi.

TRANSLATED SOURCES

NIZĀM AL-MULK, *Siyāsat-Nāma*, Eng. tr. H. Darke, *The Book of Government or Rules for Kings*, London, 1960. A handbook of advice compiled about 1086 by the great Wazir for the instruction of Malik-Shah, and a characteristic statement of Persian political theory and practice.

'UTBĪ, *Kitāb i-Yamīnī*, Eng. tr. J. Reynolds, London, 1858. A history of Mahmud of Ghazna written by his court historian who died about 1036. *Yamin al-Dawla,* 'Right Hand of the State,' was a title of honour given to Mahmud and his house by the Caliph. The original text is in Arabic: the English translation was made from the Persian.

X

The Christian Counter-attack

A REMARKABLE change in the balance of forces between Latin Christendom and the Islamic world took place in the eleventh century. Up till 1000 the West was a poor, backward and illiterate region, precariously defending itself against the assaults of barbarous nations by land and sea. The Vikings raided all along the Atlantic coasts and far inland, while the Magyars pushed their nomadic ravages as far west as northern Italy and the Rhineland. All this while, for nearly four centuries, Islam enjoyed an internal peace and security, untroubled save for domestic wars, and was thus enabled to build up a brilliant and impressive urban culture. Now the situation was dramatically transformed. Around 1000 the Vikings and Magyars were converted to Christianity, and so far as the West was concerned, the age of barbarian invasion was over. Trade and commerce revived; towns and markets sprang up; the population increased, with a resulting rising demand for food and clothing, and the arts and sciences were cultivated on a scale unknown since the days of the Roman Empire.

At this very time the immunity of Islam from external attack came to an end, and a storm of nomadic violence broke over it from Transoxiana to the Maghrib. In 1031 the Omayyad Caliphate in Spain collapsed, and after a terrible interval of anarchy, during which the Christian kingdoms pushed their frontiers southwards across the central plateau, the Spanish Muslims were forced to appeal for succour to the Murabits, or Almoravids as they were known to European writers, a Berber confederacy from southern

Morocco whose leaders landed troops in Spain in 1086 and whose rough and semi-civilized fanaticism came to dominate the Muslim West. In 1050 the Zirids, whom the Fatimids had left behind as viceroys in North Africa when they departed for Egypt in 969, repudiated their Alid suzerains and transferred their spiritual allegiance to the Abbasid Caliph of Baghdad. To punish this treachery, the Fatimid Government let loose upon them two half-barbarous Arab Bedouin tribes from upper Egypt, the Banu-Hilal and the Banu-Sulaim, who mercilessly ravaged all the open country of the once-prosperous region north of the Atlas range, destroying villages, canals, dams, orchards and plantations and turning cultivated farmland into pasture for their sheep and goats. The great religious metropolis of Kairawan was sacked by them in 1057. The Zirids clung to the towns on the coast, but the hinterland was ruined, and 300 years later the Tunisian historian Ibn Khaldun could assert that his native land had never recovered from the effects of this devastation. In the East the defences of the Oxus broke down with the fall of the Samanids, and through the breach poured the Seljuks and their fellow Turks, flooding the civilized lands of the Persians and Arabs. These nomadic newcomers were indeed Muslims, not pagans, but they inflicted wounds (serious in the case of the Banu-Hilal, less so in the case of the Seljuks) which were never properly healed. The Pax Islamica was over.

These developments had curiously contrasting effects on the two halves of the Christian world. The battle of Manzikert in 1071 dealt a deadly blow to Byzantine power, and delivered the greater part of Asia Minor to Islam. In the West the Saharan nomads were little danger to the Christian States, but by weakening the civilized Muslim principalities, they gave an advantage to the nations of Western Europe who were now emerging from the Dark Ages and building up their military and naval strength. As early as 972 the Muslim pirates were driven from their lair at Fraxinetum in Provence, from which they had so long terrorized the Mediterranean coasts of France and Italy. In 1016 the fleets of Pisa and Genoa regained possession of Sardinia, and in the same year the warlike and adventurous Normans made their first appearance in South Italy. The Zirids, frantically striving to stave off their Bedouin enemies, were unable to keep hold of Sicily: in 1072 Palermo fell to the Normans, and by 1091 the whole island had been recovered for Christendom.

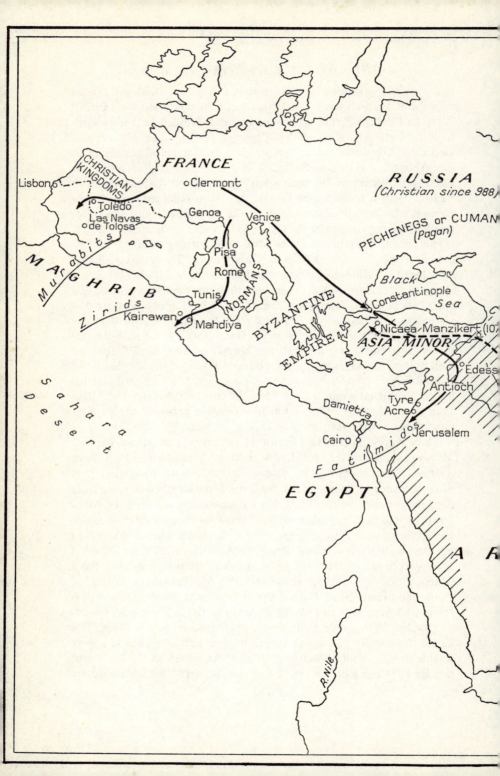

CHRISTIAN
KINGDOMS

Lisbon

FRANCE

Clermont

RUSSIA
(Christian since 988)

Toledo
Las Navas
de Tolosa

Genoa

Venice

PECHENEGS or CUMAN
(Pagan)

MAGHRIB

Murabits

Pisa

Rome

Black

Constantinople

Sea

Tunis

NORMANS

Zirids

Kairawan

Mahdiya

BYZANTINE

Nicaea Manzikert (107

ASIA MINOR

EMPIRE

Edess

Antioch

Sahara

Desert

Damietta

Tyre

Acre

A R

Cairo

Jerusalem

Fatimid

EGYPT

R. Nile

CHRISTENDOM & ISLAM
AT THE TIME OF THE CRUSADES

Main lines of Latin Christian advance against Islam →
Main line of Seljuk Turk advance -->
Seljuk Territory ⊞

BULGHARS (Muslims)

R. Volga

OGHUZ TURKS

Lake Balkash

UIGHURS (partly Christian)

Aral Sea

SELJUKS (Muslim since 956)

KARA-KHITAI (Pagan)

KHWARAZM

TRANSOXIANA

R. Jaxartes

Kashgar

Caspian Sea

R. Oxus

Merv

Caucasus

Nishapur

Alamut

Kumm

PERSIA

Ghazna

PUNJAB

Baghdad

Ghaznavids

Multan

R. Indus

Delhi

R. Ganges

ABIA

Somnath

INDIA

Indian Ocean

In 1085 the Spanish Christians drove the Muslims from the old Visigothic capital of Toledo and conquered most of the Castilian uplands. In 1087 an Italian naval force, consisting chiefly of Pisan and Genoese ships, raided the old Fatimid capital of Mahdiya, freed the Christian slaves there, and extorted a formidable ransom from the Zirid governor. In 1090 the Normans captured Malta, thereby giving the Christian Powers control of the straits separating Europe from Africa.

All this created the conditions which made possible the initial success of the Crusades. The West rejoiced in its new-found strength; it was provided with encouraging evidence of Muslim weakness and disunity; and the re-opening of the sea routes across the Mediterranean multiplied the number of pilgrimages to the holy places, which fixed the attention of the Latin world more sharply than ever on Jerusalem. When the Byzantine Emperor Alexius I despatched appeals to the West for volunteers to help stem the advance of the Turks through Asia Minor, Pope Urban II at the Council of Clermont in 1095 skilfully utilized this plea to call for a great independent military expedition designed not so much to aid the Greek Christians as to expel the Muslims from Palestine, the cradle of the Christian faith. The First Crusade was launched in an atmosphere of intense religious emotion, and was conceived as part of the grand counter-offensive against Islam which was already being conducted on two fronts, in Spain and across the central Mediterranean towards North Africa. A third front was now to be opened in the Levant. The response to the Pope's appeal was remarkable: from a mixture of motives ranging from pure religious idealism to the lure of plunder and riches in the East, thousands took the Cross, and whole armies were raised in France and Germany and elsewhere which set out in 1096, made their way down the Danube to Constantinople and thence across Asia Minor to Syria and Palestine. After bitter fighting, Jerusalem fell into Christian hands in 1099 for the first time since the Patriarch Sophronius had surrendered the city to Omar in 638.

The ineffective resistance opposed by the Muslim princes to the Crusading armies has often occasioned surprise. No doubt it is to be explained partly by the very suddenness and unexpectedness of this unprovoked assault by the 'Franks' of the distant West. A more cogent reason is the state of anarchy in which Syria had fallen after the death of Malik Shah in 1092 and his brother Tutush in 1095. Syria was always a country difficult to govern, being a hilly land in whose nooks and crannies so many racial and religious minorities found refuge, but at the close of the eleventh century it was in an unusual state of confusion. The unity of the Seljuk Empire was no more; Tutush's sons Ridwan and Dukak, who controlled respectively Aleppo and Damascus, were quarrelling over their father's inheritance; ambitious Turkish *amirs* were striving to carve out baronies for themselves; the undisciplined Turkomans raided and plundered at will; Arab tribal chiefs had set up petty principalities in northern Syria and Iraq; the towns were often obliged to look to their own defences, and the racial feuds of Arab, Turk and Kurd added to the disorder. In such a condition of affairs not only was no organized and vigorous opposition to the intruders to be expected, but their progress was facilitated by the desire of one Muslim faction to use them in its strife with the others.

It might have been expected that the strongest stand against the Franks would be made by the Fatimids of Egypt, who had recovered Jerusalem from the Turks in 1095 or 1097, only to have it wrested from them by the Crusaders in 1099. But the government of Egypt had fallen into incompetent hands after the death of the great Armenian wazir Badr in 1094. His son Afdal, who succeeded his as wazir, was indolent and pleasure-loving, and not only frittered away the resources of the State but involved the Isma'ili movement in a fresh schism. The aged Caliph Mustansir died in 1094, a few months after Badr; his adult heir Nizar was set aside by Afdal in favour of a younger and more pliable son, Musta'li, and when the latter died in 1101, his son, a child of five, was made Caliph under the title of al-Amir. These arbitrary proceedings, clearly designed by the wazir to perpetuate his power, aroused strong reprobation; Nizar's adherents refused to recognize the puppet Caliphs in whose name Afdal exercised dictatorial authority; outside Egypt the Fatimid regime was widely repudiated by the Isma'ilis, and the claims of the rightful Imam were taken up by the most extraordinary of all Alid sects, the Asssassins, whose murderous activities divided and distracted Islam and contributed to the consolidation of Frankish rule in Syria and Palestine.

About 1077 Hassan i-Sabbah, a Persian *da'i* from Kumm, long a centre of Shi'ite activity, visited Egypt, probably in the hope of persuading the Fatimid leaders to sponsor an anti-Seljuk rising in Western Asia. He found, no doubt to his disappointment, that Fatimid Isma'ilism, once a world-wide revolutionary movement, had shrunk to the confines of a dynastic State: if the cause of Ali were to be saved, it could be done only by the independent action of the Persian Seveners. In 1090, by a clever stratagem, he seized the fortress of Alamut, in the hills of Dailam, an old Shi'ite district whence the Buyids had sprung nearly two centuries before, and in the confusion following Malik Shah's death in 1092, Hassan's armed bands snatched control of several castles and strongholds in northern Persia, from which the warring Seljuk princes were unable to dislodge them. In 1094 Hassan refused to recognize the substitution of Musta'li for Nizar as Fatimid Imam, and in true Isma'ili fashion proclaimed himself the deputy of the captive or hidden leader. A man of fanatical devotion, will-power and organizing ability, he ruled his people from Alamut for thirty-four years until his death in 1124. He called his movement the New Preaching or Propaganda; his followers were strictly Nizari Isma'ilis, but to the world at large they became speedily known by the opprobrious name of Assassins.

Whatever might have been Hassan's original hopes, he failed to destroy the power of the Turks or to set up a territorial State comparable to that of Fatimid Egypt. The appeal of Shi'ism had waned; the new *madrasas* were teaching a rigorous orthodoxy, and the greatest of Muslim theologians, al-Ghazali, was effecting an alliance between Sunnite legalism and Sufi mysticism which boded ill for heresy. The cities were as a rule strongly Sunnite; the Isma'ilis rarely gained a footing outside remote country districts or mountain valleys, and it was never possible for them to wage open war with the Turkish or Arab authorities. Hence they were obliged to resort to terrorism, the weapon of the weak. In the early days of Islam, the Kharijites had pronounced their enemies apostates and therefore liable to the death penalty, and Hassan now followed their example. A murder campaign was launched which spread all over Western Asia and even into Egypt, whose chiefs were considered traitors to the Alid faith. Dedicated *fida'is* sacrificed their own lives to kill the foes of their sect, and caliphs, generals, governors, ministers and judges fell victims to their daggers. The fear and fury thus aroused gave rise to the wildest tales and legends, some of which reached Europe many years later through the reports of Marco Polo.

The commonest told how the *fida'is* were stimulated to their evil deeds by the use of the drug *hashish,* or Indian hemp; hence they were nick-named Assassins.

From an Islam torn by political and religious dissension, the Franks had little to fear save for some sporadic, local resistance. When Antioch fell to the Crusaders in 1098, the Caliph Mustazhir appealed to Malik Shah's son Berkyaruk (1095-1104) to take the field against them, but the Sultan was busy fighting competitors for his throne and defending Khurasan against the Ghaznavids, and nothing was done. The Seljuks of Rum, warring against the Byzantines, had no time to spare for Syria. The Franks, on the other hand, could count on the co-operation of many Eastern Christian communities, especially of the Armenians and the Maronites of Lebanon, and the fleets of the Italian republics rendered invaluable assistance in the capture of the Syrian coast towns. Tripoli capitulated in 1109, Beirut the next year, and operations against Aleppo gave rise to violent demonstrations in Baghdad demanding a holy war against the infidel invaders of Dar al-Islam. The new Seljuk Sultan, Berkyaruk's brother Muhammad (1104-1118), responded by appointing one of his ablest officers Mawdud as governor of Mosul with a commission to organize an offensive against the Franks. Mawdud is the first leader of the Muslim revanche: he besieged Edessa, and inflicted a sharp defeat on King Baldwin of Jerusalem at Tiberias in 1113, but his murder at Damascus in the same year, possibly by the Assassins, postponed for thirty years any serious attack on the Crusaders' principalities. Meanwhile the Franks in 1118 launched the first of several invasions of Egypt, and although this came to grief in the marshes round Pelusium, the murder of Afdal in 1121 disorganized the Fatimid State, and the remaining Egyptian-held positions in Syria fell one by one to the Crusaders, Tyre surrendering in 1124. The chaos in Muslim Syria was augmented by the intervention of the Assassins, who won over to their Nizari sect a large number of Syrian Isma'ilis, whose party was weakened by the Druze schism. Their strategy was, as usual, to gain control of hill strongholds, and Masyaf, on the slopes of the Jabal Nusairi, captured in 1140, became their principal headquarters, the Alamut of the West.

The Crusaders were, however, a nuisance rather than a serious menace to the Islamic world, and the Muslim chroniclers devote much less attention to them than might be expected. The Frankish

States were strung out in a thin line along the Syrian coast, and never included any of the great Muslim cities, not even Damascus. The heart of Islam was scarcely aware of them, and the Seljuk Sultans were far more concerned with the threat to Transoxiana and Khurasan from the pagan Kara-Khitay, who dealt a crushing blow to Seljuk power near Samarkand in 1141 and overran all the Muslim territories north of the Oxus. The task of driving out the Western intruders would have to be undertaken, not from divided Syria or decadent Egypt, but from northern Iraq, where there were ample reserves of manpower. Mawdud had shown the way, and after a long interval the path he opened was followed by the *atabeg* Zengi, a Turkish officer appointed governor of Mosul by the Sultan in 1127.

The long struggle with the Franks, began by Mawdud in 1110, was carried to a successful conclusion by three brilliant soldiers and statesmen—the Turks Zengi and his son Nuraddin and the famous Kurd Saladin. All operated from Iraq; all had to pick their way carefully amid the feuds of sultans and caliphs and local amirs, and all had to face the murderous enmity of the Assassins. Zengi, having taken Aleppo and built up a strong military position in the north of Iraq, struck at the Frankish County of Edessa, the most easterly of the Crusading States, which thrust a deep wedge into Muslim territory. The city of Edessa was besieged and captured in 1144, and the whole principality overrun by Zengi's armies. Its fall spread consternation in Europe; St. Bernard of Clairvaux preached a new crusade; the Emperor Conrad and King Louis VII of France took the cross, and Western forces again reached the Levant. This second expedition was, however, hopelessly mismanaged; a plan, sensible in itself, to take Damascus and thereby gain control of the Syrian hinterland and afford greater protection to the kingdom of Jerusalem, went awry; Damascus resisted the Christian besiegers, and the retreat of the two Western sovereigns in 1148 emboldened the Muslims and humiliated the Franks. Zengi did not live to see this; he was murdered by one of his slaves in 1146, but his son Nuraddin (properly Nur al-Din, 'Light of the Faith') who succeeded him, devoted his life to the furtherance of his father's policy and in a reign of nearly thirty years (1146-1174) shook the whole foundation of Frankish power in the East.

The reputation of Nuraddin rests as much on his personal

character as on his military achievements. 'I have studied the lives of past rulers,' says the historian Ibn al-Athir, 'and since Omar II I have found none who led a purer life or had greater enthusiasm for righteousness.' In administering justice, he never punished on mere suspicion; the booty of war was always bestowed on pious foundations and not used to enrich himself; he was a generous patron of scholars, and he made the brotherhood of Islam a reality and a political benefit by treating the races within his dominions on a footing of equality. The Kurds were surprised to find favour and justice from a Turk, and two Kurdish officers, Ayyub and Shirkuh (the former the father of Saladin), rose to high command to the ultimate advantage of Sunnite Islam. Notwithstanding difficulties with the Assassins, the Seljuks of Rum, and minor amirs, Nuraddin succeeded in uniting under his rule nearly all Muslim Syria, his most striking single victory being the acquisition of Damascus in 1154. A powerful Muslim State, uniting Iraq and eastern Syria, now interposed an impassable barrier to Frankish expansion and was in a position to exert counter-pressure against the Christian-held coastlands. Both sides sought to tip the balance in their favour by seizing control of Egypt.

By the mid-eleventh century the Fatimid regime was in full decay. The Caliph Amir, an unpopular tyrant, was murdered by the Assassins in 1130, and was succeeded by his elderly cousin Hafiz, who vainly strove to quell the disorders of the Turkish and Sudanese troops. On his death in 1149, his son Zafir, a youth of sixteen, was set on the throne; in five years his reign ended in a bloody *coup* engineered by his wazir Abbas and the latter's son Nasr, who killed the Caliph and his brothers and proclaimed Zafir's little son Fa'iz sovereign, the poor child having been an eye-witness of the massacre. The populace of Cairo rose against the criminals, who were put to death, and a new wazir, Ibn Ruzzik, restored some degree of order. But Ascalon, the last Fatimid post in Palestine, fell to the Crusaders in 1153; Ibn Ruzzik perished a victim of a harim plot in 1160, and the enfeebled condition of the country invited the intervention of foreign Powers. The Franks were eager to occupy one of the richest kingdoms of the East; its large Christian minority, Copts and Armenians, might welcome their co-religionists, and the establishment of a Christian regime in the Nile valley would deal a deadly blow to Islam and perhaps enable the Crusaders to open up connections

163

with the isolated churches of Nubia and Abyssinia. Nuraddin for his part realised that if he could beat the Crusaders in the race for Egypt, he could extinguish the heretic regime and earn the plaudits of Sunnite Islam, as well as encircle the Frankish States and drive the Western invaders into the sea.

The first step was taken in 1163, when rival wazirs in Cairo sought external help, one from Nuraddin and the other from King Amalric of Jerusalem. Shirkuh, along with his nephew Saladin, was sent to Egypt, and though obliged to withdraw, he saw enough to be able to report that it was a country 'without men, and with a precarious and contemptible government.' In 1167 he re-appeared, as did the Franks; after indecisive fighting, both parties evacuated the land. A third expedition in 1168 gave Shirkuh the mastery of the Nile valley; the Caliph Adid, the last of his line, was compelled to accept him as wazir, and upon his sudden death in 1169, Saladin was appointed as his successor. The brave, humane and generous young Kurd won the affection of the people, who had long suffered from civil strife, foreign invasion, and the excesses of the slave troops and had never really accepted the tenets of Isma'ilism. Saladin put down a rising of the negro soldiery and repulsed a Franco-Byzantine attack on Damietta. His position now unchallenged, he resolved to set aside the Fatimids, and in 1171 the name of the Abbasid Caliph Mustadi was inserted in the public prayers in the place of his Shi'ite rival Adid, who was ill and died a few days later in ignorance of this silent revolution, which Egypt received with tranquil indifference. So the Fatimids passed out of history. They are among the more attractive of Muslim dynasties: their rule on the whole was tolerant and enlightened, they made Cairo into one of the world's most beautiful cities, they encouraged art and learning, and though their luxurious palaces have long since disappeared, some of the mosques they built survive to testify to their zeal for architecture. Devoid of bigotry, they made no attempt to force their peculiar tenets on their subjects, so the people of Egypt remained loyal to orthodoxy, and the country's reunion with the Sunnite world was effected with little disturbance. Except for the Yemenis and the Assassins in their Persian and Syrian castles, Isma'ilism as a politico-religious force was dead, and it was an Islam stronger and more unified than it had been for nearly three centuries which now confronted and encircled the Crusaders' principalities in the Levant.

Using Egypt as his base, Saladin was able to build up the power necessary to expel the Franks. His brother Turanshah reduced the Nubians to submission and conquered the Yemen, while Saladin himself repulsed a big naval attack on Alexandria in which the Franks of Jerusalem, the Assassins and the Normans from Sicily all participated. In 1174 Nuraddin, who had watched the rise of his lieutenant with suspicion and misgiving, died, leaving a child as his heir, and Saladin managed, by an adroit mixture of war and diplomacy, to gain control of the Zengid inheritance, Mosul itself being reduced to vassalage in 1186. Meanwhile the final Byzantine attempt to recover Asia Minor from the Seljuks of Rum came to grief at Myriocephalon in 1176, and the death of the Emperor Manuel in 1180 opened a new series of dynastic struggles in Constantinople, one consequence of which was a breach between Byzantine and the Italian republics. Venice and Genoa began to seek markets in Egypt; Saladin encouraged this commercial intercourse, and boasted to the Caliph that the Franks were selling him arms which he could use against other Franks. With nothing to fear from the Byzantines, with the Christian Powers divided against themselves, enjoying the homage of orthodox Islam and formal investiture of the governments of Egypt, Syria and northern Iraq from the Caliph of Baghdad, his position was mightier than any Muslim rulers since the days of Malik Shah. Using Reginald of Chatillon's piracies in the Red Sea as a *casus belli*, he invaded the kingdom of Jerusalem in 1187 and shattered King Guy's army at Hattin. Palestine was overrun in a few weeks; Jerusalem passed back into Muslim hands, and only Tyre, where the garrisons of other captured forts sought refuge, held out against the Muslim revanche. The loss of the Holy City horrified Europe: the Emperor Frederick Barbarossa, Philip of France and Richard of England took the cross, but the third Crusade accomplished little more than the capture of Acre or Akka, and the peace of Ramla in 1192 left to the Christians only the narrow coastal strip from Acre to Jaffa, and the right of unarmed pilgrims to visit Jerusalem. Saladin died at Damascus in 1193, the hero of the Muslim world and respected by his Christian foes as a model of Eastern chivalry.

Saladin's Empire stretched from the borders of Tunisia to the mountains of Armenia, and his family, named Ayyubids after his father Ayyub or Job, governed it for nearly sixty years after his death. Never a centralized State, it was a kind of semi-feudal federation, the provinces of which were ruled by vassal princes of the blood. Though its subjects were mostly Arabs, it was defended by a Kurdo-Turkish army, whose officers were paid out of the revenues of *iktas,* landed estates of varying size and wealth. The Egyptian navy, so formidable under the Fatimids, languished under the Ayyubids, and Crusading expeditions were able twice (in 1218 and 1248) to effect landings in the Nile Delta. Egypt remained the richest part of the Empire, largely because of its overseas commerce; the conquest of the Yemen gave it mastery of the Red Sea and a big share of the trade of the Indian Ocean; the Karimi, an association of merchants, managed the marketing of spices and other oriental products, and the Venetians and Genoese, who bought these goods for re-shipment to Europe, provided a good deal of the customs revenues of the country. So anxious were the Italians not to risk the loss of their profits that they skilfully diverted the next Crusade, planned as an attack on Egypt, against Constantinople and secured a big share in the partition of the Byzantine Empire.

A century after the opening of the grand struggle between Islam and Western Christendom the gains and losses were fairly evenly balanced. If the Muslims had won nearly all Asia Minor, which the Latin chronicles of the twelfth century begin to refer to as 'Turkey', they had been driven from three-quarters of Spain. The Second Crusade of 1147, though it failed before Damascus, succeeded in capturing Lisbon, and in 1212 the Spanish Christians inflicted a crushing defeat on the Muslims at Las Navas de Tolosa, after which Islam was cooped up in the extreme south of the Peninsula. If Zengi, Nuraddin and Saladin steadily drove the Franks back to the coasts and wiped out almost all the gains of the First Crusade, the West retained naval control of the Mediterranean and its islands, and after the fall of Constantinople in 1204, its influence spread into the Aegean and the Black Sea, while the acquisition of Cyprus by the Franks in 1191 provided them with a useful base from which to threaten Syria and Egypt. Saladin's attempt to conclude a naval alliance with the Almohads of the Maghrib, in order to repel attacks on North Africa from Norman Sicily, was unsuccessful, and Egypt was exposed to Western naval assault on several occasions during both the Ayyubid and Mamluk periods. On the other hand, the bitter quarrel between the Greeks and Latins, culminating in the overthrow of Byzantine power in Constantinople and the establishment of a Latin Empire in 1204, destroyed the last chance of a Christian united front against Islam and broke in pieces the imperial State which had so long barred a Muslim entry into the Balkans and eastern Europe. But neither was the unity of Islam unbroken. Saladin put an end to the Fatimid schism, but he was unable to extirpate the Assassins, whose power for mischief was augmented during his lifetime by the uncanny skill of Rashid al-Din Sinan, the leader of the Syrian Isma'ilis for thirty years (1163-1193), whose Arabic sobriquet *Shaikh al-Jabal* was translated by the Franks as 'the Old Man of the Mountain.' Sinan held his own among the diverse communities of Syria by playing off one against the other; Saladin was twice wounded by the daggers of his *fida'is*, and the Crusaders benefitted not a little from this continuing and venomous feud within the household of Islam.

On the intellectual and cultural plane, the Crusades achieved but little. Only in Spain and Sicily did positive good come from the clash of faiths. The capture of Toledo in 1085 brought Western Christendom into contact with the rich accumulation of Hellenic-Arabic learning; a school of translators was set up there, and Arabic treatises on science and philosophy, and Arabic versions of Greek thinkers like Aristotle were turned with Jewish help into Latin and circulated in the rising schools of the West. The sophisticated urban culture of Muslim Sicily also instructed its Christian conquerors, and Oriental art and scholarship radiated its influence deeply into Italy, thereby contributing something to the later Renaissance. But in the Levant the Crusaders were far removed from the chief cities of Islam, and intellectuals among them were few: to the Muslims, the knights and barons of the West were not only infidels but barbarians. The adherents of the rival religions did not reach mutual understanding. Muslims had long been familiar with Christian minorities in their midst, and felt they had nothing to learn about the faith of the 'Nasara'. As for the Western Christians, disappointment with the ultimate failure of the Crusades drove them into an attitude of bitter antagonism, and though the Koran was translated into Latin in 1143, late medieval literature displays small knowledge of Islam but many fantastic errors and misconceptions, not the least whimsical being the belief that Muhammad's iron coffin was suspended in midair at Mecca by the action of powerful loadstones!

BOOKS FOR FURTHER READING

ATIYA, A. S., *Crusade, Commerce and Culture*, London, 1962.

CAHEN, C., *La Syrie du Nord à l'époque des Croisades*, Paris, 1940. Includes a detailed critique of the Arabic sources for the history of the Crusades.

DANIEL, N., *Islam and the West*, Edinburgh, 1960. Excellent full discussion of the relations between the Latin and Muslim worlds in the time of the Crusades.

GROUSSET, R., *Les Croisades*, Paris, 1944. This short book is in many ways superior to his longer history of the Crusades.

HODGSON, M. G. S., *The Order of Assassins*, The Hague, 1955. The only critical modern account of the Nizari Isma'ilis.

LANE POOLE S., *Saladin and the Fall of the Kingdom of Jerusalem*, London, 1898; 2nd. ed. 1926. Still the best biography of Saladin in English.

LANE POOLE, S., *History of Egypt* (as before).

RUNCIMAN, S., *A History of the Crusades*, 3 vols. Cambridge, 1951-54. Now the standard English work on the subject.

SETTON, K. (ed.), *A History of the Crusades*, 2 vols., Philadelphia, 1955-62 (in progress). An American co-operative work, designed to be completed in five volumes. The Muslim side is dealt with in valuable chapters by leading Arabists.

SOUTHERN, R. W., *Western Views of Islam in the Middle Ages*, Harvard, 1962. Short but useful survey.

STEVENSON, W. B., *The Crusaders in the East*, Cambridge, 1907. Based largely on the Arabic sources: not yet superseded.

WIET, G., *L'Égypte arabe* (as before).

TRANSLATED SOURCES

ABU SHAMA, *The Book of the Two Gardens*, Fr. tr. Barbier de Meynard, 2 vols., Paris, 1898-1906. A history of the reigns of Nuraddin and Saladin. The author was a Damascus scholar who died in 1268. He made full use of original documents.

BAHA AL-DIN, *Life of Saladin*, Eng. tr. C. R. Conder, London 1897. The biographer, otherwise known as Ibn Shaddad, died in 1234. As Saladin's secretary, he was well placed to write his life.

IBN JUBAYR, *Travels*, Eng. tr. R. J. C. Broadhurst, London, 1952. A vivid account by a Spanish Muslim of a journey through the Middle East in 1183-85, shortly before Saladin's invasion of the kingdom of Jerusalem.

IBN AL-QALANISI, *The Damascus Chronicle of the Crusades*, Eng. tr. H. A. R. Gibb, London, 1932. One of the few surviving contemporary accounts of the First Crusade from the Muslim point of view by a Damascus civil servant who died in 1160 at the age of ninety.

USAMAH IBN MUNQIDH, *Memoirs*, Eng. tr. P. K. Hitti under the title of *An Arab-Syrian Gentleman and Warrior in the Period of the Crusades*, New York, 1929. Autobiographies are not common in Islam: this one was written by a member of an Arab princely family from Shaizar in northern Syria. He fought under Zengi and Nuraddin, and died at Damascus at a great age in 1188. He was at once soldier, poet, man of letters and sportsman.

WILLIAM OF TYRE, *A History of Deeds done beyond the Sea*, Eng. tr. Badcock and Krey, 2 vols., New York, 1943. The finest contemporary Frankish history of the Crusades, by a man who was born in 1130 in the Latin kingdom of Jerusalem and died Archbishop of Tyre about 1186.

XI

The Mongol Disaster

At the opening of the thirteenth century the prospects of Sunnite Islam were relatively favourable. The Fatimid schism, which had disrupted the Muslim world for close on three hundred years, was healed, and revolutionary Isma'ilism survived only in isolated pockets in Persian and Syrian castles, a nuisance rather than a menace. Orthodoxy had been deepened and defined; law and theology as interpreted by the four canonical schools, were taught in the *madrasas*, and the 'university' of al-Azhar in Cairo, purged by Saladin of its Shi'ite taint, was to become the principal centre of Muslim higher learning. The Franks, if not totally expelled, clung precariously only to a few strong points on the Syrian shores. The Byzantine Empire, against which the Muslims had battled for so many centuries, was shattered to fragments by the Latin Crusaders themselves, and Asia Minor was made safe for Islam. A vigorous military State, that of the Ayyubids, dominated the Arab lands. In Persia, the Seljuk Empire finally disintegrated on the death of Sultan Sanjar in 1157, but its power was in great part inherited by a new State founded by its former vassals, the Shahs of Khwarazm. Apart from Transoxiana, which had fallen to the Kara-Khitay in 1141, no portion of Dar al-Islam was lost to heathen nomads. In the West, though most of Spain was irretrievably gone, and North Africa still bore the scars of the ravages of the Banu-Hilal, the situation had stabilized itself with the coming of the Berber Muwahhids (Almohads—'Unitarians'), ardent devotees of the unity of God against what they considered to be anthropomorphic corruptions, who starting from

170

Morocco about 1120, erected within forty years an empire embracing the whole of the Maghrib, which enjoyed for two generations a peace and well-being it had not known since Roman times. Islam was spreading along the caravan routes southwards across the Sahara; it was slowly creeping down the coast of east Africa as far as Sofala, and up the Nile into hitherto Christian Nubia.

Yet the Muslim world was in fact on the eve of its greatest disaster. The thirteenth century was the age of the Mongol conquests, the last and most dreadful of all the nomadic assaults on civilization. China, Europe and Islam were all to suffer, but the appalling avalanche of destruction which rolled over a vast segment of the globe from Korea to Germany nearly engulfed Islam completely. Much of the responsibility for what happened must rest, however, on the Khwarazmian Shahs, whose task was to defend the eastern marches of Dar al-Islam and who lamentably failed, not simply because of Mongol military superiority but through their own errors and follies.

Khwarazm (modern Khiva) was a region of great fertility and commercial importance along the lower Oxus. An intricate system of canals and dykes spread the waters of the river over a wide area; rich pastures supported large herds of cattle and sheep, and travellers expatiated on the extent and productivity of the fields, orchards and vineyards. Caravans moved across the steppes to buy furs and slaves from the Khazars, Bulghars and other Turkish tribes in exchange for fabrics of cloth and wool, and southwards to sell their wares in the markets of Transoxiana and Khurasan. Almost encircled by desert and steppe, and connected only by a narrow cultivated strip with these provinces, Khwarazm's isolation was its chief security, and in time of danger the dykes could be breached and an invading army halted by the rising floodwaters. Malik Shah gave the governorship of Khwarazm to one of his Turkish slave-officers, whose descendants, after the fashion of the times, maintained a semi-independent rule by adroitly playing off the Seljuks against the Kara-Khitay, a people from the borders of China who had routed Sanjar at Samarkand in 1141 and seized Transoxiana. The advance of these invaders dislodged a number of Oghuz Turkoman clans, who spread beyond the Oxus into Khurasan, and when Sanjar tried to check their ravages, he was defeated and taken prisoner by them in 1153. Escaping from captivity in 1156, he was so horror-struck at the sight of the ruin the Oghuz had wrought in his capital of

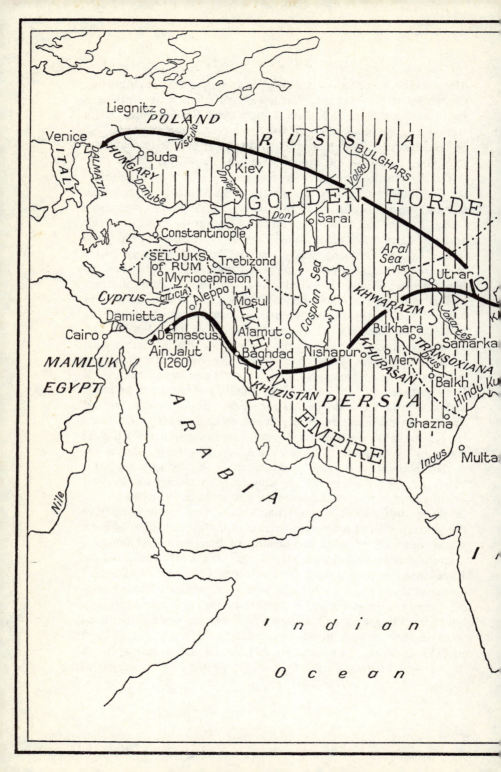

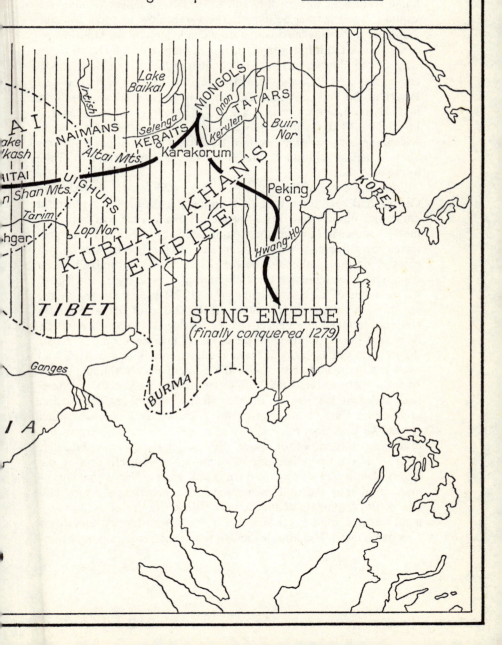

THE MONGOL CONQUESTS

SHOWING THE MAIN MONGOL THRUSTS

The Mongol Empire in 1260

Lake Baikal

Irtish

MONGOLS

Onon

TATARS

NAIMANS

Selenga

KERAITS

kerulen

Buir Nor

Altai Mts.

Karakorum

ake 'kash

UIGHURS

HITAI

n Shan Mts.

Peking

KOREA

Tarim

KUBLAI KHAN'S

Lop Nor

EMPIRE

Hwang-Ho

hgar

TIBET

SUNG EMPIRE
(finally conquered 1279)

Ganges

BURMA

I A

Nishapur that he sickened and died in 1157. With him the effective rule of the Seljuks in Persia came to an end.

The Khwarazmian governors, who bore the old Iranian title of Shah, were able to turn this and other circumstances to their advantage. Their former Seljuk suzerains were now of small account. To the east the Ghaznavids had been challenged by the Ghurids, recently converted hillmen from the upper valleys of the Hindu Kush, who sacked Ghazna in 1149 and conquered their rivals' Indian possessions as well. The way was clear for the creation of a great new Power in the Persian lands. Takash, who became Khwarazm-Shah in 1172, occupied Khurasan, crushed the Oghuz, and defeated and killed Tughril II, the last Seljuk Sultan, at Ray in 1194. This brought Khwarazmian power into western Persia and involved the ambitious Shah in a clash with the Caliph Nasir, the last able sovereign of the house of Abbas.

Since the entry of the Buyids into Baghdad in 945, the Abbasid Caliphs had been little more than puppets in the hands of powerful amirs and sultans. The advent of the Seljuks in 1055 had improved matters somewhat in that the Commander of the Faithful was 'protected' by an orthodox Muslim instead of by a heretic, but he still enjoyed no real authority. As the Seljuk Empire crumbled away, an opportunity to revive the Caliphate presented itself, and Nasir, whose reign of forty-five years (1180-1225) is the longest in the annals of his dynasty, set out to create a kind of 'Papal State' in Iraq and to make more effective his headship of the Muslim *umma*. Now that the Fatimids were gone, the chance had come to repair the divisions of Islam, and Nasir made overtures to the Alids and even reached some accord with the Isma'ilians of Alamut, whose Imam in 1210 restored the *Shari'a,* cursed his predecessors as heretics, and sent his mother on the Mecca pilgrimage. The Caliph organized a kind of order of chivalry, known as *futuwwah,* which seems like European freemasonry of a later time to have grown out of artisans' fraternities for mutual aid, with himself as grand master, in order to rally popular support round his throne. His armies, the first a Caliph had commanded for many years, cleared the Turkomans from Iraq and took possession of the province of Khuzistan, one of the fragments of the defunct Seljuk Empire. This development was not at all to the liking of Takash, who fancied himself as a second Tughril Beg and demanded from Nasir recognition of himself as Sultan in Baghdad. The Caliph, having no desire to sacrifice his newly-won independence, refused, and by the time of Takash's death in 1200 the Abbasids and the Khwarazmians were at open enmity.

Takash's son Muhammad (1200-1220) continued his father's policy. By the lavish purchase of Turkish slaves from the Kipchak tribe of the lower Volga, he built up a formidable military establishment; the Ghurids were driven beyond the Indus, the Kara-Khitay were subdued, and all Persia was gathered up in this expanding empire. As the Caliph still refused to grant the Sultanate to the Shah, Muhammad resolved to make an end of the Abbasids. In 1217 he proclaimed Nasir deposed, selected an Alid as anti-Caliph, and marched on Baghdad. An early winter checked the advance of his army, and forced him to postpone his offensive to a more convenient season. He was now outwardly the most powerful Muslim prince in Asia, yet his rule in fact rested on the most fragile foundations. The Khwarazmian State was a thoroughly artificial construction: the swollen army of Kipchak slaves oppressed the people and exhausted the treasury; the bureaucracy was alienated by their exactions, the religious leaders were disturbed by the rupture with the Caliph, the commercial classes resented the rising burden of taxation, and the Shah could depend on the loyalty of few of his subjects. An apparently trivial incident precipitated catastrophe. In 1218, as Muhammad was preparing for a final reckoning with Nasir, a caravan of merchants arrived at the frontier post of Utrar, whose governor, probably on the instructions of his master, arrested them and put them to death as spies. The men had come from the dominions of Chingiz Khan; the Mongol chief swore revenge, and the next year the storm burst over Khwarazm, the opening of a forty years' conflict which devastated western Asia and almost brought Islam to ruin.

The Mongols, destined to be a name of terror to most of the inhabitants of the globe for a hundred years, had their home in the forest land of the upper Onon and Kerulen rivers, east of Lake Baikal; to their east, in the region of Buir-Nor, lived the Tatars, probably Mongolized Turks, whose name was to be forever associated with them and which in Europe received its second 'r' from a supposed identification with Tartarus, the classical Hell, and to their west the Keraits and Naimans, apparently peoples of Turkish speech and origin. These tribes were in different stages of cultural development. The Mongols and Tatars were hunters and fishers in the lakes and forests (though the former were not unfamiliar with pastoral life), and in religion primitive shamanists: the Keraits and Naimans were horse- and cattle-breeders of the steppes, who had been largely converted to Nestorian Christianity, the Kerait chief, who bore the title of Ong- or Wang-Khan, being probably the original 'Prester John', the Christian prince who supposedly held sway over a vast kingdom in the heart of Asia. Islam had as yet no hold on any of these peoples, but Manichaean missionaries, who had been active among them before the Nestorians arrived, had taught them writing as well as religion, and their language was written in an alphabet derived from Syriac. A similar alphabetic script was devised for the Turkish Uighurs, who had been partially Christianized since the eighth century.

The Mongol explosion, which shook the globe, was not the effect of a religious stimulus or traceable to climatic change which set the nomads looking for better pastures: its origin is still obscure, but it owed most to the military and organizing ability of Chingiz Khan, the Napoleon of the steppes and a far greater man than Attila. Born about 1167 on the banks of the Onon and named at first Temujin, he lost his father as a boy, his spirited mother made a valiant attempt to hold the tribe together until he reached manhood and began to display both valour as a warrior and political skill in dividing and circumventing his enemies. A master of detail and a shrewd judge of men, he made a carefully selected guard the nucleus of his army, and from its trained and tested members were drawn the generals who conquered kingdoms in his name. Before opening a campaign, he collected from merchants, travellers and spies exact information respecting conditions in the enemy country; roads and bridges were kept in constant repair to ensure rapidity of movement and communication; prisoners of war were employed to transport supplies and keep open the highways and if trained artisans and engineers, to construct and maintain the siege machinery which battered down the walls of towns all over Asia. The grimmest feature of his military policy was the deliberate use of terror to frighten his foes into submission. If a place surrendered without resistance, it was commonly spared; if the garrison refused to capitulate, it was massacred and the civilian population driven out into the fields while the town was given up to plunder, but if the populace as a whole manned the ramparts or a city once taken revolted against its Mongol governor, every man, woman and child was put to the sword, and in one case the very cats and dogs as well as human beings were slaughtered in the streets.

Temujin's first military efforts were devoted to bringing the pastoral tribes of Mongolia and Turkistan under his sway. The Keraits were subdued in 1203, the Naimans in 1206, after which a *kuriltai* or tribal assembly hailed him as Chingiz Khan, a title probably meaning 'universal king.' He then embarked on his amazing career of foreign conquest, invaded a divided China, breached the Great Wall, and in 1215 captured Peking. A Naiman chief named Kuchluk, who had fled to the Kara-Khitay and had been accepted by them as their leader, was making trouble in the west: this brought Chingiz back from China, the Kara-Khitay were crushed, and the Mongol frontier was carried as far as the domains of the Khwarazm-Shah. Chingiz seems to have wished for peaceful commercial intercourse with Muhammad, but the Utrar massacre made war inevitable, and the Mongol forces, augmented by troops from various Turkish peoples who had submitted to the Khan, assembled on the Irtish in the spring of 1219. The Shah, realising too late the peril he was in and distrusting his people and army, sought to evade pitched battles and dispersed his troops throughout the towns of Transoxiana and Khurasan, doubtless expecting that the Mongols would find the siege of so many fortified places slow and laborious. But Chingiz had brought with him a corps of Chinese engineers, and Mongol siegecraft proved excellent; Bukhara and Samarkand fell in 1220, and the unhappy Muhammad, losing heart, fled in panic and took refuge in an island in the Caspian, where he died in lonely misery. His son Jalal al-Din, who was made of sterner stuff, courageously undertook to stem the avalanche. Breaking through the Mongol cordon, he reached Ghazna and began to raise fresh armies, while Chingiz crossed the Oxus, and Merv and Nishapur perished in blood and flame. Jalal al-Din actually routed a Mongol detachment sent in pursuit of him, but when Chingiz arrived with his main army, the young Shah was driven back to the banks of the Indus and only escaped capture by riding his horse into the river and swimming to the opposite side. Satisfied with the punishment he had inflicted, the Khan in 1222 made his way slowly back home, returning to Mongolia in 1225. Two years later he died at the age of about sixty while warring in the Kansu province of western China.

There followed a lull so far as Islam was concerned. Jalal al-Din ventured back to Persia in 1225, found there was no hope of regaining Transoxiana and Khwarazm, and tried to carve out a new kingdom in the west. He occupied Azerbaijan, invaded the Caucasus, clashed with the Seljuks of Rum, and was then obscurely murdered by a peasant in a Kurdish village in 1231. His soldiers lapsed into brigandage, and roamed about Iraq and Syria, plundering and ravaging. Meanwhile Chingiz's son Ogedai had been elected Great Khan in 1229 and had despatched his nephew Batu to complete the conquest of the Eurasian steppelands. Crossing the Urals in 1237, Batu swept over the plains of southern Russia, crushing resistance so mercilessly that, as a Russian chronicler put it, 'No eye remained open to weep for the dead.' Pressing forward through Poland into Silesia, the Mongols annihilated a German army at Liegnitz, poured over the Carpathians into Hungary, chased King Bela from his country, and by the end of 1241 were on the shores of Dalmatia. Nothing seemed capable of halting their advance; Europe was seized with terror, and the Emperor Frederick II sent desperate appeals to his fellow-sovereigns to unite with him for the salvation of the rest of Christendom. Then the storm subsided as suddenly as it had arisen. Ogedai died in December 1241, and Batu, anxious to influence the choice of his successor, withdrew his forces back beyond the Volga. Europe breathed again, and her leaders began to consider if this frightful menace might be neutralized by the forces of religion. Here was a mighty world empire, whose pagan chiefs might perhaps be won over to Christianity and whose military power be turned against Islam. The prospect of a Mongol-Christian alliance started to dazzle the minds of popes and kings, the more so as the hopes of a victorious outcome of the Crusades were steadily fading. Egypt was now the chief focus of Muslim power, but a Western assault on the Delta in 1218 failed and the Christians were obliged to evacuate Damietta, their only conquest. The Emperor Frederick II, a shrewd and secular-minded prince, resolved to try what diplomacy could do, and entering into negotiation with Sultan Kamil (1218-1238), Saladin's able nephew, he actually secured the retrocession to the Christians of a demilitarized Jerusalem in 1229. Kamil was motivated by a desire to avoid further crusades in view of the growing

isolation of Egypt. The fall of Constantinople in 1204 and the decay
of the Almohads in the West deprived the Ayyubids of two potential
allies, while Jalal al-Din and his Khwarazmians were imperilling
their position in Syria and Iraq. The Christians did not, however,
long retain control of the holy city, for it was snatched from them
again in 1244 by the marauding Khwarazmians and never recovered.
This quickened the resolve of the West to explore the possibility of
converting the Mongols and getting them to deliver a coup de grace
against Muslim Western Asia. Missions went out from Europe to
Karakorum, the new Mongol camp-capital in Mongolia.

The first overtures were not favourably received. The Mongols
were at their most arrogant, and to a letter from the Pope the new
Khan Kuyuk replied by requiring the Christian chiefs to come and
submit to him in person and he would then consider their proposals!
He implied that his people had been commanded by God to conquer
the world. But a year or two later, when Louis IX of France was in
Cyprus preparing a new descent on Egypt, a Mongol embassy
arrived there to discuss a joint offensive against Islam. What seems
to have happened was that Uighur Nestorian Christians had gained
the ascendancy in the Mongol councils and were influencing the
Khan's policy in an anti-Muslim direction. The Mongol language
was now written in Uighur characters; the Mongol chancery was
staffed with clerks and secretaries from the partly-Christianized
peoples of Turkistan; Mongol princes had married Christian wives,
and Chingiz's grandson Mongke or Mangu, elected Great Khan in
1251, was reported, perhaps erroneously, to have been baptized. To
find out the real position, Louis IX sent a Flemish Franciscan,
William of Ruybroek, to Karakorum in 1253: the report of this
shrewd and observant envoy is the source of much of our knowledge of these extraordinary world conquerors on the eve of their
fateful offensive against Islam.

Before despatching this mission, the French king launched from
Cyprus yet another naval attack on Egypt. After the death of Kamil
in 1238 the Ayyubid State fell into decline, owing to quarrels among
the ruling family, the Mongol threat from the east, and the ravages
of the Khwarazmian hordes. The situation seemed favourable for a
new Crusade. For the second time in thirty years the Franks landed
in Egypt and occupied Damietta; they advanced up the Nile to
Mansurah, but the defenders cleverly collected a flotilla of boats,

carried them by camel across country, and refloated them on the
river in the rear of the Crusaders. Caught between two fires, Louis
attempted to retreat, and on failing to cut his way through, was obliged to surrender with all his officers. While negotiations about a
ransom were in progress, mutiny broke out in the Egyptian army,
whose Turkish mamluks had long been discontented with the favour
shown by the Ayyubids to their fellow-Kurds; the Sultan Turanshah was brutally killed, and the slave troops, led by two Turkish
generals Aybeg and Baybars seized possession of the government.
Thus the Ayyubid dynasty was overthrown in Egypt, though
branches of the family continued to reign for some time longer in
Syria and northern Iraq. The new regime in Egypt was a naked
military dictatorship of the Kipchak Turk soldiery, but the Mamluk
Sultanate, as it is known, deserved well of Islam, which it saved
from ruin at the hands of the Mongols.

The revolution in Egypt took place in 1250: five years later the
Great Khan's brother Hulagu or Huleku moved across the Oxus at
the head of a mighty army designed to annex all Muslim Western
Asia to the Mongol world empire. At Karakorum the decision had
been taken to subdue east and west, and Mongke's brothers Kublai
and Hulagu were despatched, the one to conquer China, the other
Persia and the lands beyond. Hulagu was bitterly hostile to Islam,
and much influenced by his Buddhist and Nestorian Christian en-
tourage. His wife Dokaz Khatun and his principal lieutenant Kitbogha or Kitbuka were Christians, and a portable tent-church travelled with him, in which mass was celebrated daily. Mongke is said
to have promised the Christian King of Armenia, who visited Karakorum in 1255, that the Mongols would restore Jerusalem to the
Crusaders when they had destroyed the power of the Muslims. The
Asian Christians were filled with extravagant hopes and expected
the rapid downfall of Islam: the European nations were less san-
guine. They noted that the Mongol leadership was still pagan, that
it had a dreadful reputation for cruelty and perfidy, and that it demanded not friendship and alliance but abject submission. The
Franks in Palestine and Syria mostly waited to see what would hap-
pen.

The Mongol army, in composition more Turkish than Mongol,
and including contingents from the Christian kingdoms of Armenia
and Georgia, was probably the largest, best equipped and best dis-

ciplined that had ever issued from the steppes of Central Asia. Hulagu first moved against the Assassins, who though they had never succeeded in creating a territorial State, had resisted all efforts to dislodge them from their castles in northern Persia. He demanded their submission and the dismantling of their strongholds. The reigning Imam, Muhammad III, a moody melancholic, favoured defiance, but his chiefs were terrified of Mongol strength and ferocity, and had him killed in a drunken sleep. His son Rukn al-Din, the last 'grand master' of Alamut, young, inexperienced and frightened, gave in; the Mongols swarmed into the Assassin fortresses, and such local or sporadic defence as was put up was savagely crushed. Rukn al-Din asked to be sent to the Great Khan; but Mongke refused to see him, and on the road back from Mongolia he was slain by his guards.

Sunnite Islam might rejoice in the extermination of the Isma'ili terrorists, but Hulagu cared nothing for the distinctions between Muslims and turned next against Baghdad. Since the death of Nasir in 1225, the Abbasids had sunk again into lethargy under his incompetent successors, and the Caliph Musta'sim (1242-1258), the last Commander of the Faithful, was the man least likely to lead a holy and heroic fight against the hordes of paganism. Confronted by the usual Mongol demand for surrender, he temporized, desperately hoping that the Muslim princes would rally to the defence of their spiritual chief. Hulagu, growing impatient, commenced military operations; his army crossed the Tigris and besieged the city; his engineers broke the dykes and flooded the Muslim camp; the inhabitants, panic-stricken, tried to flee, many being caught and drowned in the rising floodwaters, and the unhappy Musta'sim in despair sent the Nestorian Patriarch to the enemy to offer capitulation. Hulagu ordered the Caliph to come in person to his camp, with his family and retinue, to tell his people to stop fighting, and to give up his wealth and treasure. His commands were obeyed, and the metropolis of Islam was abandoned to the merciless bloodlust of the conquerors. The palaces, colleges and mosques were plundered and burnt; the cultural accumulation of five centuries perished in the flames, and the appalling figure of 800,000 is the lowest estimate given of the number of men, women and children who were slaughtered in the streets and houses. The Christians, gathered in a church under their patriarch, alone were spared. Musta'sim and his sons

were taken to a village outside Baghdad, and there killed in cold
blood: according to report, in view of the Mongol superstition
about shedding with the sword the blood of sovereign princes, they
were rolled in carpets and trampled to death by horses. So ended
miserably the Abbasid Caliphate and the glories of medieval Baghdad.

The Christians of the East hailed the ruin of Baghdad in the
spirit of the 'Babylon is fallen, is fallen!' of the Book of Revelation,
and looked forward to the end of half a millennium of Muslim domination. Hulagu's armies were soon in Syria: Aleppo resisted, was
stormed and the non-Christian population massacred; Damascus
gave in without a fight, three Christian leaders (the Mongol commander Kitbogha, the King of Armenia and the Frankish Count
Bohemund of Antioch) riding through its streets and forcing Muslims to bow to the cross; it was expected that the Mongols would
soon be in Jerusalem and Cairo, and the usual peremptory summons was addressed to the Mamluks in Egypt to surrender or perish.
If Egypt, the last important centre of Muslim power, fell, the position of Islam would be grave indeed. The Mamluks were under no
illusions: they must fight or go under. They resolved to resist, and
were favoured by good luck. Early in 1260 Hulagu received at Aleppo the news that his brother the Great Khan Mongke had died in
China the previous December. He favoured the candidature of his
other brother Kublai for the succession, but another claimant started
up, who received the backing of Hulagu's cousin Berke, the Mongol
commander in Russia. Berke had embraced Islam, and was shocked
at Hulagu's destruction of the Caliphate: he also feared his own
power was in danger from his cousin's supposed ambition to create
an independent Western Mongol Empire. In this situation Hulagu
felt obliged to shift the bulk of his army to the Caucasus to watch the
movements of Berke, leaving only a light screen of troops in Syria.
The Mamluks, themselves Kipchak Turks from the Russian steppes,
were aware of all this, and acted accordingly. Appealing for a *levée
en masse* of faithful Muslims against the heathen enemies of Islam
and the murderers of the Caliph, they advanced into Palestine, led
by their Sultan Kutuz and his general Baybars, and came up with
the Mongols under Kitbogha at Ain Jalut ('Goliath's Spring') near
Nazareth. After a furious battle (September 1260), the depleted
Mongol army was routed and scattered; Kitbogha was slain, and

the spell which the great Chingiz had cast upon the world was broken forever.

Ain Jalut was one of the world's decisive battles. It put a stop for good to the Mongol advance westwards; it saved Cairo from the fate of Baghdad, and Islam itself from possible destruction; it ruined the last hope of a Christian restoration in the Near East; it doomed the remaining Crusading positions in Syria, and it raised Mamluk Egypt to the status of leading Muslim Power and the home of what was left of Arabic culture. It did not, however, recall the Caliphate to life. The Mongols remained in possession of Baghdad and Iraq; a Mamluk attempt to restore the Abbasids by sending an expedition under an uncle of the murdered Caliph was an utter failure, and Baybars, who seized the throne of Egypt on the morrow of Ain Jalut by deposing and killing Kutuz, contented himself with setting up a shadow-Caliphate at Cairo. The Abbasid line was prolonged in Egypt until the Ottoman conquest in 1517, but these puppet Caliphs were mere names and existed solely for the purpose of providing a symbol of the unity of Islam and confirming the legal sovereignty of Muslim princes, who long felt it necessary to secure diplomas of investiture from the Vicars of the Prophet.

The extinction of the Caliphate marks the close of the classic Arabic phase of Islamic history. The disappearance of this strange, unique institution prompts some reflections on its nature, character and failure. The Caliph was neither Pope nor Emperor: he was the successor of Muhammad in nothing but a secular sense, the protector of the Islamic community. He could not represent an independent civil power, for none such existed in Islam: he was head of an *umma*, not of a territorial State. He was the vice-gerent of the Prophet, not of God: divine revelation had ceased on the death of Muhammad, and the Caliph's business was to enforce the Law, not to expound, modify or interpret it, his functions being thus executive and not legislative. The Fatimid attempt to elevate the Imam to the position of an infallible, inspired and divinely-guided mouthpiece of God was and remained a deviation from the Islamic norm. Being strictly neither monarchy nor papacy, the Caliphate failed to maintain an imperial position in either a spiritual or a political capacity. After the cessation of the conquests, its power rapidly ebbed. To the Arabs there was something unnatural and displeasing about its drift towards kingship: to the Persians it lacked the national and patriotic character of the old Sassanid Shahdom. Baghdad had none of the aura of a sacred city; it was merely a court, an administrative centre, not to be compared with Mecca, Medina or Jerusalem. Technically, the Caliphate remained elective to the end, and the jurists (or some of them, for there was no generally accepted doctrine on the matter) enumerated as qualifications for the office moral integrity, experience and judgment, physical soundness (a deposed Caliph, like a deposed Byzantine Emperor, was commonly blinded, so that he could never resume the throne), and descent from the Kuraish, but it was never clear who the electors might be, and in practice Persian influence strengthened the trend towards hereditary succession from father to son, brother to brother, uncle to nephew, or cousin to cousin. As the vast Empire disintegrated, the Muslims learnt to rate religious unity higher than political. When the Buyids occupied Baghdad in 945, the Caliphate as an effective political force ceased to exist; a century later the Seljuks brought with them a new institution, the Sultanate, which took over most of the powers formerly exercised by the Commander of the Faithful, and the belated attempt of Nasir, after the fall of the Seljuks, to reclothe the Vicariate of the Prophet with real authority was short-lived and foredoomed to failure. The Mongols destroyed an institution which had long been moribund, and since 1258 Islam has had no single focus of politico-religious loyalty. Yet the memory of the glories of the Omayyads and early Abbasids has never faded from the Muslim consciousness, and in our own age proposals have occasionally been made to revive the Caliphate as a symbol of unity linking together the many new Islamic nations which have emerged from the debris of the European colonial empires in Asia and Africa.

BOOKS FOR FURTHER READING

BARTHOLD, W., *Turkestan* (as before).

GOTTSCHALK, H. L., *Al-Malik al-Kamil von Egypten und seine Zeit*, Wiesbaden, 1958. A biography of the Ayyubid Sultan Kamil (1218-1238).

GROUSSET, R., *L'Empire des Steppes*, Paris, 1939; 4th. ed. 1952. An excellent piece of French *haute vulgarisation*, dealing with the rise and fall of the nomadic empires of Central Asia. See also his *L'Empire Mongol*, 1941, and *Le Conquérant du Monde*, 1944.

THE MONGOL DISASTER

HOWORTH, H .H. *History of the Mongols,* 3 vols. London, 1876-88. The most detailed treatment in English, but lacking in critical scholarship.

LANE-POOLE, S., *History of Egypt* (as before).

OHSSON, M.D', *Histoire des Mongols,* 4 vols. The Hague, 1834-35. Still of value, despite its age, being based on a thorough study of the Arabic and Persian sources.

RUNCIMAN, S., *History of the Crusades* (as before).

SETTON, K. (ed.), *A History of the Crusades,* vol. 2, Philadelphia, 1962. Contains chapters on the Ayyubids, Mongols and Mamluks.

SPULER, B., *Die Mongolen in Iran,* 1939; 2nd ed. Berlin, 1955, and *Die Mongolenzeit,* 1957; Eng. tr. 1960. Two valuable studies by a leading German specialist.

VLADIMIRTSOV, B. J., *Life of Chingiz Khan,* 1922; Eng. tr. London, 1930. Standard biography.

WIET, G., *L'Égypte arabe* (as before).

TRANSLATED SOURCES

ABU' L-FARAJ, *Chronographia,* Eng. tr. W. Budge, 2 vols. Oxford, 1932. A universal history down to 1286. The author, sometimes known as Bar-Hebraeus ('son of the Hebrew'), was a Jacobite churchman who lived mainly in Iraq and died in Azerbaijan in 1286. He gives an Eastern Christian view of the Mongol invasions.

GREGORY OF AKNER, *A History of the Nation of the Archers,* Eng. tr. Blake and Frye, Harvard, 1954. An Armenian account of the Mongols, compiled about 1313.

JUWAINI, *The History of the World Conqueror,* Eng. tr. J. A. Boyle, 2 vols. Manchester, 1958. Juwaini was a member of the Persian official class who entered the service of the Mongols and accompanied Hulagu on his campaign in the West in 1255. After the fall of Baghdad he was made governor of the city and of Iraq. He died in 1283. His book is more than a life of Chingiz: it contains a history of his successors down to 1256, and of the Khwarazm-Shahs and the Assassins, and is one of the most valuable historical works of the period.

NASAWI, *Histoire de Sultan Djelal ed-Din,* Fr. tr. O. Houdas. Paris 1895. A well-documented life of the last Khwarazm-Shah Jalal al-Din (1220-31), written by his secretary.

SADEQUE, S. F., *Baybars I of Egypt,* Dacca, 1956. Text and translation of a life of Baybars by his secretary Muhyi al-Din, otherwise called Ibn Abd al-Zahir.

WILLIAM OF RUYBROEK (RUBRIQUIS), *Journey,* Eng. tr. W. W. Rockhill. London, 1900. Vivid description of the Mongol court and people by the Flemish Franciscan sent by Louis IX to Karakorum in 1253. The book includes a translation of a similar narrative by the Italian John de Plano Carpini, who visited Mongolia at the behest of the Pope in 1245-47. The best European accounts of Asia before Marco Polo.

English translations are planned of two other primary sources, *The Secret History of the Mongols*, compiled in the second half of the 13th century, and the *Universal History* of the Persian official Rashid al-Din Fadlallah, who served the Mongol khans of Persia until his execution for treason in 1318. Rashid al-Din was one of the finest of Islamic historians, who included in his survey sections on the Chinese and the Franks, thus making his work the first truly world history.

XII

The Civilization of Medieval Islam

For some four centuries (roughly between 800 and 1200 A.D.) the lands conquered by the Arabs were the soil from which grew and blossomed one of the most brilliant civilizations in the history of humanity. To give it a suitable name is a matter of some difficulty. It has been variously styled Arab, Muslim, Islamic and Arabic. The first is clearly a misnomer, implying as it does that this culture was created or dominated by men of Arab race, which was by no means the case; the second and third define it too narrowly in religious terms, whereas many of its most distinguished figures were Christians, Jews or pagans, and not Muslims at all. 'Arabic' seems open to the least objection, since it draws attention to the fact that the literature of this particular civilization was written almost wholly in the Arabic language and acquired its characteristic unity largely from this circumstance.

The causes of the rise and fall of civilizations are often hidden from us, and the questions which start to mind are more easily framed than answered. Why were the German invasions of Western Europe in the fifth century followed by a long 'dark age' of barbarism and ignorance, while the Arab invasions of the seventh century were followed by a general rise in the cultural level of the countries affected by them? So startling a contrast demands explanation, which must take the form of showing that certain conditions favourable to the growth of the arts and sciences were present in one case and absent in the other.

1. The Arab conquests politically unified a huge segment of the globe from Spain to India, a unity which remained unbroken until

187

the fall of the Omayyads in 750. The disappearance of so many dividing frontiers, above all the one which had so long separated Rome and Persia, was a useful preliminary to the building of a new civilization.

2. As the Arabs overran one country after another, they carried their language with them. But that language possessed a unique status: to every Muslim it was not just one form of human speech among others, but the vehicle through which God had chosen to deliver his final revelation to men. Arabic was 'God's tongue', and as such enjoyed a prestige which Latin and Greek and Hebrew had never known. The Koran could not, must not be translated: the believer must hear and understand and if possible read the divine book in the original, even though Arabic were not his mother tongue. To study, illustrate and elucidate the text became a pious duty: the earliest branch of science developed by Muslims was Arabic philology, traditionally founded at Basra in the late Omayyad age. The further Islam spread among non-Arabs, the further a knowledge of Arabic spread with it. A century or so after the conquests even Christians, Jews and Zoroastrians within the Caliphate found it convenient to speak and write Arabic. Thus to political unity was added the widespread use of a common language, which immensely facilitated the exchange of ideas.

3. The first conquests of the Arabs were made in lands which had been the home of settled, urban civilizations for thousands of years, that is, the river valleys of the Nile and the Tigris-Euphrates. The fighting here was relatively brief (Syria was conquered in six or seven years, Egypt and Iraq in two or three), and the physical destruction was light. The native population was akin to the Arabs in race and speech, and stood aside from a struggle which was essentially between the invaders and the Byzantine or Sassanid ruling class. The local officials often stayed at their posts, and administrative continuity, at least at the lower levels, remained unbroken. From motives of policy, the Caliphs cultivated friendly relations with the Jacobite and Nestorian Christians, who constituted the bulk of the people, and who during the long period of Roman rule had learnt a good deal of the science and philosophy of the Greeks. This learning, translated into Syriac, a Semitic tongue closely related to Arabic, was at the disposal of the newcomers, who were impressed by the rich and ancient culture of the region, and it was this region, and not

Arabia proper, which was the birthplace of the Arabic civilization.

4. Once invasion and re-settlement were over, the lands brought under the sovereignty of the Caliphs enjoyed immunity from serious external attack for three or four centuries. There was plenty of fighting on the frontiers and many internal revolts and disturbances, but no prolonged and ruinous barbarian assaults such as the Latin Christian West had to endure from the Vikings and Magyars. Under the shield of the *Pax Islamica,* which may be compared with the Augustan and Antonine Peace of the early Roman Empire, the arts and sciences rose to a new and flourishing life. Not until about 1050 did this peace begin to break down: Islam was then exposed to a series of attacks from the nomads of the steppes and deserts, culminating in the dreadful Mongol explosion of the thirteenth century.

5. The creation of the vast Arab Empire, besides levelling barriers and abolishing frontiers, brought into existence a great free trade area, promoted safe and rapid travel, and gave a tremendous stimulus to commerce. During these four centuries (800-1200) international trade was more vigorous than at any time since the heyday of imperial Rome. Merchants from the Caliphate were found in places as far apart as Senegal and Canton. The hoards of Arabic coins dug up in Scandinavia reveal the brisk exchange of goods between Northern Europe and the cities of Iraq and Persia via the great rivers of Russia. The negro lands south of the Sahara were drawn into the stream of world commerce. The ancient Silk Road through the oases of Central Asia which carried the products of China to the West had never been so frequented. Cities expanded, fortunes were made, a wealthy middle-class of traders, shippers, bankers, manufacturers and professional men came into being, and a rich and sophisticated society gave increasing employment and patronage to scholars, artists, teachers, physicians and craftsmen.

6. The pursuit of knowledge was quickened by the use of paper and the so-called 'Arabic' numerals. Neither originated in the Islamic world, but both were widely employed there by the ninth century. The manufacture of paper from hemp, rags and tree-bark seems to have been invented in China about 100 A.D., but it remained unknown outside that country until some Chinese prisoners of war skilled in the art were brought to Samarkand in 751. In 793 a paper manufactory was set up in Baghdad; by 900 the commodity was being produced in Egypt, and by 950 in Spain. The Arabic

numerals, despite their name, are probably Hindu, and may have reached Islam through the translation of the *Siddhanta,* a Sanskrit astronomical treatise, made by order of the Caliph Mansur in 773. The oldest Muslim documents employing these signs date from 870-890: the zero is represented by a dot, as has always been the case in Arabic. These innovations multiplied books and facilitated calculation, and the rich scientific literature of the next few centuries undoubtedly owes much to them.

Such are some of the possible causes of the rise of the Arabic civilization. To attempt a detailed description and analysis of that civilization would be impossible, but certain notable features or peculiarities of it may be considered : —

1. It was not specifically Muslim. Islam provided it with a framework and a universal language, but its only creations which possess a definitely Muslim character are Arabic grammar, law and theology. All else came from non-Muslim sources, even Arabic poetry and belles-lettres, which were based on a literary tradition going back to pre-Islamic times, the 'days of ignorance' of the sixth century.

2. The biggest single influence which helped to shape it was Greek science and philosophy, but this reached it indirectly, chiefly through the medium of Syriac. Of course, the great days of Hellenism were long over by the time of the Arab conquests: Greek science went out with Ptolemy in the second century, and the noble line of Greek thinkers ended when Justinian closed the schools of Athens in 529. But if nothing new was being created or discovered, the work of preserving and transmitting what had already been accomplished went on among the Byzantine Greeks and their Syriac-speaking pupils in Syria, Egypt and Iraq, and when the Arabs broke into these lands most of the leading works of Greek medicine and metaphysics had been translated into Syriac by scholars of the Oriental Christian communities. Established in an educated society, the invaders grew ashamed of their ignorance, and the Caliphs encouraged learned Christians and Jews to turn these books into the dominant language of the Empire. This translating went on for some two centuries (800-1000), at the close of which educated Muslims could read the masters of Hellenic thought in Arabic versions of Syriac translations of the Greek originals.

3. As the Syriac-speaking Christians spread through the Islamic

world a knowledge of Greek thought, so the Persians introduced to it much of the lore of Sanskrit India. Hindu influences had travelled west in late Sassanid times: the game of chess and Sanskrit medical writings are said to have reached Ctesiphon in the reign of Khusrau Nushirvan. When the Abbasids moved the metropolis of Islam to Iraq, Persian scholars were given every facility to pursue this quest. At the command of Mansur, Fazari translated the *Siddhanta;* Ibn al-Mukaffa turned into Arabic the famous *Fables of Bidpai,* an Indian collection of animal stories which has gone round the world, and the celebrated mathematician al-Khwarizmi, from whose name the European word 'algorism' (the old term for arithmetic) was derived, founded the science of algebra (Arabic *al-jabr,* a restoring, literally, setting a bone) on the basis of Hindu mathematical achievement. Translation from Sanskrit into Arabic went on till the time of the great Persian scientist al-Biruni (973-1048), who among numerous learned works left an admirable sociological description of India. The double and simultaneous impact of Greece and India provided a powerful stimulus to the building of the Arabic civilization.

4. The centre of Arabic intellectual life was long fixed in Iraq, the ancient home of culture, 'a palimpsest (as it has been styled) on which every civilization from the time of the Sumerians had left its trace.' A meeting-place of Hellenic and Iranian culture, it had been the heart of the old Persian monarchy and was the seat of the Caliphate from 750 to 1258. Baghdad became a greater Ctesiphon, the capital not simply of a State but of a world civilization. Perhaps in no other region of its size could such an extraordinary variety of belief and speech have been found. Jews and Zoroastrians, Nestorian, Monophysite and Greek Orthodox Christians, Gnostics and Manichaeans, the pagans of Harran and the strange baptist sect of the Mandaeans, all mingled in the same province. In the Arab camp settlements of Basra and Kufa the Muslims first found leisure to devote themselves to things of the mind: here was inaugurated the study of Arabic philology and Islamic law. In Baghdad the Caliph Ma'mun, the son of a Persian mother, founded and endowed as a centre of research the Bait al-Hikma, or House of Wisdom, which was at once a library, an observatory and a scientific academy. Men of many races and faiths contributed to the fame of Baghdad as a home of scholarship, and Arabic civilization never recovered from the sack of the city by the Mongols in 1258.

5. The culture of medieval Islam was multi-racial. Arabs, Syrians, Jews, Persians, Turks, Egyptians, Berbers, Spaniards, all contributed to it. One of its leading philosophers, al-Kindi, was an Arab of the tribe of Kinda (as his name implies), al-Farabi, a Neo-Platonist and commentator on Aristotle, a Turk from Transoxiana, Ibn Sina or Avicenna, perhaps the finest scientific thinker of Islam, a Persian from Bukhara, and Ibn Rushd, best known under his Europeanized name Averroes, a Spanish Moor from Cordova. A remarkable feature of Arabic philosophical literature is that much of it was written by Jews. As the Jewish religion, like the Christian, was a tolerated one among Muslims, Jews were found settled in almost all the great cities of Islam, where they learnt to write Arabic and to share in the vigorous intellectual life around them. In Spain they acted as mediators between the Muslim and Christian Spanish cultures, helping Christian scholars to translate Arabic works into Latin and so making them available to the then backward West. Spain was also the birthplace of Maimonides, 'the second Moses,' perhaps the acutest Jewish thinker before Spinoza, who was born in Cordova in 1135 and died in Cairo in 1204, and whose *Guide for the Perplexed,* a bold attempt to reconcile reason and religious faith, finds readers to this day.

6. By far the biggest share in the construction of the Arabic civilization was taken by the Persians, a people whose recorded history was already more than a thousand years old when the Arabs broke into their land, and who found in their cultural superiority compensation for their political servitude. Persia has been described as 'the principal channel irrigating the somewhat arid field of Islam with the rich alluvial flood of ancient culture': Sufism was virtually a Persian creation, and the Persian al-Ghazali was the greatest of Muslim theologians. In secular learning the Persians were predominant. 'If knowledge were attached to the ends of the sky, some amongst the Persians would have reached it,' was a traditional saying. Among the famous men of the age sprung from this gifted race were Razi (Rhazes), the great physician who first distinguished smallpox from measles, Tabari (died 923), the Arabic Livy, whose *Annals of Apostles and Kings* provided us with our chief source of information on early Muslim history, Ibn Sina, whose medical writings instructed the world for centuries, Biruni, a many-sided genius whose fame now rests chiefly on his description of medieval India.

Omar Khayyam (died 1123), more celebrated in the East for his mathematical achievements than for his poetry, Shahrastani (died 1153), whose *Book of Religion and Sects* is really a pioneering study in comparative religion, Nasir al-Din al-Tusi (died 1274), a distinguished astronomer who collected valuable data at his observatory at Maragha in Azerbaijan, and Rashid al-Din Fadl Allah (died 1318) author of the first world history worthy of that name. If to these scholars and scientists we add the poets (Firdawsi, Sa'di, Rumi, etc.), who shone lustre on their country's literature, the picture is even brighter.

7. The core of the scientific studies of medieval Islam was medicine. Socially, the medical profession had always stood high in the East: whereas in the Greco-Roman world doctors were often freed slaves, in Persia and Babylonia they could rise to be the prime ministers of kings. At the time of the Arab conquests the classical medicine of Hippocrates and Galen was being studied by Egyptian Greeks in Alexandria and Nestorian Christians at Jundi-Shapur, in south-west Persia. The Caliphs employed graduates of these schools as their personal physicians: members of one Nestorian family, the Bakht-yashu (a name meaning 'happiness of Jesus') served in this capacity at the court of Baghdad for several generations. Nestorian medical professors translated most of Galen and other authorities into Arabic, and by 900 the science of medicine was being assiduously cultivated by Muslims all over Islam. Razi was the first of their faith to acquire world fame through his vast medical encyclopedia, the *Hawi* (best known under its Latin title *Continens*), which was filled with long extracts from Greek and Hindu writers and displayed a knowledge of chemistry most unusual in that age. A similar work by Ibn Sina, the *Canon*, attained even greater celebrity and was treated for centuries as a kind of medical Bible. The branch of medicine most successively investigated was ophthalmology, eye-diseases being sadly common in the East, and the *Optics* of Ibn al-Haitham, court physician to the Fatimids in Cairo where he died in 1039, remained the standard authority on its subject till early modern times, being studied with profit by the astronomer Kepler in the seventeenth century. It was through the medical schools that many of the natural sciences found their way into Muslim education, the curricula including instruction in physics, chemistry and botany as well as in anatomy and pathology, and it was in this field

that the Arabic writers made their greatest contribution to human knowledge. They added substantially to the achievement of the Greeks in the theory and art of healing disease; they founded hospitals and invented new drugs, and they filled libraries of books with detailed and accurate clinical observations. Their long superiority is proved by the fact that most of the Arabic works translated into Latin in the twelfth and thirteenth centuries were medical writings and that these were among the first to be printed at the time of the Renaissance. Razi, Ibn Sina and Ibn al-Haitham in their Latinized form continued to be 'set books' in the medical schools of Europe till as late as the mid-seventeenth century.

8. Like all civilizations, the Arabic was highly selective in its borrowings from outside. Human societies take over only those elements which seem well suited to fill a conscious gap, and disregard those which conflict with their fundamental values; thus in modern times Russia has appropriated the science rather than the humanism of the West, and China has borrowed Marxism and rejected almost all else of European origin. Islam drew extensively on Hindu mathematics and medicine, but took small notice of Hindu philosophy, which being the reflection of a polytheistic society and of belief in the world as *maya* or illusion, was wholly repugnant to the teachings of the Koran. It helped itself to a good deal of Greek (chiefly Aristotelian) logic and metaphysics, in order to clothe its religious doctrines in a form more acceptable to a sophisticated society and enable it to defend them against philosophically trained opponents, but though it knew Aristotle's *Poetics* and *Rhetoric,* it ignored the Greek poets, dramatists and historians as spokesmen of a pagan past it had no desire to investigate. In architecture it was ready to use Byzantine and Persian models, but painting and sculpture were virtually banned because the Prophet was alleged to have pronounced representational art a temptation to idolatry. Of classical Latin literature it knew nothing: the only Latin work ever translated into Arabic is said to have been the *History* of Orosius.

That the Arabic culture was merely imitative, that it copied and transmitted what it learnt at second-hand from the Greeks, and lacked the ability to strike out on independent lines of its own, is a judgment no longer accepted. It certainly borrowed freely from the Greeks—so did the West later—but what it built on these foundations was truly original and creative, and one of the great achievements of the human spirit. For more than four hundred years the most fruitful work in mathematics, astronomy, botany, chemistry, medicine, history and geography, was produced in the world of Islam by Muslims and Christians, Jews and Zoroastrians, pagans and Manichaeans. Neither the collapse of the Caliphate nor the Isma'-ilian schism checked the process, for the local dynasties which sprang up on the ruins of the old Arab Empire competed with one another to attract scholars and artists to their courts, and the possession of a common language far outweighed the loss of political unity.   Yet this brilliant culture, which shone so brightly in contrast to the darkness of the Latin West and the stagnation of Byzantium, began to fade from the thirteenth century onwards. Arabic philosophy was dead by 1200, Arabic science by 1500. The nations of Western Europe, once sunk in barbarism, caught up and overtook the peoples of Islam. How did this come about? The question has hardly yet received a complete and satisfactory answer, but some tentative suggestions may be offered:—

1. The collapse of the *Pax Islamica* after about 1050. The end of the long peace was marked by wave after wave of nomadic invasion, the Banu-Hilal in North Africa, the Turkomans and Seljuks in Western Asia, and the mighty Mongol devastations which inflicted such irreparable damage on so many Muslim lands between 1220 and 1260. Cities were sacked and burnt, wealth dissipated, libraries destroyed and teachers dispersed. The loss to culture in the fall of Baghdad alone is incalculable. The Christian West escaped all this, since after the Northmen and Magyars had been tamed and converted around 1000, it had nothing more to fear from barbarian attack, and the Mongols never got farther west than Hungary and Silesia.

2. The decay of city life and economic prosperity. The Arabic civilization was essentially urban, and its material basis was the vigorous commercial activity which once covered an area extending as far as Scandinavia, China and the Sudan. This activity was much diminished when nomad raids and invasions threatened the security of the caravan routes. From the eleventh century onwards the volume of international trade contracted, urban wealth declined, and social and economic conditions in the Muslim world underwent drastic change. Princes, finding their revenues falling, were obliged to pay their civil and military officers out of the rents and

produce of landed estates: hence the growth of the *ikta* system, which has been compared, rather loosely, to Western feudalism. Owing presumably to the prevalence of slavery, which assured a plentiful supply of labour, there was no stimulus to technological progress and invention, which might have provided some compensation for the loss of distant markets. Nor did the cities of Islam ever develop self-governing institutions or combine in defence of their interests like the Lombard League or the Hansa in contemporary Europe: it was not that civic patriotism was wholly lacking (Arabic literature contains many town histories and biographical dictionaries of famous citizens), but that in this society the primary loyalty of a man was to his religious community, and in cities where Muslims, Christians and Jews lived together in separate quarters, it was not easy for the inhabitants to feel and act as a united body. Thus the middle classes (merchants, traders, shippers, shopkeepers and craftsmen) had little defence when the economic basis of their position weakened, and the decline of the town was almost certainly related to the falling off of intellectual capacity and output.

3. The loss of linguistic and cultural unity. In the days of its widest expansion, Arabic was written and understood wherever Islam prevailed, but its intellectual monopoly was threatened and finally broken by the revival of Persian in the lands east of the Tigris. The fall of the Sassanid Empire reduced the native tongue to the level of Anglo-Saxon in England after the Norman conquest, but under the Abbasids it began to re-emerge in an altered form, its vocabulary swollen with Arabic words and the old Pahlawi script replaced by the Arabic. With the rise of native dynasties after the disintegration of the Caliphate, Persian experienced a literary renaissance; the Samanids and Ghaznavids in particular were generous patrons of poets and scholars, and Firdawsi's great epic, the *Shah-nama*, or Book of Kings, finished in 1010, gave the new Persian a position in world literature it has never since lost. Fewer and fewer Persians wrote in Arabic, though the sacred language of the Koran continued to be used for works of theology, law and devotion. When the Turks entered Islam *en masse* with the Seljuks, it was the Persianized provinces that they first occupied, and it was on Persian officials that they relied for the administration of their Empire. Deeply affected in consequence by Persian culture, the Turks carried it with them westwards into Asia Minor and eastwards into northern India: by

contrast, they set little store by Arabic, except for purely religious purposes. The Mongol invasions, the fall of Baghdad and the destruction of the Caliphate dealt a fatal blow to Arabic in eastern Islam, where in the field of secular learning and literature it was steadily overshadowed by Persian and Turkish. Never again was the Muslim world to be dominated by a single language.

4. Probably the biggest factor was the strongly religious character of Islam itself and the absence of a vigorous pre-Islamic secular tradition. Behind Christian Europe lay the science and rationalism of classical Greece: behind Islam lay nothing save the cultural poverty of 'the days of ignorance.' The Muslims did, as we have seen, borrow a good deal from Greece, but in a limited and indirect fashion: the Greek past never *belonged* to them in the sense in which it did to Christendom, and there was never a joyous acceptance or recovery of it as took place in the West at the time of the Renaissance. The spirit of Islam was not rational in the Greek sense of the term, in that God is beyond reason and his ordering of the universe is to be accepted rather than explained. True knowledge is that of God and his Law, and the Law embraces all human activity: secular learning for its own sake is to be strongly discouraged, and intellectual pursuits are permissible only insofar as they further a deeper piety and understanding of religious truth. Such an attitude was implicit in Islamic thinking from the outset, but it became explicit only at a later stage, largely in consequence of the reaction against the Isma'ilian heresy and of a fuller realisation of the dangers to orthodoxy lurking in Greek philosophy. The shift in outlook became noticeable in the Seljuk age. The great Ghazali devoted his life to the defence of Koranic truth against what he regarded as the insidious encroachments of unbelief. Islamic dogma was linked with Sufi mysticism. Muslim education was geared to the new orthodoxy by the founding of *madrasas*, where the religious sciences alone received intensive study. The Shari'a came to dominate Muslim life as the Torah had dominated post-exilic Judaism. The door was closed against further borrowings from outside: philosophy was repudiated as a danger to the Faith, because it was alleged to deny a personal God, creation *ex nihilo*, and the resurrection of the body. The attempt of Ibn Rushd (Averroes) in Spain to answer Ghazali and defend the pursuit of secular science fell on deaf ears and exposed him to the charge of teaching atheism. How far the reaction went can be seen from the

attitude of Ibn Khaldun (1337-1406), often regarded as Islam's profoundest thinker, who dismissed all knowledge unconnected with religion as useless. Plato (he says) admitted that no certainty about God could be attained by the reason: why then waste our time on such futile inquiries? Truth is to be sought only in divine revelation. The profane sciences, which had always operated on the fringe and had never been free from the suspicion of impiety, were largely and quietly dropped as 'un-Muslim.'

BOOKS FOR FURTHER READING

From the enormous literature on this subject it is possible to cite only a few titles.

ARBERRY, A. J., *Reason and Revelation in Islam*, London, 1957. Short but useful summary of the 'science versus religion' issue in Islam.

BOER, T. J. DE, *A History of Philosophy in Islam*, Eng. tr. London, 1903. Standard work.

BROWNE, E. G., *A Literary History of Persia*, 4 vols. Cambridge, 1906-28. A classic.

BRUNSCHVIG & VON GRUNEBAUM (ed.), *Classicisme et déclin culturel dans l'histoire de l'Islam*, Paris, 1957. Valuable symposium by a number of leading European Arabists. A serious attempt to explain why Arabic civilization decayed after so brilliant a beginning.

ELGOOD, C., *A Medical History of Persia*, Cambridge, 1951. A full and detailed account of the achievement of Arabic medicine.

GIBB, H. A. R., *Arabic Literature*, Oxford, 1926; 2nd. ed. 1963. The best short introduction.

GIBB, H. A. R., *Studies in the Civilization of Islam*, London, 1962. A selection from the work of the distinguished British Arabist.

GRUNEBAUM, G. VON, *Medieval Islam*, Chicago, 1946; 2nd. ed. 1953.

GRUNEBAUM, G. VON, *Islam. Essays in the Nature and Growth of a Cultural Tradition*, Wisconsin, 1955. Stimulating discussion of many aspects of Arabic civilization.

KREMER, A. VON, *Culturgeschichliche Streifzüge auf dem Gebiete des Islams*, Vienna, 1873; Eng. tr. Khuda Bukhsh, *Contributions to the History of Islamic Civilization*, Calcutta, 1905. A pioneer work, not yet really antiquated.

Legacy of Islam, The, Oxford, 1931. A collection of essays by different hands.

LEVY, R., *The Sociology of Islam*, Cambridge, 1957. Encyclopedic in its treatment.

MACDONALD, D. B., *The Development of Muslim Theology, Jurisprudence and Constitutional Theory*, London, 1903; reprinted Lahore, 1960. Standard work, perhaps a little outmoded.

NICHOLSON, R. A., *A Literary History of the Arabs*, Cambridge, 1907. A classic.

O'LEARY, DE LACY, *How Greek Science passed to the Arabs*, London, 1949. The only monograph of its kind in English, but not very accurate.

RENAN, E., *Averroès et l'Averroisme*, Paris 1852, often reprinted. A famous work, not yet superseded. Of wider scope than the title would imply.

SARTON, G., *Introduction to the History of Science*, 3 vols. in 5, Washington, 1927-48. A vast accurate bibliography, in which the development of Arabic science can be traced from century to century. Comes down to 1400.

WALZER, R., *Greek into Arabic, Essays on Islamic Philosophy*, Oxford, 1962.

WATT, W. MONTGOMERY, *Islam and the Integration of Society*, London, 1961.

TRANSLATED SOURCES

IBN KHALDUN, *The Muqaddimah*, Eng. tr. F. Rosenthal. 3 vols. London, 1958. The introductory section of the famous Tunisian's *History*. The world as seen and interpreted by a great Muslim thinker at a time when Arabic civilization had passed its zenith.

Epilogue

THE classical age of Islam ended with the fall of Baghdad. Muslim Asia, seemingly on the verge of ruin, made, however, a surprising recovery. Ain Jalut destroyed the Mongol reputation for invincibility and kept the pagan hordes out of Egypt and the Maghrib, and the invaders, chastened by defeat, developed a respect for the Muslim faith. The Mongol leaders in South Russia had already embraced Islam: by 1300 the descendants of Hulagu, the Il-Khans of Persia, after long hesitation, chose Muhammad instead of Christ. This was decisive. The future of Islam was assured, and Christian hopes of evangelizing Asia faded and died. Nestorian and Latin churches maintained a precarious existence in Turkistan, Persia and China for a few years longer, but by 1400 they had virtually disappeared. The Crusades petered out in failure; the Mamluks ejected the Franks from Syria, and mass-defections to Islam left the native Christian communities in the Near East the tiny minorities they are to-day.

When the Mongol storm had blown itself out, Islam embarked on a fresh wave of expansion which lasted for four hundred years (1300-1700) and carried it from Hungary to Indonesia. This second age of conquest has been curiously neglected or belittled by Arabic and Persian writers, probably because it was dominated by peoples of Turkish origin, who ruled nearly all the great Islamic empires of the time, nor has it ever been adequately studied by European historians, who usually look no further than the Ottoman Turks and their relations with the nation States of Western Europe.

The four leading Muslim States of this period were Mamluk Egypt, Ottoman Turkey, Safavid Persia and Mogul India. The Mamluks ruled the Levant for more than two and a half centuries (1250-1517): they preserved and protected the remnants of Arabic culture in Egypt, expelled the Crusaders, and re-opened the offensive against the Christian positions in the eastern Mediterranean. The

Ottoman Turks, starting as a small clan in north-western Asia Minor around 1300, crossed into Europe in 1355, spread through the Balkan peninsula, took Constantinople in 1453 and Belgrade in 1456, overran most of Hungary, and twice (in 1526 and 1683) besieged Vienna. Since the original Arab invasions of the seventh century, Christendom had never been in graver peril. The Mediterranean threatened to become a Turkish lake; Rhodes, Cyprus and Crete fell into Ottoman hands, and only Spanish naval power, operating from Sicily as well as from the Iberian peninsula, stopped the further advance of Islam westwards. The Ottomans were strong enough to challenge their Muslim neighbours also; Syria and Egypt were wrenched from the Mamluks, who had neglected to make adequate use of the new weapons of war, gunpowder and firearms, but their advance in and beyond Iraq was halted by the resistance of the Safavids, who gained control of Persia in 1500 and created, for the first time since the days of the Sassanids, a kind of Iranian national State and gave it a peculiar moral flavour by adopting as the national religion the Twelver variety of Shi'ism. Meanwhile Babur, an adventurer of genius of mixed Turkish and Mongol blood, descended from the Afghan hills into the plain of Hindustan, and founded in 1525 the Mogul or Mughal Empire, which brought in time almost the entire Indian subcontinent under Muslim sway. This blow to Hinduism in its own land was matched by its defeat in Indonesia, where in rather obscure circumstances Islam gained the ascendancy by 1500, the Hindu faith surviving (as it does to-day) only in the island of Bali.

Islam's second imperial age differed markedly from the first. The Arabs, now a subjugated race under Ottoman rule, played little or no part in it; the new triumphs of Islam operated beyond their purview, and were never appreciated by them. It was not accompanied by a great florescence of science and thought, as in the classical days of the Omayyads and Abbasids. In art and literature indeed new heights were reached, but the culture of the Ottomans and Moguls was largely Persian, and the ancient Arabic learning was neglected. Moreover, the battle between 'faith' and 'philosophy' had long ago been fought and won, and while Christian Europe during the Renaissance was re-discovering the pagan Hellenic sources of its civilization, Islam turned in on itself, and extruded the Greek elements its thinkers had once striven to incorporate in its system. Complacently convinced of its superiority, contemptuous of the West, reluctant to take anything from unbelievers (the printing-press was not introduced into Turkey until 1722), Islam grew intellectually stagnant and even lost a good deal of the knowledge it had acquired in more mentally vigorous times.

The next two centuries (1700-1900) were the most dismal of Islamic history. There was no catastrophe comparable to the Mongol conquests of the thirteenth century, but political decay and collapse almost everywhere under the relentless pressure of the Western powers, whose science, industry and technology gave them temporarily the mastery of the world, and what was more serious, a challenge to Islamic fundamentals on the intellectual plane. The decline of Ottoman might was registered by the peace of Carlowitz in 1699, and the Sultan's European dominions steadily contracted. The death of Awrangzib in 1707 ended the glory of the Moguls. The extinction of the Safavid dynasty in 1722 left Persia a prey to invasion, disorder and misgovernment. Napoleon's invasion of Egypt in 1798 was the first great military assault by the West since the Crusades. Before the nineteenth century closed nearly the whole Muslim world had passed under the political control or economic exploitation of the European powers, the British in India and Egypt, the French and Italians in North Africa, the Germans in Turkey, the Russians in Central Asia. Spiritually, Islam was now threatened from two sides, from internal reactionaries like the Wahhabis of Arabia, who demanded a 'return to the Koran,' the purifying of the faith from all later 'corruptions', and from the liberal rationalism of the West, which put reason before faith and saw in the achievements of physical science the noblest victory of the human mind over ignorance and superstition.

The two World Wars of the twentieth century registered the decline of Europe and the release of the Islamic peoples from foreign domination. The Ottoman Empire fell to pieces in 1918, and after a brief period of Anglo-French control disguised as 'mandates', the Arab lands recovered an independence they had lost in the early sixteenth century. Persia, under the new Pahlawi dynasty which came to power in 1925, began to climb out of the slough in which she had long lain. After the Second World War the European colonial Empires disappeared with astonishing rapidity. Two new Muslim States of great potential strength arose in Pakistan and

Indonesia, and the freeing of the Maghrib from French rule culminated in the establishment of the Algerian Republic in 1962. Only the Turkish-speaking Muslims of Central Asia remained under the sway of a European Power, in this case Soviet Russia.

Yet political emancipation has not so far produced a new sense of Muslim unity or an Islamic renaissance. The Ottoman Sultans had long claimed to be also Caliphs, but Sultanate and Caliphate alike were abolished by the Turkish Republicans under Kemal Ataturk, and proposals to revive the Caliphal office elsewhere came to nothing. Dreams of building a new Arab Empire on the ruins of Ottoman power went unrealised; the Arab countries quarrelled among themselves, resented the efforts of Egypt to lead them, and not even the intrusion of the Jewish State of Israel in 1948 could induce them to sink their differences. The Turkish Republic disquieted Muslim opinion everywhere by disestablishing Islam, repudiating the *Shari'a,* and declaring itself a secular State. This did not imply that the Turks had ceased to be Muslims (they had always interpreted Islam in their own fashion), but the Kemalist reforms intensified Turkish-Arab hostility. Persia remained wedded to Twelver Shi'ism, and therefore out of step with Sunnite Islam. The attempt of the new Muslim States to import and work the parliamentary institutions of the West have been almost universally unsuccessful; the only political theory of Islam has been passive obedience to any *de facto* authority; 'government with the consent of the governed' is a concept unknown, and dictatorships, often headed by army officers, have replaced cabinets and elected assemblies.

Spiritually and intellectually, the future of Islam remains doubtful. The efforts of men like Jamal al-Din Afghani, Muhammad Abduh, and Muhammad Iqbal to re-formulate Islamic law and doctrine in a manner more acceptable to the modern world have won little support or favour from the *ulama,* who like all such bodies tend to be strongly conservative. Some social reforms have been achieved: slavery and concubinage, both sanctioned by the Koran, have vanished over a large part of the Muslim world, and here and there the veil has been discarded and the right of divorce granted to women. Western-type schools, colleges and universities are multiplying, and even at al-Azhar, the citadel of orthodoxy, the curriculum has been expanded and modernized. But the West both attracts and repels. Islam has not only not assimilated Western industrialism and liberal rationalism, but is by no means certain that it ought to do so. The humanist and scientific tradition is lacking; the Muslim who is distressed by the material and technological backwardness of his society and humiliated by Western airs of superiority may nonetheless feel that ultimate truth and wisdom is in Islam and not in the West.

Index